Teach Yourself®

Present with Impact and Confidence

Amanda Vickers
Steve Bavister

For UK order enquiries: please contact Bookpoint Ltd,
130 Milton Park, Abingdon, Oxon OX14 4SB.
Telephone: +44 (0) 1235 827720. Fax: +44 (0) 1235 400454.
Lines are open 09.00–17.00, Monday to Saturday, with a 24-hour
message answering service. Details about our titles and how to
order are available at www.teachyourself.com

Long renowned as the authoritative source for self-guided
learning – with more than 50 million copies sold worldwide – the
Teach Yourself series includes over 500 titles in the fields of
languages, crafts, hobbies, business, computing and education.

British Library Cataloguing in Publication Data: a catalogue record
for this title is available from the British Library.

This edition published 2010.

Previously published as Teach Yourself Presenting

The **Teach Yourself** name is a registered trade mark of
Hodder Headline.

Copyright © 2007, 2010 Amanda Vickers and Steve Bavister

Typeset by MPS Limited, a Macmillan Company.

Printed in Great Britain for Hodder Education, an Hachette UK
Company, 338 Euston Road, London NW1 3BH, by CPI Antony Rowe,
Chippenham and Eastbourne.

The publisher has used its best endeavours to ensure that the URLs
for external websites referred to in this book are correct and active
at the time of going to press. However, the publisher and the
author have no responsibility for the websites and can make no
guarantee that a site will remain live or that the content will remain
relevant, decent or appropriate.

Hachette UK's policy is to use papers that are natural, renewable
and recyclable products and made from wood grown in sustainable
forests. The logging and manufacturing processes are expected to
conform to the environmental regulations of the country of origin.

Impression number   10 9 8 7 6 5 4 3
Year   2014 2013 2012 2011

Front cover: © D. Hurst/Alamy

Back cover: © Jakub Semeniuk/iStockphoto.com, © Royalty-
Free/Corbis, © agencyby/iStockphoto.com, © Andy Cook/
iStockphoto.com, © Christopher Ewing/iStockphoto.com,
© zebicho – Fotolia.com, © Geoffrey Holman/iStockphoto.com,
© Photodisc/Getty Images, © James C. Pruitt/iStockphoto.com,
© Mohamed Saber – Fotolia.com

Contents

Meet the authors

Welcome to *Present with Impact and Confidence*!

We enjoy presenting. You might even say we love it. There's
not much that beats the buzz you get when you sit down after
speaking to a large or responsive group. In fact, we enjoy it
so much we get withdrawal symptoms when we don't get to
present for a while. Happily, that's not very often these days,
as we get plenty of opportunities to speak in public. We love
the big occasions most of all – and the feeling of the adrenalin
pumping and a successful outcome.

The idea of enjoying a presentation may be hard for some of
you to imagine. Maybe you think that's for someone else but
not for you. For most people it's a matter of enduring, not
enjoying, a presentation. That's certainly how it was for us
in the beginning. The way we are now is very different from
how we were then ...

When I (Amanda) first started work at the age of 16 I was
shy and didn't speak to anyone unless they spoke to me first.
After a while I settled in and opened up to people I felt safe
with. As the years went by I became more self-assured but,
even in my early 20s, when anyone asked me to speak in public
I'd do almost anything to get out of it.

I recall the first time I had to stand in front of 40 people and
speak. All eyes were on me. My knees turned to jelly and I
was convinced the people at the front would be able to see me
shaking. Somehow I got through it. I decided there and then
that I was going to learn how to overcome my fear and become
a good presenter. One of the first lessons I learnt is that it's
possible to alter your emotional state by changing the thoughts

inside your head. It's a hell of a lot easier to present well when you have an internal cheerleader rather than an internal critic.

I've come a long way since those days and I'm glad I experienced them. It helps enormously for me to understand and support others who are wracked with nerves when they have to present. I get enormous satisfaction from helping others to realize that they can do it too.

My (Steve) story is similar but different. I've always been reasonably confident as a person – able to chat easily with most people and comfortable in most situations, even when they're new to me. But when I first started to present in a formal setting – I was working for an international media company at the time – I learnt what it means to have a fear of public speaking.

My 'baptism of fire' involved giving the same presentation over breakfast, lunch and dinner to senior people in the photographic industry – around 30 in each group. To say I was terrified would be an understatement. The success of the magazine relaunch I was involved in depended on my ability to sell it to this influential group of people. Somehow I got through it, and it went well, but I realized there would be more to come, and I set out to conquer my nerves and master the required skills. These days I love standing up in front of large and even challenging groups of people.

If we can go from enduring to enjoying, so can you. We've helped literally thousands of people to improve their confidence and impact when presenting in the courses we run and the coaching we do. We wrote this book to share what we've learnt from working with every possible concern and challenge someone can have.

We know it will help you present with impact and confidence in any situation.

Amanda and Steve

Only got a minute?

Because many people have little or no experience of giving formal presentations they get nervous at the thought of doing so – even though they're often better at speaking in public than they think they are.

Presenting is a skill that can be developed through practice, not a talent you are born with. The more you do it, the better you become – and the more confident you feel. Preparation helps as well. The better you know your material, the more comfortable you'll be.

Start by being clear about your outcome. Avoid focusing too much on giving information and seek to influence your audience. Make sure your presentation is audience-centred. What are their wants, needs, interests and concerns?

Next decide what to include and leave out. The secret of success is 'less is more' and 'keep it simple.' Brainstorm all possible content. Organize it using a spider diagram or by writing points on cards. As you move things around, a structure will emerge.

Think about managing the audience attention span so people don't zone out. Grab them from the word go – and tell them what your presentation will do for them. Give an overview of the content, the agenda, and your key messages. Keep people alert throughout with examples, case studies and stories to bring ideas to life. Close with impact by summarizing, repeating your key messages and calling them to action.

Notes, if you use them, should be short. If you have slides, you shouldn't need notes as well. To avoid 'Death by PowerPoint' have no more than six bullet points on a slide and no more than six words per line – and use images whenever possible.

Fear of something going wrong is common. It's an emotional response that arises from taking a perfectionist approach. It doesn't matter if you make the odd slip. Be yourself, and don't put on a performance. Make eye contact with everyone. Preparing for the Q&A session gives you greater confidence too.

Think of your presentation as dialogue, not monologue – as a conversation. Find a comfortable resting place for your hands just above the navel and gesture normally as you would when chatting with someone. You'll create a positive impression if you stand tall and still, with your legs shoulder width apart, and then move purposefully and deliberately. Project your voice and pause between sentences. This also helps eliminate 'ums' and 'ers'.

Presenting with impact and confidence depends on a handful of principles: prepare and practise (it's a skill not a talent); be yourself (don't put on a performance); engage with your audience (go for dialogue not monologue); bring your ideas to life with examples; and keep it simple, because less is more.

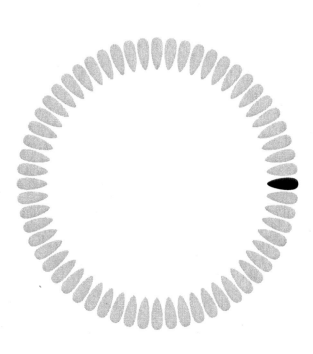

5 Only got five minutes?

Presenting with impact and confidence is a skill not a talent.
That's the first thing you need to know – and probably the most
important thing.

Many people look at charismatic presenters such as Barack Obama,
John F. Kennedy and Martin Luther King and think: 'It's easy for
them, they're just naturals. I don't have their talent – I'll never be
any good at public speaking.'

But reliable, objective, credible research proves this to be a myth.
In his book *Talent is Overrated*, Geoff Colvin demonstrates
beyond doubt that it's practice, not talent, that leads to success in
most fields of endeavour.

You could be as good as Barack Obama, John F. Kennedy,
Martin Luther King or whoever you hold up as a model of
excellence. Really, you could. They've just had more practice than
you have. Presenting with impact and confidence is a skill not
a talent. It's no different from learning a musical instrument or
learning to ski. You wouldn't play in public or ski down an advanced
slope without doing your homework and learning the ropes first.

The problem facing many people who want to be able to
present with impact and confidence is that they don't have much
experience of speaking in public. They get nervous just at the
thought, and have often spent a lifetime avoiding situations where
they might have to 'stand up and say a few words'.

This is clearly a Catch-22 situation. You can't present because you
don't have the skills – and you can't develop the skills if you don't
present. How do you get out of this double-bind? You have to 'feel
the fear and do it anyway' – be courageous and give it a go.

The good news is that you already have some experience of presenting – albeit informally. Whenever you offer an opinion in a meeting, you're presenting. Whenever you describe what you do at a networking event, you're presenting. Whenever you sit down one-on-one with a colleague, you're presenting. In business, every conversation is a presentation – and being able to present with impact and confidence is an essential business skill.

One thing we've learnt from training thousands of business people in presentation skills is that most people are better at speaking in public than they think they are. We all tend to amplify our weaknesses and minimize our strengths, which gives us a distorted perspective on how we come across to others. Most people have areas of development – they may 'um' and 'er' or read too much from their slides – but are capable of delivering a competent presentation.

The secret to feeling confident when you first start presenting seriously is preparation. The more you prepare, up to a point, the more confident you'll feel. Preparation means knowing not only your material, but also the 'story' you're telling, and the sequence of your slides, if you're using them.

Where many people go wrong when starting out is being unclear what their outcome is in giving a presentation. All too often they focus on giving information – often filling their slides with endless data – rather than seeking to influence the audience by winning support or getting buy-in.

Equally important is making sure the presentation is audience-centred – that it takes account of their wants, needs, interests and concerns. If you don't get that right, and those you're speaking to consider your message irrelevant, you're unlikely to achieve what you want. So ask yourself what's important to them when you're pulling together your content and putting together your structure. What do they know about the subject already? What's their attitude? What expectations do they have?

Once you've defined your outcome and thought about the audience, you're in a position to decide what to include and what to leave out. Most people put too much into their presentation – because they know so much about their subject. And those listening get overwhelmed by a torrent of information. One of the secrets of success can be summed up in six words and two phrases: 'less is more' and 'keep it simple'.

Many novice presenters seem to find it hard coming up with a structure, but it's relatively straightforward if you take a systematic approach. Start by brainstorming all possible content. Then organize it using either a spider diagram or by writing the key points on index cards and shuffling them around. An intuitive approach often works best. What needs to go near the front? What needs to go towards the end? As you move things around, a structure will often emerge, without you needing to force it.

With longer presentations – more than about 15 minutes – you need to think about managing the audience attention span. People can easily lose focus and zone out, so you need variety to maintain their interest. Start with a 'bang' – something that grabs them from the word go – and then tell them exactly what you're presentation will do for them. Everyone will be tuned to the same channel – WII FM (What's In It For Me). Give a quick overview of the presentation, briefly mention the agenda, and summarize your key messages.

During the middle part, where interest can easily drift, do everything you can to keep people alert: ring the changes with your voice, body language and slides. Don't just recite facts at them, use examples, case studies, illustrations and stories to bring your ideas to life.

Many presentations just run out of steam – they end with a whimper not a bang. So make sure you have a strong, impactful ending: summarize, repeat your key messages and, if there's something you want them to do, give a powerful call to action. Don't leave the audience in any doubt about what you want them to do.

When they first start presenting, many people like to use notes, so they can remember what they're going to say. But all too often these 'notes' are strings of sentences – and they become a script that gets read out. While it's certainly better to do a good presentation with notes rather than a bad one without, when someone reads aloud the result is generally stilted and wooden – and the audience quickly loses interest. If you do plan to use notes, make sure they are just that: short points that act as a prompt rather than every word you plan to say.

PowerPoint is considered de rigeur when presenting in many organizations, and if you have slides, you shouldn't need notes as well – the points on the slides will help you keep on track. The secret to avoiding 'Death by PowerPoint' is to have no more than six bullet points on a slide and no more than six words per line – and use images whenever possible so it's not just endless words.

The most important thing with PowerPoint is not to read from the slides. How on earth do you do that when all the information is on them? Easy. You use the Read, Rotate, Repeat system. You look at the slide, copy the point you want to make to your short-term memory, and then turn back to the audience and talk around it. You might think of the bullet point as a hyperlink that opens a page of information in your mind.

When the presentation is particularly important, or you're in the early stages of developing your skills, it's crucial that you practise and time it. That way you'll know you won't run short or run over, and you'll feel more confident because the material will be more familiar. The more confident you are, the more impact you'll have.

Everybody gets nervous to some degree when they have to give a presentation, but some people grow extremely anxious and some even come close to a full-blown panic attack. We know from the thousands of people we've trained there's no point in simply saying 'calm down'. The fear of the presentation going badly wrong and ending in embarrassment or even humiliation is an emotional rather than a rational response. To overcome this fear, you have to tackle the thoughts that create it. Is the audience really out to criticize you? Surely they want you to do well. And does it really spell failure if you make a couple of mistakes? Only if you take a perfectionist approach to presenting, which some people do. This is where the fear comes from. But when you're more realistic, and know you'll make the odd slip, and that it doesn't really matter, you can start to feel more comfortable.

The secret of successful presenting is to be yourself, and not put on a performance. You can only get stage fright if you put yourself on a stage. Don't do it.

What's crucial, when you're delivering the presentation itself, is to engage with the audience – and that means making good eye contact. Use the principle of 'one thought, one person': connect with each individual for two to four seconds as if they were the only person in the room. Move your gaze around randomly, making sure, over a period of time, everyone is included.

Think of your presentation as dialogue, not monologue – as a conversation, even if you're the only person speaking. You can tell how well you're doing by 'reading' your audience, especially their body language and facial expressions. Are they responding to you? Or do they seem disinterested?

Keep your energy high, because if your energy drops, so will the energy in the group. That's where your body language comes in. You need to gesture normally, so it seems like a conversation. Find a comfortable 'baseline' resting place for your hands – a good location is just above the navel – and then gesture as you would if you were chatting with someone at the water cooler or coffee point.

But while movement in the upper body is a good thing, you don't want too much movement below the waist. Many people step back and forth, as if practising their salsa moves, or pace around like caged tigers. A better impression is created if you stand still, with your legs shoulder width apart, and then move purposefully and deliberately from time to time.

Be aware of the 'silent messages' you're sending and how they might be interpreted by your audience. Stand tall and you appear to others to be standing with confidence – and that maximizes the impact you make.

Not everyone will be looking at you all the time you're presenting, but they will be listening most of the time, so your voice is of crucial importance. You need to make sure it projects into the room, but without shouting. If it's too quiet or soft it gives the impression you lack confidence. It's the same if you rush: people who are comfortable when speaking in public give a sense of having all the time in the world.

One simple way of having more vocal impact is to pause between sentences. This can also help eliminate the 'ums' and 'ers' which beset more than 50 per cent of the population when they speak in public, and which can give the impression of being uncertain or uncomfortable.

Many presenters are fearful of the question and answer session, because they believe they might 'get found out'. Who knows what issues might be raised that would reveal the speaker's lack of knowledge or expertise? Other presenters relish the opportunity to get away from their planned material and engage in a dialogue with members of the audience.

Whatever your perspective, careful preparation will enable you to feel more confident. What questions are people likely to ask? What issues would you most hate them to raise? Once you have answers prepared you'll go into the session with greater confidence. If you don't know the answer to a question, just say so. You can't possibly know everything. Say you'll get back with an answer as soon as possible.

It's what could go wrong that troubles many presenters, but in practice the worst rarely happens. And it's easy to 'catastrophize' the result if something unexpected did occur. All you can do is take it in your stride, and get on with presenting your ideas as effectively as possible.

In the end, presenting with impact and confidence comes down to a handful of simple principles: prepare and practise (it's a skill not a talent); be yourself (don't put on a performance); engage with your audience (go for dialogue not monologue); bring your ideas to life with examples; and remember to keep it simple, because less is more.

1

Everything is a presentation

In this chapter you will learn:
- *why presenting is an essential business and life skill*
- *that everything is a presentation*
- *about the ten faults audiences hate most.*

A crucial business skill

No ifs. No buts. No maybes. If you want to be successful in business these days you need to be able to present effectively. It's not optional – a nice-to-have – it's an essential professional skill.

That's because everything's a presentation. Unless you're an artist holed up in a garret, or Robinson Crusoe with no Man Friday, you're constantly interacting with other people, putting forward ideas and trying to influence and persuade them to do what you want them to do.

Maybe you've always considered presenting to be someone standing in front of a group, perhaps using PowerPoint. It's certainly that. But such formal presentations are only part of the picture. Just the tip of the iceberg. In fact, most people give many presentations during the course of a day but they don't always put them in that category.

Every interaction is a presentation. Whenever you're in a professional situation, with one or more person, and you're speaking, you're presenting. That means meetings and discussions, chatting to colleagues and customers, telephone and face-to-face conversations, pitching and selling, inspiring and motivating a team, and a whole lot more.

Meetings in particular are important arenas where presentations are given. For many business people, especially those at a senior level, the working day consists of one meeting after another. And the talent and ability of those attending will often be judged on the basis of their contributions, namely the presentations they make. Often these will be informal, unplanned – 'Hey, Sarah, what do you think?', 'Give us your perspective on this, Simon' – but they're presentations nonetheless.

Presentations of any type are your opportunity to showcase your skills, talents and knowledge. When you can command an audience you're also demonstrating your leadership ability. If you're in line for promotion and there is someone else vying for the position, the decision may just swing in favour of the person who can demonstrate the best communication skills.

That's why an increasing number of people are coming on the presentation skills training courses we run. They recognize that to get on in business and be a success you need to be able to communicate your ideas clearly, concisely, credibly and compellingly. It's not just a matter of connecting a USB cable from your head into the heads of those in the audience and downloading data. You need to interest, engage and inspire them.

And, most of the time, when you're presenting, what you're actually doing is selling. You may not think of it like that, but that's the reality. Sometimes you'll be selling products and services, but more often you'll be selling ideas, looking to gain commitment and buy-in.

As one CEO of a global household brand said recently at the beginning of one of our courses, 'If you can't present effectively, you won't get very far in this company'.

An essential life skill

Actually, we'd go further than saying presenting is an essential business skill. It's also an essential life skill. If you can't present effectively, many doors will probably be closed to you in your personal endeavours as well. So the benefits you gain from reading this book will almost certainly improve your relationships, enhance your communication skills and increase your confidence in all areas of your life.

What you'll learn in this book

Our aim in this book is to give you a thorough grounding in the theory and practice of presenting, and to prepare you to be able to go as far as you want in any company. We focus primarily on formal presentations, but the content will be relevant to informal presentations as well.

In the next chapter we start by asking you to consider what it means to be a competent presenter. We look at what good presenters believe and how that drives their behaviour. You will also be able to find out where you are on the journey to becoming a competent presenter.

The importance of preparation is highlighted in Chapter 3. You'll discover why preparation is essential for success and why it's important to prepare not only the content but also your delivery style.

Being clear about your outcome and having measures of success are crucial when it comes to presenting. Chapter 4 not only explains this but also goes on to discuss why good presenting motivates people to change.

Chapter 5 tells you how to carry out effective research on the people who will attend your presentation. How do you go about 'getting inside' the collective mind of your audience? We also look at how understanding different behavioural styles allows you to analyse your audience and adapt your approach.

Being able to create a clear structure that's easy to follow is one of the principal skills of successful presenting. Chapter 6 introduces a tried and tested way of doing this and goes on to explain how to manage the audience's attention span.

Different ways of opening your presentation with impact so you grab your audience's attention from the outset are described in Chapter 7. We also advise on how best to conclude your presentation effectively.

Chapter 8 includes innovative and creative ways of bringing facts to life and making them memorable, such as stories, anecdotes, case studies, examples, metaphor and humour.

When should you use a script and when are notes better? And how do you present successfully and remember what you're going to say if you don't use notes? These are just some of the questions we answer in Chapter 9.

Death by PowerPoint – that's something too many presenters inflict on their audience. In Chapter 10 we show you how to get the best from this program, as well as a range of other visual aids.

Chapter 11 is all about rehearsing and timing, part of the preparation process that's often neglected, but which is essential if you're to deliver well.

Many people get nervous when presenting, some have full-blown panic attacks. How do you cope with nerves and develop a feeling of confidence and ease? We reveal all in Chapter 12.

Final preparations can make the difference between success and failure, so in Chapter 13 we give you a checklist of things to think about, including how to work with different room layouts and how to handle logistics.

Chapter 14 is all about getting off to a good start and engaging the audience. How do you build rapport with a group and get them on your side? By using eye contact, smiling and being personable.

What do you do with your hands? And how should you stand and move? Chapter 15 will tell you everything you ever wanted to know about posture, body language and movement but were afraid to ask.

Using your voice well is central to communicating your ideas well, but what exactly does that mean? In Chapter 16 we look at how to sound interesting and engaging by varying your volume, pitch, rhythm, pace and intonation.

Language matters. It's not just the way that you say it, it's what you say as well. Chapter 17 is all about the words we use, and how to make them as concise, clear, credible and compelling as possible.

Any questions? That's what most presenters say when they've finished speaking. But what do you say when you don't know the answer? And how do you get people to ask questions in the first place. Find out in Chapter 18.

Into every life a little rain must fall, but you don't want problems when you're presenting. In Chapter 19 we help you deal with some of the common challenges you're likely to encounter when speaking in public.

In Chapter 20, we look in more detail at how to get the best from a range of presentation situations then in the final chapter we provide a list of resources for those who would like to take things further.

Insight

We've helped thousands of people, at all levels of ability and experience, to improve the way they present and speak in public. Presenting provides you with the perfect opportunity to make a positive impact and raise your profile. Investing time in learning about public speaking will make you more successful.

Ten faults audiences hate most

Now, before you turn the page, and as a way of getting you thinking about presenting, we would like you to reflect for a moment on presentations you've seen. What turns you off? What really drives you crazy? How many of the items on your list match our top ten faults?

1 **No clear purpose** *This may seem obvious, but all too often presenters leave their audience wondering what it was all about.*

2 **Not knowing your audience** *Delivering a presentation that's not appropriate or relevant to the audience leaves them wondering why they wasted their time. There has to be a benefit to them in listening and you need to make this clear.*

3 **Death by PowerPoint** *Many presenters fall into the trap of having too many slides filled with too much information.*

4 **Monotone delivery** *There's nothing worse than a voice that drones on at the same pitch, pace and volume. This fault's guaranteed to send people to sleep.*

5 **Lack of preparation** *If you haven't prepared it shows and they think you can't be bothered to make the effort.*

6 **Lack of structure** *If there's no clear path to follow, or flow of information, your audience will switch off.*

7 **Not connecting with the audience** *Some presenters are so focused on themselves they don't build rapport with the audience.*

8 **Offering weak evidence** *If you don't support your ideas with evidence you'll lose credibility, so do your homework.*

9 **Running over time** *If you go on too long boredom sets in and they stop listening. Prepare something slightly shorter than the time available and make sure you leave time for a proper ending.*

10 **Using jokes inappropriately** *When in doubt leave jokes out. Use humour instead.*

If you avoid these classic errors you're on the road to delivering successful presentations. The chapters to come reveal ways to ensure you don't fall into these traps and set you on the path to becoming not just competent but a great presenter.

Insight

One of the best ways to make sure a presentation doesn't over-run, says Amanda, is to rehearse first. People often miss this step out or think it's enough to go through it in their heads. When you say the words aloud you can time it.

TEN KEY POINTS TO REMEMBER

1 *Presenting is an essential business skill.*

2 *To be successful in your career you need to be good at presenting.*

3 *Everything's a presentation – meetings, networking events and formal speaking opportunities provide a chance to present.*

4 *Meetings are a great place to practise and showcase your presentation skills.*

5 *Presenting gives you the ideal platform to raise your profile and make an impact.*

6 *To communicate effectively you need to be clear, concise, credible and compelling.*

7 *When you present you're selling ideas and seeking to get buy-in.*

8 *The skills of presenting can be used in many areas of your life.*

9 *This book gives you a thorough grounding in the theory and practice of presenting.*

10 *Once you're aware of the ten most common errors that turn an audience off you can avoid them.*

2

Becoming a competent presenter

In this chapter you will learn:
- *what it means to be a competent presenter*
- *what good presenters believe and how that drives their behaviour*
- *how to hone your skills.*

Confidence to competence

Maria avoids making presentations unless she really has to. When her boss asks her to present a summary of the monthly accounts she'll come up with any excuse she can think of to get out of it. She hates being in the spotlight with all eyes on her and would never dream of volunteering to speak in public.

Some people only present under protest. They avoid doing so whenever they can because they get anxious and feel uncomfortable. Fear of speaking in public is probably the most common fear there is, so Maria is far from unusual. But it's a fear that can be overcome, relatively easily, opening the door to becoming a competent and capable presenter. Happily, not everyone is held back by their insecurities.

Henry's scared of presenting but knows it will help him progress in the company. He's willing to have a go in low key situations, such as speaking to the rest of the team, and spends ages trying to get it right. When Henry does present it goes okay, and he breathes a sigh of relief when it's all over. He doesn't believe it's something he might ever come to enjoy. For him it's a necessary evil.

Some people give presenting a go even if it frightens them because they recognize the value they can gain from it. They don't dare believe they'll be any good at speaking in public, let alone great. That's for other people, not them. On our courses people often laugh at the idea that they one day may come to think of presenting as pleasurable. What they don't yet know, or believe, is that it's possible to make this shift.

What gets in the way?

What prevents us from feeling confident and fulfilling our potential? Why does our performance often fall some way short of what we're capable of achieving? Tim Gallwey, in his influential book *The Inner Game of Work*, says the situation can be summed up in one simple equation:

$$p = P - i$$

Our performance (p) always falls short of our potential (P) because of interference (i). This is certainly true of presenting. We all have the potential to be great but things get in the way. Interference often takes the form of conversations taking place inside our head. 'You're not very good at this', we may say to ourselves, or 'This is going to be difficult', with the resulting negative feelings causing us to under perform or achieve only average results. We may use 'fillers' such as 'er' and 'um', talk too fast, or display nervous body language such as shuffling our feet or fiddling with a ring.

The good news is that fear of public speaking can be overcome, whether you've had a bad experience in the past or are simply worried about making mistakes. If you have a serious issue with

confidence and have a presentation coming up we suggest you
read Chapter 12 now.

Starting out with confidence

Lena leaps at the chance of presenting at team meetings.
She sees this as an opportunity to shine and raise her profile.
Although she's only presented a few times, she watches other
people and believes she can do it just as well as them, with
a little practice.

Some people are confident from the outset. They're willing to 'step
up to the plate' and give it a go. When we have high self-esteem
and believe in ourselves it's much easier to imagine a successful
outcome in anything we take on. The more we practise the better
we become, and the less stressful we find the experience.

Good presenters focus on continually improving what they do
because small changes lead to big results. If you only present
occasionally you won't build up much experience or confidence,
so take any opportunity you can to have a go.

The four stages of learning

Some people find speaking in public easy. At the drop of a hat
they can stand up and hold a room spellbound for as long as they
want. Were they born that way? While it might seem as if they
have a natural 'talent', in fact it's something they have learnt to do.
Many of the world's most revered speakers have received lots of
training and coaching. They didn't have the 'wow' factor when
they started out.

Presenting is a skill, like playing a musical instrument or driving
a car. If others can learn to do it, so can you. It's just a matter of
understanding the principles and putting in the practice. You may

never have thought of it, but when we learn something new we go through four distinct stages that take us from incompetence to competence.

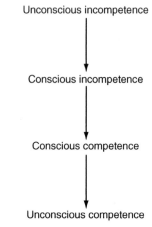

Figure 2.1 The four stages of learning.

1 Unconscious incompetence
In this stage not only do you not know how to do something, you don't even know you don't know. It's often not until a person is asked for the first time to give a presentation they realize they have little or no idea what to do – and that's when they decide to come on one of our courses!

2 Conscious incompetence
It's at this stage you realize you don't know how to do something – you become conscious of your incompetence. It may be one of the reasons you're reading this book. Maybe you gave that presentation and discovered there were lots of gaps in your abilities. Perhaps someone gave you some negative feedback or you simply realized that it didn't go very well. You are becoming increasingly aware of all the things you don't know how to do and want to learn how to do them.

3 Conscious competence

But knowing what you need to do will only take you so far. You can 'know' how to play the piano – it involves moving your fingers up and down the keyboard – but if you don't sit down and practise you won't ever become competent. It's the same with presenting. You start to stand well, gesture more effectively, pause for emphasis and make better eye contact. But it's 'clunky' to begin with. You have to remember to do it consciously, and you sometimes forget. If you've ever learnt to drive a car you'll know that practising new skills during this stage requires plenty of concentration. You can also feel self-conscious when trying out new presentation skills, because what you are doing is in public, and at first it doesn't feel natural.

4 Unconscious competence

We quickly learn new habits. And after a couple of driving lessons we're able to change gear and use the indicator without having to think. We have developed unconscious competence. It's the same with presenting. It doesn't take long before everything becomes second nature, and we automatically implement what we've learnt, becoming a competent presenter in the process.

Insight

One of the challenges when you've achieved unconscious competence is maintaining it, says Amanda. It's all too easy for bad habits to creep back in. The secret of success isn't to become complacent. You need to keep reassessing your presentation skills and seek ways to continually improve.

WHERE ARE YOU ON THE JOURNEY TO COMPETENCE?

Complete the quiz below to assess where you are on your journey to competence. It will help you to get a better understanding of where to focus your attention as you read the rest of this book. Tick or circle the letter that most accurately reflects your current experience of presenting.

1

a I generally feel anxious before presenting and continue to feel nervous when I speak

b I sometimes feel a little nervous when presenting but am able to channel my nervous energy

c I am generally relaxed about the idea of presenting and occasionally experience nerves in certain situations such as big occasions, large or hostile audiences

2

a I have limited or no experience of presenting

b I have some experience of presenting

c I have wide experience of presenting in a variety of situations

3

a I understand the importance of preparation and am not sure of the best method

b I know preparation is important and sometimes prefer to 'wing it'

c I always put time aside to work on and rehearse presentations

4

a I include lots of detail to make sure I don't miss out anything important

b I pick out the key points I want to convey and use specific evidence to support the facts

c I only use information that supports my key messages and put details in supporting documents

5

a I put my presentation together in the order important ideas occur to me

b I structure my presentation in an orderly sequence with one thing following another

c I structure my presentation in a logical way using clear transitions that make it easy for the audience to follow

6

a I use visual aids as a prompt in case I forget what I want to say

b I sometimes use visual aids to act as a reminder of what comes next

c I only use visual aids to help the audience understand a key point using a graph or diagram or where it will make my presentation more engaging. I sometimes choose to present without them

7

a I stick to the facts I need to get across

b I use examples and case studies to bring ideas to life

c I tell stories and anecdotes as well as use case studies to make my presentation engaging

8

a I don't know what a rhetorical technique is

b I've heard of rhetorical techniques but never attempted to use one

c I incorporate rhetorical techniques into my presentation to add impact

9

a I'm not sure how to stand or what to do with my arms

b I know posture is important and use some gestures when I present

c I move and stand well using gestures appropriately to add emphasis

10

a People say my voice is soft, quiet or monotone

b When people comment on my voice they suggest ways to improve it such as projection, pitch or pace

c I'm able to vary the way I use my voice to add emphasis and engage the audience

11
 a I know I use a lot of 'fillers' such as 'um', 'er', 'okay', 'you know', 'kind of', 'actually' or 'basically', when I present
 b I'm aware of using some 'fillers' when I'm not well prepared or talk too fast
 c I use pauses for impact and rarely use 'fillers'

12
 a I'm afraid the audience will catch me out by asking something I can't answer
 b I prepare for questions and know how to manage the question and answer session effectively
 c I take questions in my stride and am able to handle interruptions and challenges easily

Award yourself one point for every **a**, two for every **b** and three for every **c**. Add up your points and then find out where you need to focus attention to develop your skills as a presenter.

If you scored between 12 and 18 you're probably new to presenting or have learnt to present without formal training. It's likely you feel uncomfortable or downright nervous when you present. This book will help you understand how to prepare a presentation effectively and feel confident you can do a good job. We also recommend you sign up for an introductory level training course to get a better understanding of your current skills.

A score of 19 to 24 suggests you've presented a few times and may have received some training in how to present or learnt what to do by watching others. You'll find it worthwhile to look back over your scores and see which areas need most attention. If your body language or voice isn't up to scratch you would benefit from signing up for an advanced level or refresher course or getting some one-to-one coaching from a good presenter. If it's your preparation that lets you down, pay close attention to Chapter 3.

A score of 25 to 30 suggests you're likely to have notched up quite a few presentations and have learnt how to present effectively. To go to the next level you may need to become more accomplished at telling stories, using humour, or incorporating rhetorical techniques. You'll find Chapter 6, Shaping Your Presentation and Chapter 8, Adding 'Flavour' to Generate Interest worthy of special attention. If you plan to get some more training we recommend signing up for a Presentations Masterclass.

If you scored between 30 and 36, frankly we're not sure why you're reading this book as you clearly know a lot about presenting. Maybe like most top presenters you recognize the need to keep your skills sharp and up to date. We think you'll find some useful hints and tips in this book to help you polish your skills, and lots of ideas for improving your presentations still further.

When you're fairly new to presenting

Hannah's been presenting every now and again over the last couple of years. She still thinks of herself as a bit of a novice because she can count on the fingers of one hand the number of presentations she's made in that time. She's just been promoted and knows she'll have to present more often from now on. While she's not as nervous as she once was, she does recognize the need to learn more about presenting if she's going to do a halfway decent job.

To become a competent presenter you need to know what 'good' is like. So, what does it mean to achieve competence? The list below contains the basic skills you need to demonstrate to be a good presenter.

- ▶ **Keep your audience interested and engaged** *Manage people's attention throughout by using examples, case studies and stories to bring ideas to life.*
- ▶ **Come across as confident** *When you present with certainty and conviction you come across with power and presence.*
- ▶ **Make your body language count** *Stand tall and don't sway or shuffle. Use gestures to emphasize points. Move with purpose and motivation.*

- ▶ **Communicate your message in a logical way** *Structure your presentation in a way that's easy for people to follow and simple to remember.*
- ▶ **Use visual aids well** *Use the minimum number of words on slides and where possible include images, graphs and diagrams – and don't talk to the screen!*
- ▶ **Project your voice** *Speak clearly, and with variation in pace, volume, pitch, rhythm and emphasis.*
- ▶ **Connect with the audience** *Make good eye contact, smile, and regard presenting as a dialogue not a monologue.*
- ▶ **Open and close with a bang** *Begin in a way that's attention-grabbing and memorable, and close in the same fashion.*

Insight

Some people who attend our courses get a nice surprise when they see themselves present on video because they're better than they thought they were. Others think they're pretty good until they see and hear themselves and then come up with a long list of things to improve. The key to success is to know what you're aiming for, recognize your strengths and build your skills from there.

A never-ending journey

Each of these topics is expanded upon in the chapters to come. We also look at what goes on behind the scenes – the preparation and planning that often make a competent presentation possible. Even when you reach the stage of being an experienced presenter there are always new heights you can go to. Learning to present is a never-ending journey. The best presenters are always finding ways to make what they do even better. By experimenting and taking a few risks you learn what works and what doesn't. Every time you present you have another opportunity to raise your game.

TEN KEY POINTS TO REMEMBER

1 *It's possible to overcome fear and enjoy presenting.*

2 *Our performance (p) always falls short of our potential (P) because of interference (i).*

3 *We all have the potential to be great and things get in the way such as a voice inside our heads telling us 'This is going to be difficult.'*

4 *Good presenters focus on continually improving what they do.*

5 *Presenting is a skill you can learn by understanding some basic principles and putting them into practice.*

6 *There are four stages that take us from incompetence to competence: unconscious incompetence, conscious incompetence, conscious competence and unconscious competence.*

7 *Unconscious incompetence is where you not only don't know how to do something but also don't even know you don't know.*

8 *When you realize you don't know how to do something you become conscious of your incompetence and can move on to consciously putting new learning into practice.*

9 *It doesn't take long before new learning becomes a habit – unconscious competence.*

10 *To become a good presenter you need to know what good is like.*

3

The importance of preparation

In this chapter you will learn:
- *why preparation is essential for success*
- *when to start your preparation*
- *why it's important to prepare not only the content but also your delivery style*
- *how much time to set aside.*

It is said that when you buy a house the three most important things are location, location and location. Well, it's a similar story when you're putting together a presentation, where the three most important things are Preparation, Preparation and Preparation.

Why? Because when most of us get up and speak in public without sufficient planning we end up rambling, repeating ourselves, and getting the timing wrong. We miss out important things. Our key messages get lost. We fail to engage the audience. This means our confidence dips even lower and we may not be asked to present again.

If you want to communicate effectively you must set aside time to plan your content and delivery. While preparation takes thought and effort, it pays off. Think of the time spent as a solid investment that will produce great dividends. When it comes to presentations you reap what you sow. If you don't bother, or skimp on it, you will suffer. You'll suffer from increased anxiety, muddled messages and a poor reputation. Lack of preparation has been known to damage people's career prospects. 'To fail to prepare', as the well-known expression goes, really is 'to prepare to fail'.

*Simon is frantically busy. He's juggling ten things at once.
When his boss asks him to deliver a high-profile client
presentation on his behalf, half of him is pleased that his
boss trusts him to do it while the other half thinks, 'How
can I pull this off and keep everything else under control
too?' He's promised to take the kids to the seaside this
weekend and already has plans to work late to make sure
he meets the deadlines on two major projects. He grabs a
set of slides that might provide a good starting point and
juggles the order around, making notes for a couple of extra
points that will make it sound sexier. He's got away with
this approach before when he's been short of time. After half
an hour of working through it Simon makes a promise to
himself that he'll mentally run through it a few times before
the day and then turns his attention to the emails that have
come streaming in and crying out for his attention. Each
time Simon delivers a presentation he feels disappointed
that it didn't go as well as he had hoped. 'If only,' he thinks,
'there had been more time to polish it.'*

Most people who deliver business presentations have numerous
competing demands that can get in the way of achieving a good result.
It may seem easier to take something you have already and throw in
one or two extra ideas but the outcome is never as effective as it could
be with more thought. Even when you're busy it makes sense not to
cut corners and instead find a way to prioritize your preparation.

*Sarah looks and feels confident when speaking in public,
whether it's to a single person, to a small group or meeting,
or standing in front of 600 at a conference. She has the 'gift
of the gab'. Words just seem to tumble effortlessly out of her
mouth and she can sometimes get so carried away she has to
slow down so others can catch what she is saying. However,
because Sarah has a talent for talking, and finds it easy to
'think on her feet', she tends to rely on natural ability. More
often than not she does the minimum amount of preparation –
maybe just scribbling some notes on a pad and throwing*

together a handful of slides at the last minute – and then 'wings' it. She knows that on the day she will be able to do enough to get away with it. Sometimes, when the situation or the outcome is particularly important, Sarah will put in a bit more effort, but it's the exception rather than the rule.

Many of those who make public speaking look easy actually work very hard on their presentations, researching, planning and structuring the material so it appears effortless and natural on the day. They recognize, and have experienced, the rewards that come when they prepare well.

There are many benefits to be gained from preparing effectively, both for you and for your audience. For a start you'll feel confident. The better prepared you are the more confident you feel. You'll know what you're talking about, you will anticipate which slide is coming next, and be able to take the whole thing in your stride. Because you have taken time to research your audience you will know precisely how to pitch your message to get the best response. Thorough preparation is good for your reputation and your career. First-rate speakers are always in demand and more successful at whatever they do.

The audience wins too. Here are five reasons why:

1 **You make it audience-centred** *Part of preparing effectively is thinking about what matters to them and delivering a message they can relate to.*
2 **You care about the quality of your communication** *People can tell when you've skimped on preparation by the poor quality of your communication. They assume you're either incompetent or can't be bothered.*
3 **You deliver a clear message** *They need a clear structure to follow and want to leave with an explicit understanding of the points you made.*
4 **You stick to the topic** *Without preparation you're more likely to go off at a tangent and confuse your audience.*
5 **You create a win–win result** *The audience gets what they want and you have them on side and willing to respond to your call to action.*

> Like most people, writes Steve, I learnt how crucial preparation
> is the hard way. Back when I worked in a FTSE-100 media
> company I had to give an important presentation to persuade
> the divisional board to back the relaunch of a magazine I was
> publishing. I'd spent weeks doing the numbers, and months
> working on the creatives, so I felt totally on top of the topic.
> As a result I didn't prepare as well as I should have. I figured
> I could wing it. I was wrong. The divisional board, like many
> executive teams, was challenging and demanding. My lack
> of structure and organization led them to lack trust in the
> relaunch, and I didn't get the backing I wanted.

What else do you need to prepare?

Preparing effectively isn't just about structure, content, and
wondering what questions the audience might ask you. It's also
about how you deliver your presentation and bring it to life.
In Chapter 8 you will discover lots of ways to make facts and
data interesting. Chapter 17 includes ideas for using language
to make your presentations engaging and memorable.

The best speakers go one step farther and plan the way they will use
their body language and voice to enhance their presentation. Their
audience may assume they're naturally gifted communicators, when,
just like top entertainers, such as Madonna and Kylie Minogue
and Robbie Williams, a lot of work goes into a seemingly effortless
world-class performance.

Plan how you want your audience to feel. This may seem an odd
thing to suggest and yet, when you present, you're like a film
director who takes people on an emotional journey that taps into
all of their senses. Plan how you will connect with them, keep their
attention, arouse interest, emphasize points, convey your point
without incurring their wrath, make them laugh or at least smile.
Know how you will change them in some way, get them to take
action or adopt a different attitude as a result of listening to you.

Getting started

How soon after you know you have to give a presentation should you get started? Why delay? The sooner you start the more time you have to research, organize, structure, add anecdotes, stories or quotes and plan your overall delivery.

It's a good idea to get started as soon as possible, for four reasons:

1 **You may need to gather some information, data or images** *If you leave it to the last minute you may not have sufficient time to pull it all together. If it's a bigger occasion you may want to commission someone to create a short video or illustration to support your message. This option isn't open to you if you wait.*

2 **You won't do your best if you do it all in one go** *You need to allow time for thoughts to settle and the dough to rise. If you start by jotting down some initial thoughts and then come back to it adding notes as ideas occur to you, you'll end up with a much richer final result.*

3 **Putting it off makes it harder to get inspiration** *When you first hear about the presentation, more often than not you get some form of briefing. If you make a start while all of that is fresh in your mind the ideas tend to come quickly and easily. If not, you may struggle to recall key points.*

4 **Other things come along and demand attention** *The closer you get to the deadline the more likely it is that unexpected tasks will land on your desk. The precious time you set aside is swiftly eaten up leaving your important preparation time squeezed into a tiny slot. This means you only end up doing the bare minimum.*

'I WORK BEST UNDER PRESSURE'

Some people, though, prefer to leave things to the last minute, and that includes presentations. 'I work best under pressure,' they say, 'I need an imminent deadline to get me focused.' That may or may not be true – sometimes there's an element of procrastination in this approach – but the result is that you create unnecessary stress for you and any other people who you have roped in to bale you out of a tight spot. With time to reflect on your first draft and then refine and improve it you will inevitably end up with a better presentation. When time is tight, as Simon's story illustrated earlier in this chapter, we tend to start with the slides. This doesn't produce the best possible result. Time is a scarce and valuable resource and needs to be used wisely because presentations place you in the spotlight and can be career or deal makers and breakers.

How long?

How much time should you spend preparing? That obviously depends on a number of factors, including how much you know about the subject already, the length of the presentation and your previous experience in creating presentations. You need to spend just the right amount of time. As a rule of thumb, some people say, ten minutes for every minute of your presentation when you know the subject well, and up to twice that if you don't. We believe it's not quite as simple as that because it depends on the complexity of the subject. You may need to spend many hours researching, gathering data and simplifying the concepts to deliver a good presentation on a complicated topic if you have an inexperienced audience who need to understand it. Another factor that affects the time you spend preparing your presentation rests on how important it is for you to succeed. If your reputation depends upon it, or there's a large piece of business that you will win if you do a good job, you're likely to burn the midnight oil to achieve the best result you can.

You need to be realistic about how long it might take. Many people are far too optimistic about what's involved. They underestimate, start too late, and then end up rushing, leaving some aspects inadequate. It's not unusual to see presentations in which the beginning is polished and prepared, then after a few minutes it deteriorates into an unstructured out-pouring of disparate ideas or a dull monologue with nothing to excite or interest the listener.

The dangers of over-preparing

There are, though, dangers in over-preparing, of trying to make sure absolutely everything is right. You can devote unnecessary time to going over and over your material. It's all too easy to start agonizing over every little detail. The truth is that your audience won't recall every word you say anyway. Another downside of over-preparing is that for many people it heightens their anxiety level.

The bottom line, whichever way you look at it, is preparation leads to success. If you leave it to chance you're more likely to feel stressed and deliver, at best, an average presentation.

Insight

The first time I had to give an important business presentation, writes Steve, I totally over-prepared. I was so concerned about forgetting what I planned to say I wrote a script and then memorized it word for word. I figured that preparing in detail would make me feel more comfortable and confident. Not so. In fact it had the opposite effect. I was so worried about forgetting my lines I ended up giving a wooden and uninspiring 'performance'. Ever since then I've prepared carefully – but never too much.

TEN KEY POINTS TO REMEMBER

1 *The three most important things in putting together a presentation are preparation, preparation and preparation.*

2 *It may seem easier to take slides you have already and throw in a few extra ideas but the outcome is never as effective as it could be with a little more thought.*

3 *Those people who make presenting look easy work hard on researching, planning and structuring their material.*

4 *The better prepared you are the more confident you'll feel.*

5 *There are five reasons why the audience wins when you present well: you make it audience-centred, you care about the quality of your communication, you deliver a clear message, you stick to the topic and you create a win–win result.*

6 *Preparation includes other things apart from structure, such as how you'll bring it to life, how you'll use your body language and voice, and how you want your audience to feel.*

7 *It's a good idea to get started as soon as possible because:*
   ▷ *you may need to gather some information*
   ▷ *you won't do your best if you do it all in one go*
   ▷ *putting it off makes it harder to get inspiration*
   ▷ *other things come along and demand attention.*

8 *As a rule of thumb you need to allow ten minutes' preparation time for every minute of your presentation when you know your subject well, and up to twice that if you don't.*

9 *If you start preparing late you may end up with a great start with the rest of your presentation gradually deteriorating.*

10 *Preparation leads to success and leaving it to chance leads to, at best, an average presentation.*

4

What's your outcome?

In this chapter you will learn:
- *why clarity of outcome is vital to success*
- *about the value of having measures of success*
- *why good presenting motivates people to change.*

> **The audience only pays attention as long as you know where you are going.**
>
> Philip Crosby

Clarity of outcome is vital to success

Have you ever sat through a presentation and wondered at the end what it was all about? If your answer is 'yes', you're not alone. When we ask that question on presentation skills courses almost everyone raises their hand. This suggests that speakers are often not clear about their outcome in giving the presentation – and if they're not clear, the audience won't be clear either.

As Stephen Covey says in *The Seven Habits of Highly Effective People*, you have to start with the end in mind. How will your audience – whether it's one person, ten or 100 – be different at the end of your presentation? What do you want them to know or think or do or believe or feel as a result of listening to you? Here are some of the things you may be seeking to achieve:

▶ **Informing/updating** *The aim of many business presentations is first and foremost to impart knowledge and information. Typical situations include describing what's happened over the last month/quarter/year, introducing a new product/ service/ procedure or outlining a change in departmental/ company direction.*

▶ **Training or educating** *The focus of some presentations is to help people develop their skills or understanding. They may learn how an IT system works or ways of developing their leadership skills.*

▶ **Explaining** *At times you'll find yourself giving reasons, explaining, perhaps even defending or justifying yourself. You might be asked to go to a regional or board meeting to account for why a target hasn't been met, challenged by a customer to say why you want to raise your prices, or required to give the rationale for launching a new product or service.*

▶ **Building a relationship** *Meetings and presentations are often as much about people getting to know each other and building a relationship as achieving something specific, so don't ignore the interpersonal side.*

▶ **Selling** *In some ways, every presentation is about selling. Sometimes you'll be selling a product or service. Sometimes it will be an idea or vision to which you're seeking commitment and buy-in. And sometimes you're selling yourself or your company.*

▶ **Exploring/debating** *The purpose here is to look at the pros and cons of a situation, invite comment, gain feedback or promote discussion about a problem.*

▶ **Challenging** *Sometimes you'll want to challenge the status quo or accepted wisdom and suggest a better way of doing things. Presentations are often designed to provoke discussion or get others to consider an alternative point of view.*

- ▶ **Influence, persuade or convince** *Many presentations are designed to win support or change people's opinions and, in some cases, attitudes. If you're to get your recommendations approved part of your purpose will be to convince others.*
- ▶ **Stimulating** *The aim of your presentation may simply be to arouse curiosity and provoke thought on a particular topic.*
- ▶ **Raising your profile** *Giving presentations can also be an effective way of raising your profile and becoming better known, both inside a company and within an industry.*
- ▶ **Inspiring and motivating** *As a leader, a manager or even a member of a team you may sometimes want to inspire or motivate. Everyone might have been through a tough, busy period, or there may be challenges ahead, and a 'thanks guys' or 'we can do it' pep talk is often what's called for.*
- ▶ **Entertaining** *Some presentations are delivered purely to entertain. This is essential for a motivational speech or an after-dinner session, but can also sweeten most other kinds of presentation.*

Insight

The problem with many of the presentations I see, writes Steve, is that the emphasis is on giving information rather than trying to influence. They lack impact, don't engage and fail to persuade and convince. The shift from information to influence is a crucial one.

A collection of outcomes

It's rare for a presentation to have just one outcome. Most of the time you'll be aiming to achieve several of the things listed above. When pitching for business, for instance, you'll often be informing, explaining, influencing and building the relationship as well as selling. When educating or training it's not enough to download facts, data, figures, details – that quickly gets boring – you also need to engage and interest people. When your aim is to persuade you'll find that people are more receptive to your message if you entertain them as well. Making a presentation fun, interesting and engaging is a great way to win over an audience.

Presenting is about change

The bottom line when presenting is to get people to change in some way. It could be their behaviour (filling in an expense claim properly) or the beliefs that drive that behaviour ('it's really important that finance is accurate'). Often it's both.

Articulate as specifically as possible how you want your audience to be different as a result of your presentation. Create a movie in your mind of what you will see and hear and feel. Some examples:

▶ *The person I am presenting to will smile, shake my hands and place an order for 100 widgets.*
▶ *My team will deal with complaints with greater empathy, listening carefully to what customers say and find ways of putting things right as quickly as possible.*
▶ *The board will grant unanimous approval to my proposal and give me the budget I need.*

The clearer you understand your outcomes, the better able you will be to create presentations that achieve them.

TEN KEY POINTS TO REMEMBER

1 *When a speaker's unclear about their outcome, the audience won't be clear either.*

2 *It's important to know what you want your audience to know, think, do, believe or feel.*

3 *Your outcome may be to inform, update, train/educate or explain something.*

4 *Outcomes aren't always about tasks. They can be about building relationships too.*

5 *Most outcomes include an element of selling, influencing, persuading or convincing.*

6 *Some outcomes are focused on exploring or challenging ideas or simply stimulating thought.*

7 *Other outcomes include inspiring, motivating, entertaining and raising your profile.*

8 *Presentations nearly always have more than one outcome.*

9 *Presenting is about getting people to change in some way.*

10 *The clearer you are about the outcomes you want, the better equipped you'll be to create presentations that achieve them.*

5

Understanding your audience

In this chapter you will learn:
- *why understanding your audience is vital to success*
- *how to research people who will attend your speech*
- *about Perceptual Positions*
- *how understanding behavioural styles allows you to analyse your audience and adapt your approach.*

Audience-centred presentations

Anna walks into the meeting room and takes up her position at the head of the table. Several of the senior management team look expectantly in her direction. The remainder settle into their chairs and send final BlackBerry messages. Anna feels her nerves jangle when she sees the company's Finance Director at the far end – she didn't know he would be there. Silence falls on the room. As the projector throws the first of her slides up on the screen, Anna begins her carefully prepared speech. Just six minutes into the proposal she's interrupted by Pat, the chairman: 'I think we know most of the background,' he says impatiently. 'Could you just give us your recommendations? We've a lot to get through today.' As she flicks through to her final slides, Anna gets a sinking feeling, realizing she's been patronizing the team by telling them things they already know. Five minutes later she's finished and is taking questions. The first is from the

*Finance Director: 'Where's the spreadsheet that backs this up?'
Not realizing he would be there, Anna hasn't included it.
On that basis, the management team can't support the
proposal, and it gets the thumbs-down. Reflecting afterwards,
Anna is only too aware of her mistake. 'If only I'd done my
homework,' she muses, 'and found out who was going to be
at the meeting – and what they knew already – I could be
home and dry now.'*

*Aftab spent several days thinking carefully about who would
be at the meeting, their current level of knowledge, and what
they would need to know to support his proposal. Then he
tailored his presentation to meet their individual needs.
Once everyone was settled he began with a story that clearly
illustrated how launching the new FX-2000 would benefit
them personally as well as the company as a whole. He went
out of his way to invite questions and address their concerns.
His passion for the product, backed up by research data and
detailed spreadsheets, started to pay dividends. Aftab realized
he was on to a winner when he saw even the biggest skeptic
in the company start to smile.*

The best presentations are audience-centred. This means the
message, and the way it's delivered, takes account of their
wants, needs, interests and concerns. When you're preparing a
presentation this should be the compass that guides you in planning
your material. Many presenters focus primarily on what they have
to say and the outcome they want. They pay scant attention to
their audience. But in his excellent book Working the Room, Nick
Morgan makes it clear that successful presenters think more about
their audience than anything else. This starts at the research stage
and continues throughout. He says, 'There is something essential
about the intellectual, emotional and physical connections a good
speaker can make with an audience.'

Insight

As I, Steve, reflect back on presentations I've given that have
gone well, and those that haven't, I would say what made

the difference much of the time was my ability to make my
message relevant to the audience.

Understanding your audience

To communicate with the people in your audience on every level
you need to know as much about them as you can, and consider
their expectations and attitudes. You want to engage them at
every stage, and have them engrossed in what you have to say,
which means you need to understand what matters to them. When
you know the people who will attend personally, that's relatively
easy. When you don't you'll need to do some research, perhaps
by asking someone who does, or by talking to the person who
asked you to speak. The more information you have about your
audience, the better prepared you'll be on the day. And the better
prepared you are, the more likely it is you'll get your message
across. This chapter explains in detail the areas you need to cover
to fully understand your audience.

Exercise

Think about a presentation you gave recently. What
assumptions did you make? To what degree did you
consider your audience?

Our experience of delivering presentation skills courses shows that
most people don't give much thought to things such as age, gender,
existing knowledge, cultural mix and attitude. Sometimes they do
consider their audience, but rather superficially, and by now you'll
have realized this isn't enough. One size doesn't fit all when it
comes to presenting. We've distilled our collective experience and
come up with four core questions you need to answer in order to
create an audience-centred presentation.

1 *Who are they?*
2 *What are their expectations?*
3 *What do they know/understand already?*
4 *What's their attitude?*

1 WHO ARE THEY?

First and foremost you need to find out how many people are due to attend. It's totally different creating a presentation for two, 20, 200 or even 2000. The more you discover about the demographics of the group, the more you'll be able to tailor your approach to meet their specific needs. Things to consider include:

▶ **Age range** *Why is age range important? Because you need illustrations and stories that connect to the world in which the people in your audience live. If on average they're older you could refer to events in the era during which they grew up. When your audience is mostly young, or you have a wide-ranging group, draw more on what's going on right now, such as current affairs or the latest cult TV programme.*
▶ **Gender mix** *The balance of males and females in a group can sometimes affect the approach you take. We don't want to stereotype here, but an all-male group may not respond well to a metaphor on dressmaking, while an all-female audience may not be inspired by a rugby story.*
▶ **Education** *If you're presenting to people who left school at 16 your approach will be different from a group with a degree. You need to pitch your message at the right level, and the more education someone has received the better able they will be at coping with complex sentence construction and abstract concepts.*
▶ **Occupation** *Sometimes you need to take account of the occupation of people attending your presentation. Accountants and PR consultants are likely to find different types of topics and styles of delivery appealing.*
▶ **Nationality** *Many companies operate on an international basis. This means you may find yourself presenting to people who don't have English as a first language. Researching*

*your audience means you're prepared and can avoid using
colloquial expressions, unusual words and jargon which
may be difficult for them to understand. You may sometimes
find yourself presenting through an interpreter and it's
vital to know this in advance so you can allow time for
the translation.*

▶ **Cultural/social/political background** *Many things influence
people's view of the world – their culture, social group, etc.
The experiences we have in life shape us and affect the way
we respond. Politics and religion in particular are issues that
need to be handled carefully in presentations as people have
deeply held views.*

▶ **Influencers and decision-makers** *When you're pitching or
selling it's essential to know who will be making the decision.
Sometimes it's more than one person. You also need to
be aware of who will influence the decision and present
effectively to them as well.*

A word of caution. Although this information helps you shape
your content and the approach you take, it's all too easy to
pigeonhole people. Take care not to make assumptions that simply
don't fit. The bottom line is that everyone in your audience is an
individual. Never forget that.

2 WHAT ARE THEIR EXPECTATIONS?

When people arrive for a presentation they bring with them
various expectations about what's going to happen. How clear
and accurate those expectations are will depend upon a number
of factors.

If it's a regular event, such as a weekly meeting or a monthly
briefing, there's often a standard format and those attending will
know exactly how things will go. It could be something like this:

On the first Friday of each month the whole company turns out at
4 p.m. to get a state-of-the-nation from the MD about how things
are going, followed by questions from the floor. The assembled

multitude expect the presentation to last around 40 minutes, be mind-numbingly boring, and illustrated with a barrage of PowerPoint slides showing the current trading position. Half a dozen people will then ask questions, get bland, defensive answers, and everyone will be streaming out the doors by 5 p.m.

But when the presentation is a one-off, or doesn't come round like clockwork, people may not have clear and accurate expectations.

Picture the scene: Sophie calls her team together with the intention of telling them they need to raise their game and start selling more. They turn up believing things are going just fine, expecting to get a pat on the back for doing a good job in a tough market. What happens when they suddenly realize it's a pep talk? Number One: it's one hell of a shock. Number Two: it's demotivating in the extreme.

Another common area where audience expectations are often dashed is over time. They arrive at 2 p.m. expecting the session to last 20 minutes and are still sitting there at three. People start to look at their watches and sit on the edge of their seats wanting to get back to their inbox or off to their next meeting.

That's why it's important to consider your audience's expectations carefully. Having a mismatch between what they think is going to happen and what actually does can be a recipe for disaster. Anticipating your audience's expectations allows you to meet them. If there's a gulf between what you're planning and what they perceive to be on the agenda, you need to manage their expectations ahead of time.

Whenever you can, let people know what you plan to cover, how long it will take, what your approach will be, and so on. If you're not responsible for organizing the presentation, find out as much as possible about what your audience has been told and what their expectations are.

Should you ever get to the stage where people are parting with their hard-earned cash to hear you speak – maybe you start running workshops and seminars – they'll expect a lot more than when they're getting it free. What's crucial is that you deliver what was promised. And that's true of every presentation you give.

3 WHAT DO THEY KNOW/UNDERSTAND ALREADY?

If you've ever sat bewildered through slide after slide crammed with technical information and unfamiliar jargon you'll realize how important it is to take account of what your audience knows, and doesn't know, already. When you're an expert in a subject it's all too easy to fall into this trap. You forget that other people don't have your level of understanding and find yourself facing rows of blank faces.

On the other hand, you don't want to patronize them. If they already know what you're telling them it won't be long before they either get restless, go to sleep or walk out.

So always take stock of what your audience understands about the topic and adapt your approach accordingly.

David has two presentations to make about his plans to use the intranet for online customer service training. One is to the IT Department, and since they're fully conversant with the intranet and how it works, David uses technical language he knows they will understand. The other presentation is to the board of directors, who have only a superficial understanding of the intranet's technology, so he keeps the jargon to a minimum and talks more in terms of the benefits to the business.

Virginie has more of a challenge. She has to present her marketing plan to everyone in the company at the annual conference. But some members of staff are seeing it for the first time, and know little or nothing about marketing, while others have played a significant part in providing analysis and figures. Knowing that, Virginie starts with the basics and then moves forward step-by-step to more complex issues and concepts, taking the audience with her.

4 WHAT'S THEIR ATTITUDE?

One of the most important issues to consider in relation to your audience is their attitude. If you misjudge it you can soon find yourself coming unstuck. You need to think about how keen they are to be there, what kind of mood they might be in, how they'll feel about your message and what their reaction might be to you as a person.

Do they want to be there?

Not everyone who attends a presentation is delighted to be there. Some may even be press-ganged into it, perhaps by their boss.

> *Helen tries every excuse she can think of to get out of going to the quarterly update. She thinks, 'It's such a waste of time. I've got more important things to do.' Matt wants to get out of it too. He's struggling to hit his monthly sales target and needs every minute to catch up. But they both know if they don't attend it will count against them.*

> *Others are looking forward to the quarterly update. Dan sees it as a chance to get a break from the same old routine. Jackie wants to network with senior people in the company. And Kylie's keen to find out how things are going.*

It's easy to present to people who want to be there. They're attentive, interested and engaged. But those who would rather be somewhere else can be resistant. Winning them over is essential if you're to get your message across. When you know, or suspect, that some people in your audience are not there entirely of their own free will, acknowledge that fact. Say, 'I'm sure you would be rather be doing something else ...' and then either find a way to get them engaged or keep the presentation as brief as possible.

What's their mood?

Even when people do want to attend, you can never be sure what kind of mood they'll be in. It depends on a host of factors, even down to what kind of day they've had.

Suppose you make a presentation to a sales team an hour after their annual bonus has been announced, and it's a record. Are you likely to receive a positive reception? What if they'd just been told that 25 per cent of them are to be made redundant in the next month? Do you think the response might be different?

Ever had to give a presentation at 4 p.m. when you're the tenth speaker of the day and the audience's energy is flagging? Then you'll know how much of a challenge it can be to combat the audience's mood.

Most of the time, though, you'll have a mix of emotions, with some people 'up' and others 'down', and the mark of a good presenter is being able to get everyone absorbed and interested in what they're saying.

Attitude to the message

Sometimes it's not so much their mood as your message. They may be doubtful about the content of your presentation, even hostile. They may come with preconceived ideas and openly disagree with you, especially if your views are at odds with theirs or you come bearing bad news.

Some people adopt an attitude to match their role. Buyers, for instance, are often skeptical when faced with a sales person making a pitch. Some attitudes can become institutionalized, such as the negative stance some union leaders take to whatever management says.

Knowing that your audience might not agree with some aspect of your speech means you can prepare persuasive arguments in advance. We once gave a presentation on the subject of charisma, founded on the principle that it's a skill that can be learnt rather than something you're born with. Some people in the audience disagreed, as we knew they would, so we had plenty of research to support our argument.

....
Insight

Sometimes it may be possible, says Amanda, to speak to people beforehand to run your recommendations or

(Contd)

proposals past them. This gives you a much better idea of their concerns which means you can adapt your approach. You may even find you create advocates and allies who will support you on the day.

Attitude to you

Something else to consider is what the audience thinks about you. Sometimes they'll know you of course – they may be your colleagues, bosses or team members. If they like and respect you, chances are you'll get a positive reception and a fair hearing, even if they disagree with you. If they don't like you or don't respect you, you'll probably have more of a hill to climb, and you'll need to present your ideas persuasively.

Even when your audience doesn't know you personally they may have preconceived ideas based on what they've heard about you or your organization. So much depends on your status, reputation and credentials. If you're an acknowledged expert in the topic you're presenting, then it's a good idea to make sure the audience is aware of the fact.

The Social Styles model

Another valuable way of thinking about your audience is in terms of the Social Styles concept developed by psychologists David Merrill and Roger Reid. Based, liked many similar models, on the work of Carl Jung, Social Styles assesses two crucial dimensions of behaviour – Assertiveness and Responsiveness. It categorizes people into four distinct types, called Drivers, Amiables, Expressives and Analyticals (see Figure 5.1).

It's useful to be aware of the different needs and preferences of your audience. By analysing the people you want to communicate with you can adapt your material accordingly.

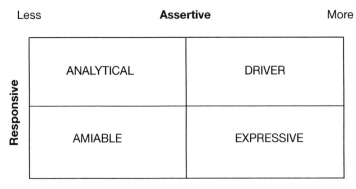

Figure 5.1 The Social Styles grid.

With small groups you can refine what you do to suit their specific
needs. For larger groups you can make sure you include things
that will satisfy people with all four styles. Presenters who are not
aware of these differences tend to deliver every presentation in a
way that matches their own style. By doing this they risk alienating
some of the audience.

Table 5.1 The assertiveness dimension

People who are Less Assertive tend to:	People who are More Assertive tend to:
speak more slowly and more softly	speak more quickly and more intensely
be more tentative in expressing opinions	be emphatic when expressing opinions
find eye contact difficult	make consistent eye contact
move slowly and deliberately	move more rapidly and energetically
avoid confrontation	be comfortable with confrontation
ask rather than tell	tell rather than ask
let others take the initiative	take the initiative

Table 5.2 The responsiveness dimension

People who are Less Responsive tend to:	People who are More Responsive tend to:
limit their use of gestures	gesture more strongly and frequently
show less facial expression	have more facial expression
come across as serious	come across as playful
focus more on facts	focus more on feelings
appear more reserved	appear more friendly
move more rigidly	move more freely
speak in a monotone	have more vocal inflection

DRIVERS

Assertive, sometimes to the point of being aggressive, Drivers are action- and results-oriented individuals who typically prioritize getting things done over building relationships. They waste as little time as possible on personal conversations, have a short attention span, and want you to get to the point without too much waffle.

AMIABLES

Combining a high level of emotional responsiveness with lower than average assertiveness, Amiables tend to be sensitive, supportive and sympathetic. They are good team players who like to get along with others. They dislike conflict and confrontation, and can sometimes be resistant to change and averse to risk.

EXPRESSIVES

Because Expressives are both emotionally responsive and assertive, they come across as confident, optimistic and extrovert. They focus on the bigger picture, rather than on details. Expressives are willing to take risks in order to seize opportunities. They tend to make decisions quickly, sometimes impulsively, without always having the necessary data.

Table 5.3 The four Social Styles at a glance

Driver	Amiable	Expressive	Analytical
decisive	patient	enthusiastic	controlled
independent	supportive	outgoing	orderly
practical	respectful	impulsive	precise
tough	mature	charming	deliberate
direct	stable	generous	cautious
competitive	trusting	dramatic	logical
determined	dependable	persuasive	analytical
assertive	willing	animated	systematic
results-oriented	persevering	optimistic	diplomatic
efficient	team person	fun-loving	serious
risk-taker	loyal	confident	prudent

ANALYTICALS

Exhibiting a low level of both assertiveness and responsiveness, Analyticals take a precise, deliberate and systematic approach to everything they do. Structure, clarity and order are important to them. They favour analysis over emotion, and require facts, data and figures to feel comfortable in coming to a decision.

Presenting successfully to the four different styles

In an ideal world you would tailor your presentation to the preferences of each style, as shown in the table on page 46.

You'll come across some groups with a collective preference for one style, according to profession or specialization. Many of those working in accountancy, engineering and IT, for example, are Analyticals, where their talents are extremely valuable. Many of those who are successful in 'people' roles are Expressives or Amiables. Expressives can often be found in sales, PR and acting. Amiables tend to gravitate to human resources, customer

Drivers	Amiables	Expressives	Analyticals
Give the big picture and get to the point. Focus on the task. Talk about goals and results. Don't go on longer than necessary	Stress the people side, have a clear structure, introduce new ideas one step at a time. Make sure they believe in you	Keep it lively, make it fun, be upbeat and positive. Don't give too much detail. Focus on the people side of things	Give lots of detail – facts and figures. Be measured and precise. Use a logical structure. Provide graphs and charts, etc

relationship management and social work. The drive and determination of Drivers means that many eventually fight their way to the top, or end up working for themselves.

When you have an audience you can identify as being of one style, you can easily adapt your approach accordingly. More often than not, though, you will have a mix of styles in the audience, in which case you'll need to balance it to meet all needs. This means you will need to take account of the task and the effect on people, describe the big picture and give enough detail to satisfy the Analyticals, and so on.

Insight

I, Amanda, presented to a small group of people in a pitch for new business. My audience included a Driver (the most senior person there), an Analytical and an Expressive. Because I'd done my homework beforehand I was able to adapt the content to appeal to all three styles and win the business.

See things from your audience's point of view

By now you'll realize that people are diverse, and to connect with an audience you need to adapt your approach. If you want to go a little deeper we recommend you use the Neuro-Linguistic Programming (NLP) 'meta mirror' technique. This allows you to put yourself mentally in someone else's shoes, moving from one 'perceptual position' to another so you understand your audience's perspective more fully.

There are three perceptual positions: first, second and third position.

▶ *First position involves seeing things through your own eyes, hearing through your own ears and being aware of the feelings in your body.*

▶ *Second or 'Other' position involves taking on someone else's perspective by imagining being them. This can work effectively even if you've never met them. The aim is to increase your awareness of how they might experience you and your presentation. You may, for instance, discover that if you step into the skin of someone right at the back of the room you seem a long way away, which reduces the impact of your message.*

▶ *Third or 'Observer' position provides a detached 'fly on the wall' viewpoint, looking down on both the presenter and audience. From there you can gain valuable insights into the dynamic between you and the group. You may, for example, realize the use of PowerPoint is hindering rather than aiding you in getting your point across.*

Some experienced presenters use this cycle several times, even sitting in audience chairs to get a feel for how they will come across. Each time they move from first to second to third and then back to first they adapt their approach until they are entirely satisfied that their planned approach will work effectively.

Insight

Being able to understand the psychology of your audience – what's important to them, what motivates them – enables you to create powerful presentations that get buy-in and bring about action.

1 *Think about a presentation you have coming up. Imagine the day has arrived and you're about to start. In your mind's eye run through the first part of your presentation. What do you see? What do you hear? How does your voice sound to you? How does your audience react? How do you feel?*

2 *Select one of the people in the audience. Imagine you're them watching 'you' standing up front ready to speak. Through this person's eyes what do you see? What do you hear as the presenter opens the session? How does it feel?*

3 *Take a detached position, as if you're a 'fly on the wall' looking down on both 'you' the presenter and the audience. What do you notice? Take stock of your experience in both second and third position. What changes do you advise the other you to make?*

4 *Imagine you're the presenter again, but this time implementing those changes. Notice how this time the outcome is slightly different. Cycle round as many times as you like, moving from one position to another until you're entirely satisfied.*

Keep researching to the last minute

There's one further stage to knowing your audience and this happens on the day itself, or sometimes the evening before. There's nothing quite like meeting the people who will actually be hearing you speak as a final check that you've pitched your presentation right. When we present at conferences we always get to the venue as early as possible, giving us plenty of time to mingle and chat with guests. If we discover that some of the impressions we had about our audience were mistaken, we quickly adapt our approach accordingly. Another advantage of doing this is that you can then weave in relevant anecdotes and mention specific people by name. When making presentations in-company, however, this is not always possible. People often arrive at the last minute, and there's little opportunity to have much of a discussion. Shaking a few hands, though, and exchanging a few words will give you a feel for the mood and make-up of your audience.

Understanding your audience is crucial

By now you will know why the best presentations are audience-centred and how important the research stage is when planning your content and approach. It's vital that you know as much about those you're speaking to as possible, from who they are to what they expect.

TEN KEY POINTS TO REMEMBER

1 *The best presentations are audience-centred. The message and the way it's delivered take account of their wants, needs, interests and concerns.*

2 *You need to know as much about your audience as you can and consider their expectations and attitudes.*

3 *Find out how many people there will be and who they are. How old are they? What's the gender mix? What's their educational background, occupation and nationality? Are they influencers, decision makers or a mix of both?*

4 *Anticipating your audience's expectations allows you to meet them or manage them ahead of time.*

5 *Take stock of what your audience knows already about the topic and adapt your approach accordingly.*

6 *It's important to consider your audience's mood, their attitude to attending and to your message.*

7 *Assess the different needs and preferences of your audience using the Social Styles model.*

8 *When you can identify an audience is made up of primarily one behavioural style you can adapt your approach accordingly.*

9 *Use NLP's 'meta mirror' technique to help you consider your audience's viewpoint.*

10 *Keep researching until the last minute by checking your audience's mood on the day up until the moment you present.*

6

Shaping your presentation

In this chapter you will learn:
- *about creating a clear structure*
- *how to gather information and decide what's important*
- *how to order your material*
- *how to identify key messages and create a central theme*
- *why managing the audience's attention span is vital to success*
- *how to maximize the value of the Primacy and Recency Effect*
- *to use the Firework Display approach.*

Why is it important to make your presentation easy to follow?

One of the things that most frustrates people listening to presentations is when the content is muddled, unfocused and hard to follow. And, sadly, many presentations are like that, either because they've been thrown together at the last minute without sufficient thought, or because the presenter wasn't clear what they wanted to communicate. If you want your audience to follow what you're saying, remember it, and act upon it, you need a logical structure. Creating one has an additional benefit. It makes remembering the presentation easier when you're up there delivering it.

When there's an established structure

Sometimes there's an established format for the presentation – it may be standard throughout the company or just your department – and it's simply a matter of flowing new material into it.

> ▶ *A presentation by the finance department of the figures for the last quarter, for instance, might follow the same sequence each time: overview → analysis of revenues → analysis of costs → review of current situation → options going forward.*
> ▶ *An update to an IT departmental planning meeting could involve a summary of issues that arose over the previous month and a proactive look forward to the following month.*
> ▶ *A product launch by a sales or marketing team might begin with an overview of the range and then detail each of the new items in turn.*

In situations of this kind you obviously don't have to worry about creating a structure yourself. All you have to do is compile and organize the information required.

Insight

Some people use a slide deck provided by their marketing department or some other source as a starting point. They may choose certain slides or topics to cover and add a few of their own. If this is true of you, make sure you step back and reassess the flow. Your presentation can easily become disjointed if you're not careful.

When you're starting from scratch

When you don't have a template to work from you'll need to start from scratch. Then you need to structure your material effectively. Sometimes you'll have a pretty good idea of how you want to sequence it. Other times it will be a matter of creating order from chaos. That means gathering the relevant information and sifting and sorting it until you have a simple, clear structure.

Focus on your messages and central theme

In Chapter 4 we stressed the importance of being clear about your outcome and what you want your audience to think, feel and do as a result of hearing you speak. This needs to be at the front of your mind as you create your structure. What are you seeking to communicate? What's your central theme – the bigger picture behind your presentation? What are your key messages – the points the audience must take away if you're to achieve your outcome?

Be careful to differentiate between key messages (what you say) and subject areas (what you talk about). 'Why customer service is important', 'Learning from mystery shopper feedback' and 'Customer complaints' might be subject areas, but they're not key messages. In this case the key messages could be:

▶ *'Good customer service leads to increased profits.'*
▶ *'Customer waiting times must be reduced.'*
▶ *'The number of complaints is increasing. We need to take action to reduce them.'*

Sometimes you'll know right from the start what your key messages are, and sometimes they only emerge as you work with the material.

Gathering information

Before you get started on the structure you need to decide what to include, and begin to gather together any supporting material, such as charts, pictures, diagrams, tables, illustrations, etc. There will be times when you have everything you need already and times when you need to request material from others or carry out research. The sooner you start the longer you have to pull everything together and structure it effectively.

What to keep? What to dump?

The challenge many novice presenters have is knowing what to include and what to leave out. Rarely do you have time to include everything you know, and even if you did it's not a good idea. The amount of information people can recall is limited. If you try to tell them too much you'll overload them and they end up remembering little or nothing.

This is particularly true when presenting to Drivers and Influencers (see Chapter 5) who prefer the big picture to lots of data. When your audience consists mainly of Amiables and Analyticals, though, you need more detail, or they'll feel short-changed. With a mixed audience it's a balancing act – you're walking a fine line between giving enough but not too much. When you find yourself wanting to include more, ask yourself these questions, 'Is this core to the success of my presentation? Would it matter if I dumped it?' If the answer is no, let it go.

Organizing information

Don't be in too much of a hurry to come up with your structure. If you like to take a logical, systematic approach to projects in general that's likely to be how you tackle presentations. Your preference might be to start at the beginning and work your way through step by step to the end. That can certainly be effective – and efficient if you're up against a deadline – but it can stop you thinking more creatively.

Some people dive straight into PowerPoint and produce the slides first. There are dangers in doing this. It's all too easy to start writing a script onto slides and end up with too many words. This is the birthplace of 'Death by PowerPoint'. Even when you have limited time, it's better to wait until you've worked out what you want to cover before you start on the slides.

Taking an intuitive approach

Some people prefer to generate ideas in a freeform way, without the constraint of having to make sense of them immediately. Brainstorming is one good way of doing this. You can either work on your own, or with others to bounce your thoughts off. Write everything that comes to mind in relation to the presentation on a large sheet of paper or tap it into a Word document. At this stage don't evaluate what comes up – that will inhibit the creative process. Just record everything. You can decide later what's valuable and what can be dumped.

This approach also helps if you occasionally get 'stuck' and experience the presenter's equivalent of 'writer's block'. Knowing that what you're putting down isn't the finished product, and doesn't have to be perfect, can make it easier to get started when your mind goes blank.

Using a spider diagram

One effective way of clarifying what you want to cover is to use a spray or spider diagram. As you write down your ideas, group and connect them in the way you naturally think. This method involves writing down a central idea – the subject of your presentation – and adding related ideas that radiate out from the centre. These can be recorded in any order, making it an extremely intuitive process.

A TYPICAL SPIDER DIAGRAM

It's easy to create a spider diagram following the steps below.

▶ *Write the subject of your presentation in a circle in the centre of a large sheet of paper. In this case 'Customer Service Excellence'.*
▶ *Draw lines radiating out from the centre. You need one for each key area you want to cover, such as 'Mystery Shopper Feedback'. These can be added as they occur to you. You don't have to list them all at the start.*
▶ *Each of these ideas can then be expanded with lines coming off them, for example 'Anecdotal feedback about attitude …'.*
▶ *Keep going until you've captured every thought. This can involve a lot of going back and forth. Sometimes you'll work on part of the spider diagram for a while, exhaust your ideas, only to return to it a short while later.*

Some people like to use colours to separate ideas or connections but it's perfectly possible to do it in black and white. You can also get spider diagram software for your computer. This makes it very easy to juggle each branch into order.

Creating a structure

One bonus of using a spider diagram is that it starts the process of creating a structure. But whether or not you've used one, all that remains is to sequence the various elements into a logical order that's easy to follow. We know from the courses we run that it's at the structuring stage where many people have problems, especially with longer presentations where there's a lot to cover. How should you start? What's the best way to end? How do you maintain interest in the middle?

There are various ways of sorting topics. Sometimes you don't need to worry about the order. It may be obvious to you what goes first.

You may have identified a problem, three possible solutions and be making a recommendation. In some situations, it's not that straightforward. One method that works well is to use adhesive notes or pieces of paper. Write a word or phrase that represents each topic on separate notes/sheets. Spread them out and move them around until you're satisfied with how they fit together.

If you've created a spider diagram, you can allocate numbers to each branch to indicate the way you want each idea to follow another. Computerized software has been designed to allow you to juggle each branch around. Once you've worked out the flow you can create a linear list of points. There are a number of standard structures you can use which are covered later in this chapter.

Insight

Another tool I sometimes use to organize material for a presentation, writes Steve, is an 'affinity diagram'. I write each of my key points on an index card or Post-it sheet and then move them round until I get the sequence I want. It saves lots of writing and rewriting on paper, and I find it extremely intuitive.

Tell 'em times three

Advice often given to novice presenters is to 'Tell 'em what you're going to tell them, tell 'em, then tell 'em what you told them'. In the case of a launch by a marketing department of some new products that would mean:

▶ *saying at the beginning something along the lines of 'Today I'm going to tell you about our new range of computers'*
▶ *in the middle giving details of each of them: 'The first computer is …', 'The next model is …', etc*
▶ *summarizing towards the end: 'So there you have it – five new computers …'*

'Tell 'em' is good advice, if rather simplistic. Because it outlines the structure and people know what to expect, they find it easier to follow your thread. It also improves the likelihood of you getting your message across by repeating it. But 'tell 'em' doesn't really go far enough.

We've developed a similar but much more sophisticated model that greatly increases the likelihood of people hearing, remembering and acting upon what you have to say. Drawing on research on audience attention span, and based on our experience of training thousands of people to speak in public with confidence and impact, the model allows you to structure your presentation so that key messages are delivered when the audience is at its brightest.

We've also systematized ways of managing the audience attention span, so people are alert more of the time. The result is a powerful method of putting together presentations that are compelling and memorable.

Understanding audience attention span

The main incentive to pay attention in conversation is the ever-present threat that you might have to speak next. As audiences know they won't have to speak until a speech is over, their incentive to listen is massively reduced, sometimes even to the point where they fall asleep.

Professor Max Atkinson

Have you ever been at a presentation and suddenly realized you haven't been listening for the last five or ten minutes – or even longer? It happens to most of us at one time or another. Maybe you have a pressing issue at work you get absorbed in, becoming totally oblivious to what's going on around you. Or you glance out of the window and notice the beautiful weather. That leads you to thinking how wonderful it would feel to be out there walking or playing golf. Or your mind simply wanders, and you find yourself thinking about where you might go on holiday or whether you have time to stop and do the weekly food shop on the way home.

All too often presentations don't hold our attention. Unless the content grabs us, the delivery captures our imagination, or we have a vested interest in the message, we quickly lose focus. Our eyes glaze over. We zone out. This can happen to even the best presenters. The moment you stand up to speak, you have the full attention of the audience. They've sent last minute email messages. They've stopped chatting. They're looking at you. But for how long can you hold their attention? You need to plan and structure your presentation so you engage your audience all the way through. You can't just leave it to chance. To do your job well you have to manage their attention actively, and that means presenting in a way that's easy to follow and simple to understand.

Figure 6.1 shows how an audience's level of attention changes over the course of time. It starts high but soon falls. How soon depends on a number of factors. The most important is how interesting you are – or how dull. Other factors include the time of day, the temperature in the room, whether there have been other presentations before yours, the emotional state of the audience, and whether they've just eaten. Sometimes attention tails off slowly. Sometimes it drops like a stone. Either way, it then bumps along the bottom until you say something like, 'In conclusion', 'Finally' or 'To summarize' and the audience sits up and listens, knowing you're near the end.

Understanding this cycle will help you construct your presentation more effectively. By taking advantage of the times when attention span is naturally high, and finding ways of lifting it when it normally dips, you can keep your audience engaged throughout. Our tried and tested model for structuring your presentation in accordance with the audience attention span has proved effective in virtually every situation.

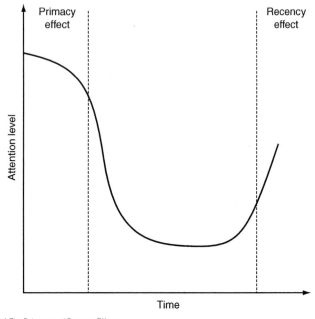

Figure 6.1 The Primacy and Recency Effects.

Making the most of the Primacy and Recency Effects

What's obvious is that the only time you can be sure the audience is listening is at the beginning and the end. This is backed up by solid research. Psychologists, including Glanzer and Cunitz (1966) and Atkinson and Shiffrin (1968), have shown repeatedly that people are best at remembering things they're exposed to first (the Primacy Effect) and last (the Recency Effect). Why then do so many presenters squander the opportunity to get their message across at the beginning and the end, and say the most important thing in the middle when there's no guarantee that anyone is listening? It makes no sense. There are certain things you need to say during the Primary and Recency periods.

Taking advantage of the Primacy Effect

Many people start by giving their name and the title of their presentation. This is sometimes described as a classical opening. But it's dull. Very dull. Kicking off with 'Good morning, my name is John Doe and today I'm going to give you an update from the Operations Team' lacks impact and starts the process of driving attention span down. If your audience doesn't know who you are, or what the title/subject of your presentation is, then you obviously need to tell them. But rarely does it have to be the first thing you say. It may be what most people do, but that doesn't make it right or effective.

You can stand out from the crowd and 'hook' the audience right from the word go by telling a story, making a bold claim, using a quote or giving a dramatic statistic, anything that gets them to sit up and take notice. It doesn't have to be long, in fact it *shouldn't* be long. Between ten and thirty seconds is ideal. You need to keep the pace lively. Long, drawn-out anecdotes are definitely out. (There are lots more ideas on how to open with a 'bang' in Chapter 7.)

What next? Well, you only have a couple of minutes before their attention starts to flag, so you need to make good use of the Primacy Effect period. Here's what you need to cover in that time:

1 *Open with a 'bang'*
2 *What's in it for them*
3 *Who am I?*
4 *Purpose/aim*
5 *Overview/agenda*

WHAT'S IN IT FOR THEM (WIIFT)

After the opening 'bang' you need to give them a reason to listen. Place their needs at the heart of your opening. Explain how what you're talking about affects them, or if they already know, remind them.

When the audience understands what they'll get from your presentation their motivation to pay attention is higher.

Think like a sales person: don't just focus on the 'features', concentrate on the 'benefits'. If you want them to know about a new computer system that's due to be installed, tell them how you can help minimize disruption and save them time when it arrives. Once they understand what's in it for them, they'll want to listen. Take care to include benefits that apply to the whole audience. The advantages for a finance team may be different from those you present to a marketing team.

Here are some ways to flag up your benefit statements:

▶ *This is important to you because ...*
▶ *What does this mean for you? (then tell them)*
▶ *Why am I telling you this? ... (then explain)*
▶ *Why should you care/listen? This will ...*
▶ *Why does this matter? It matters because ...*

Insight

Most people in business want to be more successful and achieve their goals, says Amanda. So if you can demonstrate, in a way they find credible, that what you're suggesting helps them do that, they'll sit up and listen. The same is true if you can show you can take problems away. Make sure you use 'you' language so they feel you're speaking directly to them.

INTRODUCING YOURSELF

It's really only at this point that you should introduce yourself, because to do so earlier will minimize your impact. By now you're somewhere between 30 and 60 seconds into your presentation. If you've got the opening 'bang' right and let them know clearly What's In It For Them you'll have their attention and be able to deliver some of the more 'boring' stuff without risk. As well as saying who you are, you should also take the opportunity, if it's appropriate, to establish your credibility. You're more likely to do this in a public speaking situation, such as when presenting to a conference, than in small group settings such as a team or client meetings, when those present already know you.

What you should aim to do whenever possible is have the audience recognize you as an authority on the subject you're speaking about. If you can, briefly state your credentials: 'I have over 20 years' experience in this business', 'I wrote a 60-page report on this subject last year'. They're more likely to believe and act upon what you say.

PURPOSE/AIM

Make the purpose/aim of your presentation clear upfront, and tell them what you expect of them. Get to the point. It's not a 'whodunnit', with the 'secret' revealed on the last page. If you delay and keep them guessing there's a chance they'll get bored, confused or frustrated. You might say something like, 'My purpose here today is to explain what the restructuring will mean for you all' or 'My aim is to persuade you to buy 1000 of our widgets'. You don't need to give chapter and verse about your purpose/ aim. Often you can sum it up in a single sentence. Sometimes your purpose/aim will include your central idea and key messages, but not always. There are times when you'll want them to emerge during the presentation. If you're trying to influence someone you may not want to give the game away at the start.

Don't be vague when presenting your purpose/aim, be crystal clear about what you're planning to do. If you're making recommendations or proposing a course of action it can be useful to say what it is right at the beginning, rather than give all the background information first.

Unless the timing has been made clear by someone else or listed on an agenda, you'll want to inform the audience about how long you'll be speaking. That way they can pace themselves and know how long they have to go if they start to feel restless.

SET THE AGENDA/OVERVIEW

The importance of letting your audience know early on in your presentation what you plan to cover cannot be overstated. If you don't, they may struggle to make sense of some of the detail because they don't have a context. It's a bit like giving someone pieces of a jigsaw puzzle without having shown them the picture on the lid of the box – they don't know where to place them in their mind. If they have an overview first they find it easier to make sense of what you say to them. It also helps if they get 'lost' because they have a route map to assist them in navigating through your presentation.

Here's where time spent planning and structuring really pays off – you'll be able to say clearly and concisely what you intend to cover. When presenting a proposal to the board, for instance, you might say, 'I'll begin with my analysis of the problem, describe various options I've considered, and give my recommendation for what I think we should do'. Another alternative is to say how many points you intend to cover: 'I have five main points I want to make', and list them briefly.

PUTTING IT ALL TOGETHER

To give you an idea of what this approach to making the most of the primacy period might mean in practice, here's a pithy, punchy way the introduction to a financial report could be structured:

> £250,000 (pause) That's how much we need to save over the next three months. £250,000 (pause). If not we'll be in trouble. We'll need to start cutting our costs and that will probably mean cutting jobs as well. None of us would be safe if we got to that stage. But if we get our act together we'll all be secure. You all know me, I'm Joe Bloggs, and over the next 20 minutes I'll tell you how I think we can save that money without damaging the business or losing people. I'll start by analysing the current situation and discussing how we got here, go on to consider various options, and make my recommendation, which is to defer some capital investment until our next financial year.

Taking advantage of the Recency Effect

The other time when you can be sure the audience is listening is at the end. The attention level generally rises when you signal you're about to bring things to a close by saying something like: 'In conclusion', 'Finally', or 'One last thought'.

Because of the Recency Effect, people are more likely to recall the last thing they hear because it's fresh in their minds, so your close is just as important as your opening. The end is where you draw together all of the threads of your presentation and tie them into a neat knot the audience can easily grasp. The conclusion is the lasting impression they will have of you and what they'll recall in the days, weeks and months that follow.

To make sure your message sticks, there are certain things you need to do as you close:

- ▶ *Give a brief summary/recap of the presentation.*
- ▶ *Run a question and answer session.*
- ▶ *Repeat the key messages and central theme.*
- ▶ *Make a call to action and/or next steps.*
- ▶ *End with a memorable message – your closing 'bang'.*

Most audiences don't appreciate it if you drag things out at the end, run over time or ramble on. They find that dull and irritating. Their minds are already moving towards the door. As you approach the finish you need to quicken the pace, be succinct and keep it punchy. That way you end with maximum impact.

SUMMARY OF KEY MESSAGES

The first thing you should do when bringing the presentation to a close is to summarize what you've covered. This is the final 'tell 'em' in which you 'tell 'em what you told them'. Quickly cover the main points, linking them together logically, so that anyone who 'zoned out' for a few minutes gets a chance to catch up. Don't add any new information at this stage. Recap only what you've already said.

QUESTION AND ANSWER SESSION

Most business presentations include a question and answer (Q&A) session at the end. But is this the best time? What happens if you don't handle the queries well or, worse, the audience is challenging or even turns hostile? The lasting memory participants will have is of you struggling to get your message across, which is not what you want.

For that reason we suggest you take questions after your recap, followed by a restatement of your key messages, any call to action and a memorable, closing 'bang'. Even if you do have a difficult Q&A session, you have a minute or two afterwards to give the audience something positive to remember. This way you get maximum benefit from the Recency Effect and increase the odds that they will recall what you said. There's detailed information on how to manage the Q&A in Chapter 18.

RESTATE YOUR KEY MESSAGES AND CENTRAL THEME

Your restatement of the key messages won't be as long as your recap but it's every bit as important. It ensures that people leave with the central theme of your presentation at the forefront of their thoughts. Spend some time planning this part carefully, and make sure you can deliver these key messages crisply and clearly, so the audience is left in no doubt about what you're seeking to communicate.

CALL TO ACTION OR NEXT STEPS

Your aim in speaking will often be to get people to take action, and just before you close is the best time to remind them what that is, increasing the likelihood of them following through. This can also be a time to 'inspire the troops', as in the following example:

> *'Let me ask you, as I close, to consider the future and the task that lies ahead of us. I know we're all committed to the success of this company and have the skills to achieve the results we want. All we need to do now is put these ideas into practice.'*

THE CLOSING 'BANG'

All that remains, then, is to make sure you have a strong close. All too often speakers get to the end of their slides, turn to the audience, and say 'That's it – any questions?' This is a limp, low-impact way of concluding. But if, as we recommend, you take questions earlier, you are free to go for a high-impact closing 'bang'. Depending on the type of presentation you're making, it can be motivational, challenging, thought-provoking or action-oriented. You can read about different kinds of close in Chapter 7.

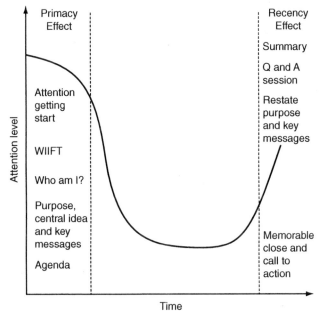

Figure 6.2 Managing audience attention span.

The firework display model

Imagine going to a firework display. The beginning is fantastic, with rockets going up and bangs going off, and at the end there's a rousing finale, with the action reaching an exciting crescendo. But what about the middle? Suppose there's only a small display of Roman Candles or someone waving a few sparklers. It wouldn't be much of a show, would it?

It's the same with presentations. There needs to be something interesting happening at regular intervals if you're to keep the audience engaged and the attention level high. If too long a period of time passes with little activity, people will start to lose focus and stop listening.

On average we speak at a rate of 140–180 words per minute and listen at 700 words per minute. And, as Professor Max Atkinson points out in his book *Lend Me Your Ears*, in everyday conversation there's a great incentive to keep awake because we know it will soon be our turn to speak. Because there's often a long wait in a presentation before the audience gets a 'turn' there's little motivation to maintain interest. When you put all of this together, it's no surprise that we get bored and trance out during longer presentations.

It's your responsibility to make sure that people stay awake by structuring the middle part effectively. Here's what the attention span curve should look like if you get it right (Figure 6.3). The peaks represent interventions by the speaker that keep the level of alertness high.

This middle 'tell 'em' is crucial, because it's usually the longest period, and the time when you're most likely to lose your listeners. It's unrealistic to imagine you could ever have their full attention all the time – even the best presenters in the world don't achieve that – but you should be able to spike it up periodically as it starts to dip.

The secret lies in having as few points as possible and a logical flow that's easy to follow. If your points seem to jump around with no obvious structure, people will struggle to make sense of what you're saying, and eventually switch off and stop listening altogether.

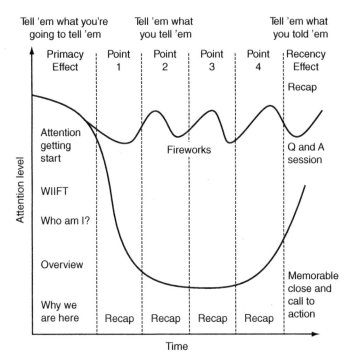

Figure 6.3 Managing audience attention span.

Your aim is to bring the ideas to life in as engaging a way as possible, by using examples, case studies, anecdotes, illustrations, photographs, videos, props, etc. – something we call 'flavour', which we describe in detail in Chapter 8.

THE IMPORTANCE OF SIGNPOSTING

When you present it's important to give your audience clear signposts that tell them where they are on the journey and in which direction they're heading. There's an easy, effective way of doing this: having finished one point you summarize it, and then move on to the next point in a way that's obvious. Don't try to be smooth and subtle. Let people know you're moving on. You might say, 'The next point I would like to make …' or 'That's not the whole picture – we also need to consider …' A middle section of a simple

presentation with four main points would, then, be structured
like this:

1 *Introduce Point 1 and bring to life*
2 *Recap Point 1 and signpost*
3 *Introduce Point 2 and bring to life*
4 *Recap Point 2 and signpost*
5 *Introduce Point 3 and bring to life*
6 *Recap Point 3 and signpost*
7 *Introduce Point 4 and bring to life*
8 *Recap Point 4 and signpost*

Insight

I know how frustrated I get, writes Steve, when I'm listening
to a presentation and there's a lack of signposting. I don't
know where I am in the 'story' and where I'm going – and
I don't like that. So I always make sure I signpost carefully,
because I figure there are other people like me in the world!

Standard structures

While it's possible to come up with a logical structure yourself,
why re-invent the wheel when there are several tried and
tested 'standard' structures that have proved their worth over
many years? They have a natural 'flow' that audiences seem to
understand intuitively, which makes it easy to maintain their
attention. Using a structure that matches your purpose and subject
will make putting your presentation together straightforward.
The following list is by no means definitive but covers the most
commonly used structures.

▶ **Chronology** *The structure of a presentation based on chronology
could not be more straightforward – events are described in the
order they happened. First this, then that, then this ...*
▶ **Points in the order of importance** *Often you'll want to
arrange your points in order of importance. When we're doing
presentations on How to Present with Impact and Confidence,*

for instance, we often start with 'being yourself', because we consider that to be the most important. We then continue by introducing other points in priority order.

▶ **Past, present and future** *This is similar to Chronology but also includes a future perspective. It contrasts three periods in time: 'Last year our sales were [£10m], now they're [£14.2m] and next year we're aiming for [£17m].*

▶ **Problem and solution** *This, as the name suggests, is where you outline a problem followed by the solution. Perhaps you need to recruit more skilled staff and are looking for ways of doing so. Often this structure has three parts – Problem, Options, Solution – with various options considered in the middle.*

▶ **Category** *Sometimes you'll organize things according to type or category. You may, for instance, be introducing a range of products and decide to sequence on the basis of price point, market sector, profitability, etc.*

▶ **Contrasts** *This is a simple structure you can use to compare one thing with another. Maybe you want to suggest having weekly rather than monthly team meetings and present your ideas by contrasting the two options.*

▶ **Theory and practice** *Here a theory is explained, followed by illustrating how it works in practice. You might explain how a computer software program works and then demonstrate it in action.*

▶ **Telling a story** *You can follow a 'story' format. This can be a personal experience, about someone else, or made up. Typically it will have a chronological flow.*

▶ **Numerical** *If in doubt you can always fall back on a numerical structure. 'There are six things I would like to cover today …'*

TEN KEY POINTS TO REMEMBER

1 *If you want your audience to follow what you're saying, remember it, and act upon it, you need a logical structure. When your company has an established structure flow new material into it. When starting from scratch gather relevant information and sort it into a simple, clear structure such as 'Tell 'em three times'.*

2 *Keep your outcome and what you want your audience to think front of your mind as you create your structure.*

3 *Differentiate between key messages (what you want to say) and subject areas (what you talk about).*

4 *When deciding what to keep and what to dump ask yourself, 'Is this core to the success of my presentation? If the answer is no, let it go.'*

5 *All too often presentations don't hold our attention. Plan and structure your presentation so you engage your audience all the way through.*

6 *The only time you can be sure the audience is listening is at the beginning (the Primacy Effect) and the end (the Recency Effect).*

7 *To take advantage of the Primacy Effect your introduction should follow this sequence; open with a 'bang', what's in it for them (WIIFT), who am I?, purpose/aim and overview/ agenda.*

8 *Presentations are like firework displays – there needs to be something interesting happening at regular intervals.*

9 *Give your audience clear signposts that tell them where they are and in which direction they're heading.*

10 *Tried and tested structures audiences find easy to follow include: chronology, points in the order of importance, past/present/future, problem and solution, category, contrasts, theory and practice, telling a story, and numerical.*

7

....

Starting and ending with a bang

In this chapter you will learn:
- *how to grab your audience's attention*
- *about different types of high impact opening and closing 'bangs'*
- *how to conclude your presentation effectively.*

How not to open

The first 30 seconds of your presentation is crucial, so don't waste it. You need to grab the attention of your audience and engage their interest from the start. Many speakers begin by giving their name and the title of their presentation. This is predictable and boring and should be avoided whenever possible. Go instead for a strong opening that gets them sitting up and taking notice immediately.

Ten great ways to open with a bang

Here are ten ways to win attention and ensure the audience is with you from the start.

1 *Make a bold claim.*
2 *Invite them to 'Imagine'.*
3 *Present a striking fact or statistic.*
4 *Ask a question.*
5 *Tell a story or anecdote.*

6   *Use an aphorism or proverb.*
7   *Be mysterious.*
8   *Introduce an analogy or metaphor.*
9   *Commence with a quote.*
10 *Crack a joke.*

1 MAKE A BOLD CLAIM

A bold statement at the beginning of your presentation is guaranteed to get you attention. The more dramatic or provocative it is the more alert the audience will be and ready to listen to what you say next.

> *In five years this industry will not exist as we know it.*
> *Within a generation most people will live to be 100.*

2 INVITE THEM TO 'IMAGINE'

Starting your presentation with the word 'imagine' places your audience in the centre of an experience. Dr Frank Luntz, in his book *Words That Work* says imagine is one of the most powerful words in the English language as 'an open, non-restrictive command – almost an invitation. Its power is derived from the simple fact that it can conjure up anything in the mind of the one doing the imagining'. The word 'imagine' makes the audience active participants in the presentation, rather than detached onlookers. It transforms the presenter's words into vivid pictures, sounds and feelings in the minds of those listening. It's like guiding them to create their own private film show.

How can you use 'imagine'? Here are just a few suggestions to get you started:

▶ *Ask them to visualize some point in the future:* Imagine what it would be like if you didn't have to give presentations yourself and you could send your personal android to do it for you …
▶ *Encourage people to put themselves in someone else's position:* Imagine you receive an email from our company telling you we've suspended your account. How would you feel?

► *Use the word to point towards a vision:* Imagine a company where everyone works together, supports each other, and is one integrated team ...

3 PRESENT A STRIKING FACT OR STATISTIC

A simple, powerful way of grabbing the attention of an audience is to present them with a striking fact or statistic. This is especially effective when it's surprising or counter-intuitive. Obviously it needs to relate to the purpose of your presentation, and not be included just for interest and entertainment value. Use accurate, verifiable numbers whenever possible and where you have credible external sources make sure you name them.

> *A recent study by Philip Zimbardo, one of the world's leading psychologists, found that 50 per cent of Americans describe themselves as shy.*

> *25,000 people die every day of hunger or hunger-related causes. That's an official figure from the United Nations.*

> *In a study of 600 firms only 21 per cent of satisfied customers intend to stay with them.*

In business presentations you can make your introductions compelling by stating company, market or competitor information. This provides a strong platform, in particular when making proposals, reviewing corporate strategy or checking performance against budget.

> *£350k – that's how far we are behind budget at the end of Q1.*

> *This is a £4.2m market. We've only got 4 per cent of it.*

Insight

Many people who are subject-matter experts in areas such as finance, surveying, IT and engineering, find numbers credible

(Contd)

and are convinced by them. So my opening, writes Steve, when presenting to those with a technical, factual preference is almost always number-based. Right from the start the audience gains confidence in me because I'm speaking their 'language' – and once I've won them over it's easier to move the presentation into other areas.

4 ASK A QUESTION

Asking the audience a question is one of the most powerful ways of getting them engaged right from the start. This is easier with small- to medium-sized groups where it's easy to converse with them, and more of a challenge with larger groups like conferences, where you need a microphone.

When delivering a presentation about a possible rationalization of office space and location, for instance, you might start by asking, *How many countries do you think we operate in around the world, and how many buildings do you think we currently own or lease in total?*

Or you might, when pitching to a new client, start by asking, *What's the most important factor for you when choosing a supplier?*

This gets the audience thinking and talking. Another alternative is to ask a rhetorical question and provide the answer yourself: *Why do so many people leave filling in their expense claims till the last minute? (Pause). Because they hate doing them.*

This is not usually as strong or engaging as a real question, but has the advantage of being quicker, and avoids the risk of getting embroiled in a long discussion.

You can also call for a show of hands. *How many of you have used the internet today?* (Presenter raises hand to encourage the audience to follow suit.)

Asking questions at the beginning of a presentation keeps people on their toes and alert because they know you may do so at any moment later on.

5 TELL A STORY OR ANECDOTE

When you start with a story you grab people immediately, especially when you share a personal experience that others can relate to. Make sure, though, that people see the relevance to the topic you are talking about.

> *Vandana, the cashier at my local bank branch, gets on well with customers. She takes a personal interest in them while they pay in or cash cheques. The other day, she was chatting to me about the new kitchen I'm having fitted. I was quite anxious about it as the bank was being slow in approving a home improvement loan and I wanted to get things started. Vandana had a word with the manager. She got approval within 24 hours. Imagine my surprise when she hand-delivered the paperwork to me on her way home. Service like that builds customer loyalty.*

Personal disclosure builds a strong emotional connection with your audience, but it can also be effective to tell stories where you have no direct involvement. You might, for instance, pick up on a story that's in the media, relate to something that you read in a book, or even describe an event that's well known.

> *Did you catch the story about the 14-year-old boy who saved a complete stranger's life after he was involved in an accident?*

> *Richard Branson was born an entrepreneur. He started his first business ...*

Keep your stories relatively brief. If you go on too long your audience may grow restless as they wait for you to get to the point.

Be especially careful when using stories to open presentations to senior people or important clients, who are likely to have a short attention span.

There is much more on storytelling in the next chapter.

6 USE AN APHORISM OR PROVERB

Proverbs, aphorisms, or familiar sayings can be a great way of opening provided they relate closely to your message. Use them carefully, though, or they might come across as tired, obvious clichés. Here are some possible ways of beginning.

> *Familiarity breeds contempt – and contempt can kill. If we're casual in our attitude towards our customers we'll kill our business.*

> *They say a chain is only as strong as its weakest link – and right now the bottlenecks in the telephone ordering system are hampering our sales growth.*

> *It's the early bird that catches the worm, which means we must get into the emerging markets now. You've heard the expression 'He who hesitates is lost'. We must act now.*

7 MAKE IT MYSTERIOUS

Audiences are easily hooked when you arouse their curiosity. In the mystery opening you give them ambiguous clues before revealing your point. You need to make sure you get the timing and delivery right because some people may be irritated rather than amused at the 'game' you're playing if you string it out for too long.

One of the most memorable examples we've experienced was in a presentation delivered by NLP guru Charles Faulkner who placed a jellybean sweet on every seat before the audience arrived. As we took our places our curiosity was immediately aroused. We didn't know whether to examine it, eat it or what. He opened by talking about the fact that we experience the world through our five senses and some while later asked us to consider the jellybean from this perspective.

8 INTRODUCE AN ANALOGY OR METAPHOR

Analogies, similes and metaphors are comparisons between two apparently unrelated items. They're a practical, engaging way of making a complex or theoretical concept easier to understand. In the film *An Inconvenient Truth*, Al Gore gives a presentation in which he uses a powerful simile to get across his message about the dangers of global warming:

> **My late friend Carl Sagan used to say that if you had a big globe with a coat of varnish on it, the thickness of that varnish relative to that globe is pretty much the thickness of the Earth's atmosphere compared to the Earth itself. And it's thin enough that we are capable of changing its composition.**

Sometimes an important business thought can be represented with a simple analogy that you then develop through the presentation: *Customers are like plants in a garden – if you nurture them they'll grow, if you don't they'll die.*

9 COMMENCE WITH A QUOTE

Quotes can be an extremely effective way of opening a presentation. They may be well known or more obscure. You might open a presentation on the challenges facing your company with the following observation from John F. Kennedy: '*When written in Chinese, the word "crisis" is composed of two characters – one represents danger, and the other represents opportunity.*'

When you're talking about quality what better opening could there be than the Gucci family slogan: '*Quality is remembered long after the price is forgotten.*'

Leo Tolstoy's comment *that 'Everyone thinks of changing the world, but no one thinks of changing himself'* could be a perfect introduction to a presentation on personal development.

Or when sharing your thoughts on leadership you might offer Sheila Murray Bethel's observation *'As leaders you know that the higher up you go – the more gently down you need to reach.'*

Remember, though, when using a quote it is common courtesy to name whoever said or wrote it.

You can also use a quote that relates directly to your business. A positive comment from the press or a remark from a satisfied customer is one option: *'I don't think of you as a supplier, I think of you as part of my team'* – that's what a customer said to me yesterday.

10 CRACK A JOKE

Many people believe it's a good idea to start – and end – a presentation with a joke, on the basis that you should get people in a good mood as soon as possible and leave them smiling at the end. There are plenty of books on the market full of material you can use to open in an 'amusing' way. Beware – this is a high-risk strategy. There's no guarantee your audience will share your sense of humour and unless you have the stand-up skills of Robin Williams or Eddie Izzard it could fall very flat indeed. This is especially true if the joke's only been 'grafted' on, and doesn't relate directly to the subject matter of your presentation.

Insight

In my (Amanda's) experience, many people push back at the idea of opening a presentation with anything other than the classic 'Hello, my name is...'. They either think opening with a joke won't be acceptable to people in their business or want to appear warm and welcoming from the outset. It's not until they try it out for real that they realize how powerful this concept is. My advice is simple: Be brave, be bold. It's easy to be better than average at presenting and this is a great way of achieving it.

Concluding your presentation with a bang

Your close is just as important as your opening. You need to make sure you bring things to an emphatic, positive, satisfying conclusion, rather than stopping because you've run out of steam. The easiest way to do that is to refer back to what you said at the start. Doing so means your opening and closing remarks act like bookends to your presentation.

So if you started with *This is a £4.2m market. We've only got 4 per cent of it*, you might end with something along the lines of *We may only have 4 per cent of this £4.2m market right now, but I am confident we'll have 20 per cent in five years' time.*

Or if you started by mentioning the Gucci family motto, you could end with, *I mentioned at the beginning that 'Quality is remembered long after the price is forgotten'. If we make sure we're the best, we'll always be remembered.*

TEN KEY POINTS TO REMEMBER

1   *Grab your audience's attention and get them interested from the start.*

2   *Avoid opening with your name and the title of your presentation because it's boring and predictable.*

3   *Ten great ways to open with a bang are:*
    ▷ *make a bold claim*
    ▷ *invite them to 'imagine'*
    ▷ *present a striking fact or statistic*
    ▷ *ask a question*
    ▷ *tell a story or anecdote*
    ▷ *use an aphorism or proverb*
    ▷ *be mysterious*
    ▷ *introduce an analogy or metaphor*
    ▷ *start with a quote*
    ▷ *crack a joke.*

4   *Make a bold, dramatic or provocative claim to alert your audience to be ready for what follows.*

5   *Opening with a question, striking fact or statistic are great ways of creating impact from the outset.*

6   *Audiences are easily hooked when you start your presentation with a story, anecdote or even a mystery.*

7   *Analogies, metaphors, aphorisms and proverbs provide presenters with a rich source of possible ways to get their presentation off to a good start.*

8   *Opening with a joke is a high-risk strategy best left to the experts.*

9   *Whichever opening you choose make sure it's relevant and aligned with your outcome.*

10 *Make sure you bring your presentation to a close in an emphatic, positive way. The easiest way to achieve this is to refer back to what you said in your opening bang at the start.*

8

....

Adding 'flavour' to generate interest

In this chapter you will learn:

- *how to bring facts to life and make them memorable*
- *practical techniques for incorporating 'flavour' into your presentation*
- *about the power of 'stacking' points to paint pictures in the mind of your audience.*

What is flavour?

Imagine what it would be like if there were no flavour in the world. Without herbs and spices meals would be bland and tasteless. Without their signature spices all the distinctive cuisines of the world – Indian, French, Thai, Italian, Chinese – would be pretty much alike. Well it's the same with presentations. If you only serve up 'meat and two veg' – all facts and figures – what you say will not only be dull but people will be unlikely to remember it or act upon it.

In Chapter 6 we stressed the importance of structure in boosting the attention of the audience's attention in the middle 'tell 'em' section of a presentation. While this is effective, it only goes so far. You can go even further by adding flavour – it's the difference that makes the difference when it comes to presentations.

Too many people reach the stage in their preparation where they've gathered their content and sorted it into order – and then stop. Going the extra mile and adding flavour will instantly catapult you into the top 20 per cent of speakers. You'll never be dull again.

Insight

Only two presentations have held my (Steve's) attention all the way through – and in both cases it was flavour that did it. The best talk I ever heard was by Guy Kawasaki, who at the time was working for Apple. His presentation to 2000 conference delegates in Dallas was called '10 Ways to Drive Your Competition Crazy'. Each 'way' was an amusing, engaging story, and all ten were bookended by a short intro and ending. Every story made a point that was easy to get, and I can still vividly remember several of them many years later.

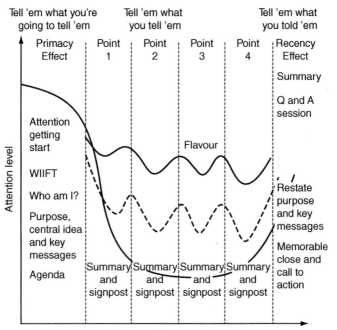

Figure 8.1 Adding flavour.

The top line in Figure 8.1 shows how much alertness can be improved when you bring your ideas to life with flavour. It's significantly higher than the level achieved by sequencing points well on its own. What exactly do we mean by flavour? Well, it's a range of ways of painting pictures in the minds of your audience so they find your presentation more engaging, interesting and entertaining. The most effective are case studies, examples, illustrations, stories, anecdotes, humour, metaphor and quotes.

The great thing about flavour is that it allows you to repeat a point several times without patronizing the audience. You might introduce one of your key messages by giving facts and figures – the basic ingredients with little or no flavour – but then go on to give a case study, offer an analogy, or introduce a relevant quote. Each says the same thing, but in different ways. 'Stacking' flavour in this way makes your messages extremely powerful, and easier for the audience to remember. When you get it right they'll have the pictures you paint in their minds for weeks and possibly months to come.

We'll come back to this idea at the end of the chapter, with some examples of how it can work in practice, once we've discussed each of the types of flavour in turn.

Using illustrations, case studies and examples

In many business presentations you'll want potential customers to understand the benefits of working with your company. One of the easiest and most effective ways of bringing this to life and making sure your message sticks is with illustrations, case studies and examples. You can even present them with an imaginary scenario to fire their imagination.

CASE STUDIES/EXAMPLES

Suppose you're selling office furniture. Having listed the features and benefits, you could then go on to give an example of work you carried out for another company. It might be something like this.

Atlas invited us to equip their new office block in Docklands with 7,200 workstations. They asked us to plan the layout as well as provide the furniture. They needed a mixture of fixed workstations, hot desk areas, and shared general utility space for storage, photocopiers, etc. We exceeded their expectations by coming up with a workable plan and installing everything in less than a month. They were delighted with the idea of our free follow-up snagging list service and surprised at how few items needed fine-tuning on such a large job.

The art of a good case study lies in choosing something that highlights the buying criteria the prospect has that you want to sell against. In this example, the presenter has identified speed of installation, quality of work and after sales service as being important. The case study is carefully crafted to illustrate each of these elements.

- *Speed of installation* We exceeded their expectations by coming up with a workable plan and installing everything in less than a month.
- *Quality of work* ... surprised at how few items they identified that needed fine-tuning.
- *After sales service* They were delighted with the idea of our free follow-up snagging list service.

ILLUSTRATIONS

Suppose you want to demonstrate why your company is renowned for excellent customer service. Rather than quoting statistics about your call rates, you can illustrate it.

When a tractor broke down in the middle of the harvesting season, one of our people drove to Cornwall to collect a part and delivered it to a farm in Carlisle on the same day. You can imagine the smile on the farmer's face when he arrived.

Illustrations are a type of story where the tale you tell is of a customer you've worked with. The example you choose will reflect the quality you, and your company, have that you want to emphasize. You can use illustrations in lots of different ways. We often work with people from charities to help them improve their presentation skills. They frequently use examples like the one shown below to highlight their cause and get businesses to sponsor their work.

> *Teresa Aoko lives in a small village in Kenya with her mother Margaret. Before she goes to school, she has to walk several miles to fetch water and then help her mother with her brothers and sisters before she walks several more miles to school. Teresa wants to become a teacher so she can help educate other children like her in the future ... Organizations like yours can help and benefit at the same time by ...*

IMAGINARY SCENARIO

Sometimes your case study or example may not exist. Instead, you paint a picture in their minds of how things could be. You encourage the audience to step into the future and experience it mentally. The more vivid it is the more impact it will have on them. This approach is especially attractive to those people with an Expressive behavioural style (see Chapter 5).

> *In the future your new office will be held up as an example of a great environment for people to work in ...*

> *Imagine what it would be like if you didn't need to have individual applications on each of your computers. Your people could log on to any machine, anywhere, saving them time and you money.*

> *Imagine what it would be like if all your people were so persuasive that your clients felt compelled to act upon what they say.*

SHARING RESEARCH FINDINGS

Some business presentations involve sharing research findings on a particular subject. If you've carried out a study, you may have lots of quantitative and qualitative data to communicate which can end up being very dry and, if you're not careful, instantly forgettable. Let's use an example to explain how this works.

> *There are three major risk factors. The first is an increase in costs relating to Health and Safety. The monthly figures show an increase of 12 per cent ...*

Instead, you can present the results with memorable examples people want to take action on.

> *There are three major risk factors. Let me illustrate the first by telling you about Kim, who works at a packing plant. She was slightly injured when she tripped over some cabling that had not been taped down. She was off work for three months. Our research shows the staff has not received Health and Safety training for over a year. Kim's minor injury cost us £8,700. Imagine that multiplied by ...*

Whatever the subject matter, you can find a way to bring facts to life. Adding a few details makes the information infinitely more memorable and engaging.

Stories and anecdotes

The storyteller takes what he tells from experience – his own or that reported by others. And he in turn makes it the experience of those who are listening to the tale.

Walter Benjamin

When you present case studies, examples and illustrations, what you're actually doing is telling a story – a story with a business message embedded in it. Stories are a phenomenally powerful way of communicating with people, which is why they've been the first choice for many leaders – political, spiritual, business – since public speaking first began. Great communicators often use stories to make their point. When someone tells a tale we often feel compelled to listen, even, sometimes, if we're not particularly interested in the subject. We get drawn in, fascinated and entranced, wondering what's going to happen next. If you want to take your presenting to the next level, and the level beyond that, it's telling stories that will enable you to do so.

WHAT'S STORYTELLING GOT TO DO WITH BUSINESS?

However, we know first-hand from running workshops that some hard-nosed business people push back at the idea of telling stories in presentations. Stephen Denning, author of *The Leader's Guide to Storytelling – Mastering the Art of Business Narrative,* makes a compelling case for using stories. They can be used, he says, to 'spark action, get people to work together', and achieve a host of other things. For people in business it is, he says, a 'critical skill'.

In their book *Made to Stick*, Chip and Dan Heath see telling stories as a crucial way of making your messages 'sticky' and memorable, burning ideas into the brains of the people you're speaking to. 'Stories,' they say, ' provide stimulation (knowledge about how to act) and inspiration (motivation to act)'. They are, as they put it, 'effective teaching tools'.

THE PERSONAL AND THE PROFESSIONAL

Some people, though, are okay with case studies, examples and illustrations, but they're less comfortable with sharing a personal anecdote in a professional setting. And we can, to a degree, understand that reticence. Some individuals like to keep their personal and professional worlds separate. But there's a power that comes from revealing something of yourself.

The best stories are based upon personal experience because vivid memories help us to visualize small details that bring them to life when we talk about them. Think back over your life and you'll find that even small and seemingly insignificant events can provide a rich source of material. It may be something you learnt while pursuing a pastime, a chance experience when buying something, a poignant moment with your family, or a universal moment we've all had such as being stuck in a traffic jam. Many presenters make a note of events as they occur and build up a stock of stories they can draw upon.

Of course the stories need to illustrate the point you're seeking to make. They're not just random insertions. You need to make sure they're relevant to the audience. But that just requires common sense and creativity. Here's an example of a personal experience used as the basis for making a business point.

> *When flying back from Rotterdam last week I was killing time at the airport when I saw two small boys and was fascinated by the way they behaved. They were only toddlers, and both still walked unsteadily. One was already there with his family when the other came in. They looked at each other warily, but with interest. One eventually walked over to the other and stood next to him. Neither was old enough to speak. After 30 seconds the second boy went back to his pushchair, picked up a soft toy, carried it over to his companion, and offered it to him – which he took. After another minute the boy with the toy toddled off to his mum, and came back shortly afterwards with a half-eaten biscuit which he passed to the other. Recognizing it as food, he took a nibble. Another 30 seconds passed in silence, after which they gave each other a peck on the cheek, and started to play as if they'd known each other all their lives. What happens to us as we grow up and lose all that childish innocence, openness, warmth and trust? How many business opportunities do we miss out on because we hold back from being the first to say 'Hello'? If we're to achieve our goals this year we need to network more effectively.*

Insight

How do you come up with stories that can be used in presentations? All you have to do is keep your eyes peeled and ears open. Every day you have experiences that can

provide the raw material you need: you get bad service in a
restaurant or someone in a call centre goes out of their way
to help you. The media – newspapers, radio, TV and the
internet – generates hundreds of stories every day, many of
which can be crafted and repurposed to illustrate a point.

USING WELL-KNOWN OR OTHER PEOPLE'S STORIES

Some presenters choose well-known anecdotes that fit the point
they want to make. If you decide to go down this route and use
someone else's story, make it your own by placing a personal spin
on it. 'I was walking down the street yesterday and saw a scene
that reminded me (story starts here) …'. Always acknowledge the
source. We once came across a speaker who failed to acknowledge
the author of some of his material and some of the audience knew
it came from the work of Robert Cialdini. Integrity goes hand in
hand with credibility. Those who knew felt short-changed.

HOW TO CREATE A CLEAR STRUCTURE

Stories work well when they have a clear structure with a start,
middle and end, and work best when there's a moral or a pivotal
moment when something changes. First you lay the foundations,
including enough information for people to understand the
context. Next comes the middle section which often includes
a critical point that changes something. Then you move on to
the conclusion and tie up any loose ends.

Another effective way of telling a story is through the eyes of one
of the 'characters' because your audience will identify with this
person, as they would if reading a novel or watching a film, and
vicariously experience the narrative as a participant themselves.

> *Sarah was constantly in trouble at school, almost from the*
> *first day. She was a bit of a tomboy, always into mischief,*
> *and her attitude seemed to annoy the teachers. It was no*
> *surprise that eventually she was suspended, nor that she*
> *ended up running away. Life on the street was harder than*

she thought it would be. But she couldn't go home. She was hungry. She was cold. She made some choices she later came to regret.

When you give people 'walk on parts' your tale comes to life. Make your characters real by using their names and saying a little about them, 'Davina is small, slender, with beautiful blonde hair and a brace on her teeth. She has no fear of approaching people she's never met before, no matter how senior they are'. You can add dialogue too. 'Davina turned to the CEO, smiled and said, "I'd like to talk to you about our plans for the next year …".' Give characters different voices by changing your voice tone.

ELICIT AN EMOTIONAL STATE WITH YOUR STORIES

When you can tell stories where your 'characters' encounter a challenge or overcome an obstacle your audience will feel something. Strong narratives trigger emotion, grab attention and stay in the minds of people for a long time, sometimes all their life. Stories connect facts and ideas with feelings. You need to win hearts as well as minds. Presentations that only contain information and logic are less likely to influence and persuade people.

Think about the emotional state you want them to experience: curiosity, pride, sadness, passion, happiness? Why should they care about your story? How will you create a connection? If you describe it in the first person, and recall how you felt at the time, it becomes more real for your listeners.

BRING YOUR STORY TO LIFE

In any good story the details, adjectives, adverbs and active language make the difference. Make the words you choose interesting – rather than 'tired' use 'exhausted', instead of a 'problem' describe it as a 'puzzle' or 'mystery'. Describe the scene. You only need a few details to add colour and depth to your story. Illustrate abstract ideas with specific details of people and places. While your story needs to be rich in detail, you need to make sure you don't ramble on at great length. Don't let your audience get bored, or wonder 'where is all this going?' The longer the story the more impact it has to have.

USE ALL OF THE SENSES

Because people have different preferences for one or two senses you need to vary your language to connect with everyone in the audience. If you use a mixture of visual (seeing), auditory (hearing) and kinaesthetic (feeling) language in your story you'll cover all of the bases. The word lists below will get you started.

Visual (seeing)

Appear, bird's eye view, catch a glimpse of, clarify, clear-cut, dark, dress up, enlighten, examine, expose, focus, glance, graphic, hazy, hindsight, illusion, illustrate, in light of, look, look into, make a scene, mind's eye, notice, obvious, outlook, perspective, picture, pinpoint, reveal, see, short-sighted, spectacle, dim view, tunnel vision, vague.

Auditory (hearing)

Audible, call, clear as a bell, clearly expressed, compose, discuss, earshot, harmonize, hear, listen, loud and clear, manner of speaking, mention, note, outspoken, remark, report, say, scream, shout, silence, sing, sound, speechless, tell the truth, tongue-tied, tune-in, voice, word-for-word.

Kinaesthetic (feeling)

Affected, bear, carry, cold, cool, crash, crawl, emotional, foundation, get a load of, get in touch, grab, grip, handle, hang in there, hassle, heated, hold, hot-headed, impact, irritate, lukewarm, motion, muddled, nail, pressure, rub, shallow, sharpen, shift, shock, slipped my mind, solid, sore, stir, stress, strike, tap, throw, tickle, touch, wring.

When you start using stories write them down first, so you're clear about the flow. Avoid using notes or people won't think they're genuine. Improvise the story as you go along, so it comes across as spontaneous. If you deliver it in a flat, monotone voice, you're unlikely to make the impact you had in mind. Imagine you're telling the story of 'Goldilocks and the Three Bears' to a small child. Adults want to be enthralled in the same way as children. And once you master the art of storytelling, you'll have the audience eating out of the palm of your hand.

Insight

I, Amanda, learnt the art of storytelling from my mother, Joyce. She's brilliant at reading children's books. She adds emphasis on key words and pauses for dramatic effect. She's a master at getting the voices of characters just right. On our courses we sometimes get people to read children's books so they get an idea of how much more engaging a business presentation can be when they move away from a flat monotone delivery.

Make 'em laugh, make 'em smile

'Humour is our ability to delight, smile and laugh at the wonder of life, as a child does.'

Jack Maguire

Sometimes your stories will have an element of humour in them. And it's worth looking for it, because people always love a presentation that makes them smile. By humour we don't mean telling jokes. Unless you have the skills of a professional stand-up comedian we strongly recommend you avoid modelling yourself on Robin Williams. Humour is about being playful, lighthearted and good humoured. It's about not taking things too seriously. It's about seeing the funny side and having an amused perspective.

If someone gives you a gushing over-the-top introduction, self-effacing humour can provide a great antidote. '*Who is this guy? I can't wait to see him!*' (Looks around for someone to appear). Using humour relaxes your audience. The safest target is you.

WHAT TO AVOID WHEN USING HUMOUR

▶ *Don't say you're going to tell a funny story ('You're going to love this') or describe an experience as funny. If you set their expectations too high they'll be disappointed.*
▶ *Don't use sarcasm – it's not humour, and can offend.*
▶ *Don't make fun of anyone in the audience unless you're absolutely sure it's okay or you've cleared it first. It's okay to make fun of yourself.*
▶ *Don't joke about race, sex, religion, politics or disability, or tease people about their beliefs and values.*
▶ *Don't say 'I don't know if I should tell this one' – it sounds like you're reheating material you've used before.*

Take care, in particular, when you're speaking to people from another culture. Humour that works well in one country may not go down so well in other places – and may not even be understood. Bear in mind, when something serious has been announced shortly before you get up to speak, that you'll need to pace your audience, and gradually introduce humour as their mood shifts.

METAPHOR AND ANALOGY

Ever found yourself banging your head against a brick wall? Seizing defeat from the jaws of victory? Swimming against the tide? Or maybe there's light at the end of the tunnel. Everything's coming up roses. You're on top of the world.

Using metaphor – directly comparing two or more seemingly unrelated subjects – is a common way for us to express ourselves when speaking or writing. It's so common, in fact, that we're often unaware we're doing it. We 'go the extra mile' for a customer.

We 'steel' ourselves for bad news from the markets. Metaphor is everywhere.

And it can be a powerful tool when giving a presentation. You can use it to get your message across in a more dramatic, more illuminating, more engaging way. Take a look at the three examples below to see how using metaphor can add impact to a presentation:

1 *The target for this month is going to challenge us.*
2 *We're going to have to stretch to reach this target.*
3 *We need to reach for the sky this April.*

The first is mundane and may not get the message across effectively. Including the word 'stretch' in the second implies the people listening will need to make some effort if they're going to achieve their goal. The third example makes it clear that everyone will have to 'pull out the stops' (to add another metaphor) if they're going to have a 'fighting chance' (enough already!) of reaching the target.

Metaphors are a great way of bringing concepts to life in your presentations. When the two things being compared are structurally identical we're able to make a connection between them. Giving shape to ideas in this way makes them easier to understand and easier to remember.

> *We're at a crossroads and we have a number of paths open to us. Do we take the motorway or do we take the country road? That's the question. If we continue as we are, meandering along the country lanes, it will take us a year to achieve our goal. The motorway, on the other hand, is fast and leads us directly to where we want to be in three months.*

Metaphor is also the language of the unconscious mind, which thinks in a more symbolic way than the conscious brain. This means it can connect with people at a deeper level than normal communication.

Metaphors don't, though, have to be as corny as the ones we opened this section with. Or clichéd 'management speak', such as 'touching base', 'singing off the same hymn sheet', 'moving the goalposts' or 'thinking outside the box'.

Insight

Sometimes people push back at the idea of using metaphor in a business presentation, says Amanda. They find it a bit 'touchy feely'. It's only when they start to reflect on how much metaphor and analogy they and other people use every day that they start to recognize the benefits this approach brings.

ANALOGY

Analogy is like metaphor in that it associates two things that are essentially dissimilar. The difference is that the comparison is made more explicit by the use of words such as 'like', 'as', 'than' or 'resembles'. Analogies provide flavour in your presentation by painting vivid pictures that people can really see, instead of abstract concepts that are hard to grasp.

> *'Sometimes it feels like we're wading through treacle – we need to find an easier way forward' is more powerful than 'sometimes it feels like we're not making much progress.'*

> *'Finding money out of what remains of the marketing budget is like squeezing the last drop of water out of a wet towel' grabs attention better than 'the marketing budget is all but used up.'*

If you're creative you should be able to come up with your own metaphors and analogies. But make sure they're not too obscure or too unusual, or you'll get some bemused looks. 'We're as reliable as a breakdown service that always turns up in an hour' may be more interesting than 'We offer a reliable service', but it doesn't actually improve communication of the idea.

Exercise

As you prepare for your next presentation, take a few moments to complete this simple exercise. Having identified the overall purpose, think of as many analogies and metaphors as you can that describe it. For example:

▶ *My presentation is like a firework display because it has enough bangs to hold the audience's attention.*
▶ *My presentation is like a hot air balloon because it will take us all to new heights.*
▶ *My presentation is like a circus because there are lots of attractions and opportunities for fun.*

Come up with at least six ideas to get you started.

My presentation is like ... because ...

You can also use this technique for key messages. For example:

▶ *My key message is like a children's story because metaphors are the secret ingredient that enthralls them for hours.*

My key message is like ... because

This exercise is designed to stimulate your thinking about how creative you can be in coming up with metaphors. Metaphors and analogies provide an elegant and articulate way of expressing ideas that is far more memorable than telling it straight.

Quotes

Quotes can be used to perk up your presentations by providing new perspectives on situations or linking ideas together. They can be well known ('We have nothing to fear but fear itself', Franklin D. Roosevelt) or unfamiliar ('If you don't risk anything, you risk even more', Erica Jong). Either way they add interest.

The shorter and more original quotes are the better. They don't have to be from famous people, they can also come from books you're reading, magazine articles, the internet and so on. Quotes from clients, people working inside your company or suppliers can be extremely effective and potentially motivating.

DOs AND DON'Ts OF USING QUOTES

Do
- *Make sure your quotes are credible, relevant to your point and appropriate for your audience.*
- *Tell the audience who said it. If you're not sure, say so.*
- *If you're using several quotes draw them from a range of sources. If they're all from one, your audience may wonder why the person you're quoting isn't speaking instead of you.*

Don't
- *Limit your quotes to dead famous white men, but choose from a diverse range of living people.*
- *Pass off a saying as one of your own if that's not the case. We came across a speaker, who will remain nameless, who did this, and for those people in the audience who recognized the omission he lost all credibility.*
- *Use too many quotes. If you use half a dozen it may come across as forced. If you have a fairly short opportunity to speak – 15 to 20 minutes – include only one or two.*

Quotes are widely available on the internet. Some websites specialize in them such as www.quotationspage.com where you can find quotes categorized under a vast array of topics such as attitude, change, progress, risk and success.

Definitions

Definitions can be useful in a presentation too. You can use them for something simple such as defining an important business term, to clarify your message or to add humour.

> *'A boss is someone who's early when you're late and late when you're early.'*

> *'An expert is someone who's called in at the last moment to share the blame.'*

Communicating customer/client testimonials

In a pitch or sales presentation you can tell a prospect about organizations that you're already working for. Some presenters merely provide a list of organizations they've done business with but including testimonials is a great way of adding flavour and finding a way of repeating your core messages. Choose testimonials that illustrate success with organizations similar to theirs. Actively soliciting comments from existing clients will give you a pool you can draw from when necessary.

> *'I'd just like to say a big "thank you" for your fantastic customer service. When we had a problem recently you put it right straight away – no fuss, no hassle. If only all companies were as responsive as you are!'*

Stacking the mix

Now you're familiar with all the different ways you can add flavour we'd like to illustrate how you can stack the mix. Stacking is like repeatedly hammering a nail – every type of flavour bangs it in farther. The deeper the nail goes the more difficult it is for people to remove it. That's how you make ideas stick so strongly they have no choice but to remember them.

Here's an example of how we sometimes stack four different kinds of flavour when pitching for business. Our key message is 'We tailor our courses to match your exact specifications', and we want to make sure that prospects are clear about this by the time we've finished speaking.

> *Speak First is a specialist communication training company that operates like Dell Computers. We don't just provide courses off the peg, we create tailored solutions to meet the specific needs of our clients. Everything is built to order. (ANALOGY)*
>
> *Let us bring that to life for you. We've worked with a number of organizations similar to yours, with similar needs. One was ABC, who wanted a Personal Impact course for their frontline staff. The company's policy was to grow by acquisition. As a result, people of many different nationalities and cultures worked together, often in a pressured environment. Some managers were in a different country from several of their direct reports, so face-to-face meetings were infrequent and often hurried. The different working and communication styles resulted in misunderstandings and conflict. The company's rapid expansion encouraged an aggressive 'can do' style among employees. We designed a tailored two-day Personal Impact course for mixed nationality groups, across Europe, incorporating many*

practical exercises based on real-life situations. The feedback was extremely positive. As the course was rolled out in different countries, and key messages about high level sponsorship for changing the culture were reinforced, participants were able to express concerns, challenge upwards and become more assertive without fear of retribution. Staff satisfaction and motivation increased dramatically as a result. (CASE STUDY)

We know we can make the same kind of difference in your company. You've said that you want something that's designed specifically to meet your needs. We have a track record of doing just that and we're excited about working with you. I guess some of you will have eaten at Burger King and be familiar with their slogan 'Have it your way'. We don't want you to have to have it our way – we want you to have it your way. (QUOTE)

But don't just take our word for it. Emma at ABC Ltd says we're flexible to work with. She likes the way we take her views on board. She says: 'Speak First are great to work with and they have some great trainers who take time to fully understand our needs.' (CLIENT TESTIMONIAL)

You may have noticed that in this final section we've used a number of analogies (nail, hammer) and illustrated it by telling you a story. What works in presentations also works in writing. When you have important messages to communicate, make sure you get them across. Flavour comes in all shapes and sizes and is only limited by your imagination.

TEN KEY POINTS TO REMEMBER

1 *Adding 'flavour' to the facts is the difference that makes the difference when it comes to presentations.*

2 *'Flavour' allows you to paint pictures in people's minds and repeat a message without patronising the audience.*

3 *Illustrations, case studies and examples are a great way of making sure your messages stick.*

4 *Some business presentations contain a lot of data which can end up very dry. Instead include memorable examples people want to take action on.*

5 *Stories are a phenomenally powerful way of communicating with people and play a crucial part in making your messages 'sticky'.*

6 *The best stories are based upon personal experience because vivid memories help us to visualize small details that bring them to life when we talk about them.*

7 *People love a presentation with an element of humour in it. Humour is about being playful, light-hearted and good humoured.*

8 *Metaphor is the language of the unconscious mind which means it can be used to connect with people at a deeper level.*

9 *Using short and more original quotes can add interest and help you link ideas together.*

10 *When you have important information to communicate 'stack the mix' so every type of flavour hammers your messages home.*

9

Using scripts and notes

In this chapter you will learn:
- *when to use a script and when to use notes*
- *how to write a script*
- *about the difference between writing and speaking*
- *how to create effective notes*
- *about conversational presenting without notes.*

Scripts vs. notes

One of the questions we're most commonly asked on our courses is 'Should I write a script or is it better to use notes instead?' Our answer is always a categorical, definite 'It depends'. There are pros and cons for each approach, and which you choose depends on factors such as the situation, your level of experience and how well you know the subject.

Sometimes reading from a script is absolutely the right thing to do – and sometimes it's completely wrong. Sometimes using notes will give you the result you want – and sometimes it won't. And sometimes it's better to speak without either – no notes, no script. Let's take a look at the advantages and disadvantages of each of these options.

Why read a script – and why not?

When politicians or senior business leaders speak in public you often see them reading from a script. And with good reason. Where there are potentially legal, contractual or political consequences it would be foolhardy to rely upon memory. A slip of the tongue or a momentary lapse of concentration could have dire financial or personal implications. It's far better to be safe than sorry. You should consider opting for a script when you have:

▶ *A specific message that must be communicated accurately.*
▶ *Lots of detail in it which it would be impossible or difficult to remember.*
▶ *A complex argument or development of ideas that needs to be in the right order.*
▶ *Memorable turns of phrase/rhetorical techniques you want to include.*
▶ *Stories, humour, anecdotes, etc. which form an integral part of the presentation.*

But there are downsides to reading a script, as anyone who's ever listened to one delivered badly will be only too aware:

▶ *Unless you're experienced in reading scripts your delivery can be stilted and lack a sense of spontaneity.*
▶ *Your voice doesn't project as well because you're looking down more of the time.*
▶ *Eye contact with the audience is greatly reduced because of the amount of attention devoted to the script.*
▶ *You can easily lose your place. We know of one senior manager who took a sip of water and then repeated a whole page of his script without realizing it!*

Why use notes – and why not?

Instead of a script that includes every word, many people use brief notes, usually written in a bullet point form, as prompts. This results in a much more conversational style of presenting. Having glanced briefly at their cards to check what they want to talk about next, they then speak naturally and spontaneously, making good eye contact with the audience and engaging and connecting with them. This approach, though, is not suitable for every situation. You need to know what you're talking about and be sure there are no risks associated with going wrong. Notes are the best option when:

▶ *You have extensive, detailed knowledge of your subject matter.*
▶ *There are no significant risks associated with missing out details.*
▶ *You want a conversational style with lots of audience engagement.*
▶ *It's not essential to include specific rhetorical techniques.*

Potential problems with using notes are:

▶ *You don't have every last detail recorded, you need to remember more yourself.*
▶ *It's easy to be indiscreet. Some CEOs have famously made inappropriate off-the-cuff remarks that are embarrassing and damaging to their company.*
▶ *You're relying on your own ability to convey the information in an interesting and engaging way.*

We have a dream – no notes at all!

Most people go through an evolutionary process when learning to present. When they start out they feel the need for either a script or detailed notes, but over time they come to feel more comfortable with just a few notes or simply use their slides as a prompt. Some ultimately reach the stage where they're confident enough to speak in public without a script, notes or slides to help keep them on track. It's like when you learn to ride a bicycle. First you have stabilizers. Then you have your mum or dad running behind holding the saddle. Then you do it all on your own.

This can seem like an impossible dream to some inexperienced or nervous presenters. They simply can't imagine being able to stand up in public without a security blanket or safety net of some kind. But some people do – and with enormous success. Of course, you need to know your topic inside out and trust in your ability to speak fluently and articulately off-the-cuff.

We believe that you should aspire whenever possible to do without notes altogether. Often they're a distraction, they get in the way, and if you know your stuff there's no reason why you can't present effectively without them. In fact, you probably do so already in situations where you feel confident and competent. If so, you'll know how much more natural, spontaneous and conversational it feels. Some people resist this approach because they're concerned about what to do if their mind goes blank or they miss something out altogether. In practice this is rarely a serious problem. Should it happen you'll quickly get back on track.

We're not saying you should never use notes. No matter how experienced you are at presenting, there will be times when you don't know the subject as well or have limited time to prepare. Our view is that it's better to give a good presentation using a script or notes than a bad one without them.

Insight

It can be scary letting go of notes when that's what you've always done. In my (Amanda's) experience it's easier than you might think once you give it a try. Many years ago when I started to speak in public I remember the sense of freedom I gained from trusting myself enough to know the subject matter and let go of my 'comfort blanket'.

DIY scriptwriting

If you decide you do need a script for a particular occasion, where do you start? One option is obviously to write it yourself. If you're experienced in putting your thoughts down on paper you should have no trouble pulling together a workable script. It's much like writing a report or a proposal. You move paragraphs around until they flow well, following the Firework Display Model described in Chapter 6. You also need to add plenty of flavour – stories, illustrations, anecdotes, examples, quotes, etc. – as discussed in Chapter 8.

The main difference is that you need to write as you speak. If you draft your speech 'correctly', as you would a formal piece of writing, you'll come across as stuffy and lacking in personality. Following these simple 'rules' will help make it sound more natural:

▶ *Use 'contractions' – 'you'll' rather than 'you will', 'we're' rather than 'we are'.*
▶ *Avoid pompous, pretentious words and phrases – go for 'use' rather than 'employ', 'I'm delighted to be here' rather than 'It is my pleasure to attend this function'.*
▶ *Go for short, sharp phrases that make their point quickly, instead of long, rambling sentences that seem to go on forever.*

You may find you're able to write your script in one sitting, but more often than not you'll need to come back to it, perhaps a number of times. Once you've finished it, put it to one side for a few days, if your schedule allows, and come back to it with fresh eyes to see how you can improve it.

Getting professional help

Don't feel you have the skills to craft a really good script? You're not alone. Some people can express themselves easily when it comes to writing, but many struggle to communicate as clearly as they would like. If that's true of you, why not ask a colleague to help or, if you work in a company where there's a communications department, see if they can offer assistance?

When the stakes are high it's worth considering engaging the services of a professional scriptwriter who is expert at getting your message across clearly and accurately. Once they've been briefed by you on what you want to achieve, along with background information, they'll craft a speech that keeps the audience interested and engaged, using tricks of the trade such as anecdotes, humour and rhetorical techniques (explained in Chapter 17). In the process they'll help you sound intelligent, articulate, compassionate, whatever impression you would like to give.

If you're not sure what you want to say, don't worry. They're used to asking questions to help you clarify your core messages and central theme. In fact, hiring a scriptwriter can be a powerful way of taking a machete to the dense jungle of information you have and creating a clearing where you can see what's important.

Producing hard copy

If you're using a script you'll obviously need to read it on the day. One option is to use an autocue/teleprompter system, which has the advantage that you don't need to look down to read – you appear to be speaking spontaneously because the words are displayed on a clear glass screen which the audience can't see (see Chapter 14 for more information on using an autocue/teleprompter).

More often than not, though, you'll be reading from the printed page, in which case you need to make sure the words are as legible as possible. If you've employed a scriptwriter they may do this for you, if not you'll have to sort it out yourself. Here are some things to bear in mind:

▶ *Even if you have legible handwriting make sure you produce a printed document. Use a clear font such as Verdana or Gill Sans and a point size 14.*

- ▶ *Don't write in capitals. Contrary to popular belief, this makes it harder, not easier, to read. Use upper and lower case text instead.*
- ▶ *Keep paragraphs short and leave space between them so you can find your place quickly and easily.*
- ▶ *Use at least 1.5 line spacing, ideally double-line spacing. It makes the words easier to read.*
- ▶ *End each page after a complete paragraph – somewhere you would naturally pause. This will give you an opportunity to move to the next page without it being obvious.*

When you do go from one page to the next, simply slide the page you've finished to the side. It's less distracting than turning it over. Don't hold your script, unless you really have to. Place it on a table or lectern. If you have it in your hands, you'll wave it around.

Using notes

Many people use notes when presenting. It's probably the most common approach, along with using PowerPoint as a prompt. There's nothing fundamentally wrong with using notes, but if you look at them frequently it can give the impression that you don't know what you're talking about. If you only glance at them occasionally it's not a big deal.

Some people use slides *and* notes, and this 'belt and braces' approach has a serious drawback. Because they're looking in two places it dramatically reduces the amount of eye contact they give to the audience.

Creating effective notes

The secret of creating effective notes is simple – less is more. Distil what you want to say into as few words as possible.

This means simple headings followed by bullet points of the main things you want to cover, or, if you prefer, a spider diagram. The only exceptions are when you need to make sure what you say is 100 per cent accurate, such as facts and figures, quotes, names or places and testimonials. Avoid writing complete sentences – you'll get drawn into reading them.

And don't use A4 notepaper. It's hard to keep track of where you are, and floppy when you move it around. A better option is to use 15 x 8 cm index/prompt cards. Because they're slightly thicker, and significantly smaller than A4, they're easier to handle.

To minimize the risk of getting confused when you're presenting, write on one side of the card only, and use a new card for each new idea. Don't use any more cards than you need to, or you'll be endlessly going from one to another.

There's nothing wrong with writing on cards by hand as long as you do it clearly and legibly. That means large letters so you can read the words at a glance. It can also help if you highlight key words and phrases so they leap out from the page, which means they're less likely to be missed.

Adding timing prompts can help you keep on track with longer presentations. Placing a number in the right-hand corner is a life-saver if you drop your cards and need to put them back into the correct sequence quickly.

USING INDEX/PROMPT CARDS EFFECTIVELY

Don't hold your cards. They limit your ability to gesture effectively (see Chapter 15). Instead, place them nearby, just in front of you, so you can glance down at them when needed. The edge of a desk or a small table works better than a lectern. When you've finished with a card just slide it sideways, rather than turning it over, which draws attention to it.

Some organizations have a standard way of presenting that is part of their organization's culture. It may be to use notes, have prompt cards held in the hand, or slides with notes pages and so on. It can, in Amanda's experience, be hard for people to go against the company norm even if they know it's getting in the way. Be courageous. Be a pioneer. If the company uses cards, by all means create them – but put them down rather than holding them, and only refer to them when you have to.

It depends

Scripts and notes form a vital part of good preparation. A script requires thought and conversational language and the secret of good notes is – less is more. Then, of course, you could follow the dream and go for nothing at all. When you come to decide whether to use notes, a script or use nothing at all, you'll know the answer – 'It depends'.

TEN KEY POINTS TO REMEMBER

1 *There are pros and cons for using scripts and notes. Which you choose depends on the situation, your level of experience and how well you know the subject.*

2 *Where there are potentially legal, contractual or political consequences it's best to use a script.*

3 *There are downsides to reading a script. Your delivery can be stilted, your voice doesn't project as well, eye contact is greatly reduced and you can easily lose your place.*

4 *Notes are the best option when you have detailed knowledge of the subject, there are no significant risks with missing out details and you want to deliver your presentation in a conversational style.*

5 *The problem with notes is you have to remember more yourself; it's easy to be indiscreet.*

6 *Notes can be a distraction and you'll come across as more spontaneous without them.*

7 *The secret of creating effective notes is simple – less is more.*

8 *Use a new card for each idea; write on one side only using large letters that are clear and easy to read at a glance.*

9 *Place cards near by so you can glance down at them when needed.*

10 *Do you use scripts or cards? Or follow the dream and go for nothing at all.*

10

Using visual aids effectively

In this chapter you will learn:
- *why good presentations don't have to include visual aids*
- *how visual aids can add impact*
- *about different types of visual aids*
- *when and how to use supporting materials*
- *how to create effective PowerPoint slides.*

Why use visual aids?

When most people think of visual aids, it's PowerPoint that comes immediately to mind. The program, developed by Microsoft, is the automatic choice of many presenters in the business world. But it doesn't have to be that way. There are many different ways to bring a presentation to life, and that doesn't necessarily mean getting out the laptop and projector.

The whole idea of using visual aids is to communicate more effectively. Many people absorb information better when, as well as listening, they have something to look at or touch. Words alone can sometimes be enough to get your message across, but the saying 'a picture paints a thousand words' is true. Showing the audience diagrams, photographs or charts will often be more effective. For many people seeing really is believing. They learn more easily by seeing a process demonstrated or by handling a sample of a product.

Your aim should be to stimulate as many of the audience's senses as possible. Most of us have zoned out at least once during a presentation, and that's usually because there's not enough going on to keep us alert. This is particularly true when the subject matter is dry, abstract or detailed.

VISUAL AIDS ARE NOT A MAGIC WAND

Visual aids, used well, can help improve attention span, but they're no substitute for a lack of content, imagination, structure or passion. *They can make a good presentation better – they can't make a bad presentation good.* If what you're saying lacks substance, no amount of PowerPoint will make it succeed. It's like dining at a beautiful restaurant with attractive table decorations, fine linen and barely edible food. You're bound to end up disappointed.

VISUAL AIDS ARE NOT ESSENTIAL

It's worth making the point that, despite what some people and many companies seem to think, visual aids are not compulsory. It's perfectly possible to give a compelling presentation without them. In fact, if anything, it's easier to give a compelling presentation without them because there's nothing to distract the audience's attention from the speaker and the message. More often than not powerful presentations involve people just talking. Certainly the ones that have stuck in our memory are like that.

Types of visual aids

Before discussing PowerPoint in some detail, let's consider some of the other options, which include flipcharts, handouts, whiteboards and props, each of which can be useful when presenting.

WHITEBOARDS AND FLIPCHARTS

The advantage that whiteboards and flipcharts have over PowerPoint is that you can use them creatively and fluidly. Starting with a blank canvas, you can build up things like diagrams, lists and processes step by step. They also make it possible to put things over more spontaneously in the moment. Slides need to be prepared ahead of time, which means they're fixed. What happens if you think of something extra you want to say once you're delivering the presentation? How can you illustrate it? With PowerPoint you're stuck. When using a whiteboard or flipchart you don't have that problem. In some circumstances presenters will use all three – PowerPoint, whiteboard and a flipchart.

Whiteboards

These can be found in the meeting rooms of many businesses, so they're available when you need them. If you think or know you'll be using a whiteboard, make sure you clean it before you start – it makes you look unprepared and potentially unprofessional if you have to clean it when the audience is in front of you. Write legibly and draw clearly so it's easy for everyone to understand without having to strain. Use proper whiteboard pens. Some marker pens aren't designed for whiteboards and it's hard to erase them afterwards. Remember to wipe the board clean before you leave so it's ready for the next presenter, especially if there's confidential information on it. Some whiteboards can be connected to a computer, which allows the information to be downloaded and stored for later distribution to the audience.

Flipcharts

Flipcharts are even more flexible than whiteboards, and ideal for small- to medium-sized groups. But don't try to use them at conferences or other large gatherings as only those at the front will be able to see what you're writing. The great thing about flipcharts is that you can tear off individual sheets and put them on the wall, side by side. The problem with a whiteboard is that once it's full you have to rub something out to continue. You should be aware, though, that some individuals and companies think of flipcharts as training tools rather than presenting tools, and consider them less professional than PowerPoint.

You can prepare flipcharts in advance or create them as you go along. Start with a blank page, or just your session title. Be sure to include break sheets (blank pages) that prevent writing underneath from showing through. One sheet may be sufficient, but when the flipchart paper is thin leave two sheets between each page. Using chisel-edged pens rather than bullet tips will give strong, clear readable results. On pre-prepared flipcharts you can fold back a small section of one of the bottom corners to help you find a page quickly. This method also creates space between the pages so they turn more easily.

Another useful tip if you're presenting on a new subject, or want to recall an important point easily, is to write 'cheat notes'. All you need to do is lightly pencil in key words on the edge of the flipchart at eye level. They won't be visible to your audience and will help you feel confident when you present. It can be useful sometimes to have two stands. You can prepare one set before and use the other to work interactively. Or just use two and move across the presentation area.

Insight

Take care when using whiteboards and flipcharts, advises Steve. I see a lot of presenters turn their back on the audience, and this not only disconnects you from them, it also seems rude. Always keep your body as open to the room as possible when writing on a whiteboard or flipchart.

OVERHEAD PROJECTORS

You still see overhead projectors in lots of places, but not many people use them any more. The idea of producing acetates rather than PowerPoint these days is like something out of the ark and if your audience sees you using overheads you'll almost certainly go down in their estimation. We strongly advise you to avoid them.

PROPS

There are endless possibilities when it comes to props. You might use a long elastic band to show how flexing your personal style creates tension. Or a tennis ball to demonstrate how far you can project your voice. Spinning plates can be used to illustrate how to balance a number of priorities at once. If you get yourself into a creative frame of mind you should be able to come up with metaphors or analogies for just about any problem or situation you find yourself facing. These can help your audience understand potentially abstract, theoretical ideas in tangible, practical ways.

Props can also be more literal. If you manufacture or sell products you might pass samples round for people to look at or handle. One clothes retailer we know uses the garments he wears to illustrate his own products. If you have a brochure or quote from a magazine you could hold that up. Take care when passing things round – you'll inevitably lose the attention of some members of the group for a while.

HANDOUTS

If you provide printed copies of your slides before you start they can be thought of as visual aids because people will inevitably look at them as you go along. This can work to your advantage, especially when you have detailed financial charts, step-by-step sequences or complex diagrams that may be difficult to read on the screen. But there are potential disadvantages as well. Some members of your audience may start to look ahead and by the time you get to a particular point or slide they're already familiar with it. Without a doubt their attention will be split and as a result they'll be less focused on you and what you're saying. If you present in a way that commands their attention, that won't be a serious problem, but it's an issue to be aware of.

Our view is that most of the time it's better not to distribute your handouts ahead of time, but you may have no choice. It's the norm in many companies and at some events such as conferences. People often like to have copies of slides so they can write notes on them and get irritated if they're not provided. If you do provide a print-out of your slides, make them easy to read and have lots of white space. We recommend you go for PowerPoint 'notes pages' handouts with two slides to a page.

PowerPoint

Let's be honest. Most people don't use PowerPoint as a visual aid to help the audience understand and recall their message. They use it as a visual prompt to help them remember what they're going to say. That's one of the reasons for the program's enduring popularity. It makes it possible to speak in public without the need to constantly refer to notes. That's why so many presenters have more slides than they need and put too much information on each slide. The end result is what we call 'Death by PowerPoint'.

Now, we don't condemn relying on slides as a memory jogger, but there's no substitute for good preparation, adequate practice time and some concise notes if you need them. The problem is that most people don't believe they'll be able to recall what they want to say without slides to rely on. This is true up to a point, but our experience of running courses, and observing lots of presentations, is that most people can remember more than they think. Besides, if you know your stuff, keep slides to a minimum and speak from the heart. You're much more likely to engage your audience.

Another reason so many presenters use PowerPoint is because they think it's professional. And it can be – but only when used well.

THE PROBLEM WITH POWERPOINT

Recent research undertaken by Professor John Sweller, (University of New South Wales, Australia) suggests that PowerPoint can actually inhibit the amount of data that people remember. He found that the human brain processes information most effectively when it's presented in either a verbal or written form, and least effectively when it's presented in both forms at the same time. Anyone who reads out exactly what's written on their slides is actively reducing the amount the audience remembers because reading and listening at the same time places too great a strain on their working memory.

Professor Sweller says, 'If you have ever wondered why your eyes start glazing over as you read those dot points on the screen, at the same time words are being spoken, it is because it is difficult to process information if it is coming in the written and spoken form at the same time.'

Repetition of this kind makes the brain 'switch off' and stop listening. Professor Sweller says that points should never be read aloud from PowerPoint. Doubling up does not double the chances of the message getting across.

'It is not effective to speak the same words that are written, because it is putting too much load on the mind and decreases your ability to understand what is being presented. PowerPoint can backfire if the information on the screen is the same as that which is verbalized because the audience's attention will be split.'

Professor Sweller says that if you say something different from what's on the slide, perhaps by elaborating on a bullet-point or even better discussing a diagram, chart or picture, you don't put the same 'cognitive load' on the working memory.

Preparing your slides

In many companies PowerPoint is so much part of the culture it would be considered an aberration not to use it, so we're certainly not going to suggest that. What we do recommend, though, is that you limit the number of slides you use, and keep the content of each to the absolute minimum.

Most importantly of all, don't plan your presentation round the slides. Do it the other way round. Create the structure first, and then consider what visuals will support or illustrate the various points. This avoids the structure of the presentation being driven by the PowerPoint, which is something that happens with great regularity.

Visual aids should add value to your presentation. Avoid producing slides that simply repeat what you're going to say. If words are all you have on them they're potentially dull and probably not going to be effective as a visual 'aid'. Add relevant pictures, statistics, diagrams, etc. Give your audience something interesting to look at which complements and reinforces the messages you want to communicate.

SETTING THE STYLE

It's essential, before you begin, to plan the overall look and style of your slides – the type style, colours and graphics you're going to use. This is good practice even if you're only producing something 'quick and dirty'. Ten minutes spent creating a consistent theme that runs though all the slides will pay real dividends in the professional look and feel you end up with.

Some companies produce strict guidelines on company branding that covers all these elements and more and it's essential you follow them to the letter. Companies create them so they can protect the way their brand is communicated. They may even have an existing PowerPoint template you can use, which makes life easier. You simply flow your content into the existing design and everything is formatted automatically for you. If you're not in a corporate role or there isn't a standard slide pack available, you'll need to come up with your own style.

MASTERING POWERPOINT

If you're not familiar with PowerPoint there's plenty of free information on the internet to get you started, or you might ask an experienced colleague to show you the basics. The PowerPoint help screens are useful too. If that's not enough, there are lots of good books on the market, such as *Teach Yourself PowerPoint*.

WHICH BACKGROUND?

If no template is provided/prescribed by your company you need to choose one yourself. Go for one that's attractive but not busy.

There are standard templates available in PowerPoint that, while quick and easy to use, are well known and widely employed. If you want to stand out from the crowd you'll ultimately want your own template. These can be bought ready-made or you might prefer to commission a company to design a unique template.

Company logos need to be displayed in the same place on each slide and should be discreet. The easiest way of doing this is to use the Slide Master which ensures consistency from slide to slide.

Colour can add vibrancy to a presentation, but too much can be distracting. If in doubt go for a white background with perhaps some slim graphic strips at the top, bottom or edges. Take care when using strong colours as subtle shades often work better. Most of the colour schemes available in PowerPoint work effectively. You're probably already aware that colours on your PC may not reproduce accurately when projected onto a screen, so it's a good idea to test them through a projector before giving a presentation. You may need to change them to achieve the result you want.

CREATING YOUR SLIDES

Once you've created your Master Slide you start with a blank PowerPoint screen page in front of you. The next stage is obviously to flow in your content. Don't try to cram too much onto each slide. Less is more. If you have some text, a photograph, quote and diagram on the same page your audience won't know where to look first and certainly won't be listening to you while they work it out. This may seem like an exaggeration but it is commonplace in many companies. When you create a slide, think of it from the audience's perspective. Be selective – only include your main points and put detailed information into a supporting document.

PRESENTATIONS VS. LEAVE-BEHINDS

One common cause of 'Death by PowerPoint' is trying to kill two birds with one stone – producing a presentation and a leave-behind at the same time. As a result both get done badly. As Jerry Weissman points out in *The Art of Winning*, there's a lot of confusion between presentations and documentation:

> **The Presentation-as-Document Syndrome represents one of the most common underlying problems that plague presentations. Presenters have become so accustomed to relying on graphics, especially PowerPoint slides, that they often think of the presentation as a mere accompaniment to those aids. In fact, many people act as if the presentation is completely dispensable. They'll say, 'I can't attend your presentation next week. But it doesn't matter. Just send me your slides!' Or they sometimes say, 'Send me your slides in advance.' The PowerPoint slides then are treated as handouts.**

You need two distinct, different, documents:

▶ *Your PowerPoint presentation, which should have as few words as necessary.*
▶ *Your leave-behind, which will have lots of background details, information and data.*

Problems often arise when a written document, such as a report or proposal, is repurposed into a presentation. If there's not much time, or the presenter isn't aware of the PowerPoint/leave-behind issue, the slides can end up containing way too much information.

Insight

Some people, writes Amanda, have limited control over their PowerPoint because it's provided by the company. Sometimes they can adapt the slides, but sometimes they're told to use the deck as it is. Often these slides are text- and detail-heavy, and not easy to present. The best workaround is to identify the key message in each slide and 'talk around' it. Using the 'hide slide' feature allows you to leave out anything you don't want to cover. The full set of slides can still form a handout.

HOW MUCH TEXT PER SLIDE?

To avoid this issue, follow the '6 × 6 rule'. Use no more than 6 words per line and 6 lines per slide. This will limit the detail you include, with the advantage that neither you nor the audience gets drawn into 'reading the slide'. Six words are usually enough to remind you of the point you want to make, but not too many to provide a distraction.

Of course, 6 × 6 is a counsel of perfection. You're not always going to be able to achieve that. Sometimes you'll have seven points, maybe eight, or you need slightly more than six words to capture the thought. Your aim, though, is to keep the number of bullets and their length to a minimum. Avoid complete sentences and chunks of text. If you end up with too much on one slide but can't leave it out, consider running it across two or more slides.

WHAT SIZE TEXT?

Readability is essential. Keep the font size reasonably large – minimum 20 point and maximum 32 point. Generally 24 or 28 point is about right for most presentations. The text needs to be large enough to read from the back of the room. Some people make the mistake of using a size that's appropriate for a written document, such as a report, which is 10–12 point. This is way too small for PowerPoint, and people will struggle to read it. A simple rule of thumb is to take the age of the oldest person in the room and divide it by two – that should be the size of your bullet points. In practice, 32 point is about as large as you can go without it appearing childish. The font you choose will affect the size too so you'll need to exercise judgement over what gives the best result.

Headings need to be around 8 points larger than the bullet points, so there's sufficient distinction in size between them. If the text is 28 point, the title needs to be 36 point, and so on.

WHICH FONT TO USE?

Don't use lots of different fonts, it looks amateurish. Stick to one ideally, two at the most. Most operating systems provide lots of fonts to choose from but many are unsuitable. Don't use them just because they're there. Serif fonts (those with small lines at the ends of the characters) such as Times New Roman are supposed to be easiest to read, but in practice sans serif faces such as Verdana, Gill Sans and Arial tend to be clearest. If there's a possibility you might need to email your slides to others in the future, choose a font that's standard on all PCs. If you decide to use a non-standard font, you'll have to embed it for the recipient to be able to read it, which can increase the file size considerably.

EMPHASIZING WORDS AND PHRASES

Sometimes you'll want to emphasize certain words and phrases – what's the best way of doing so? Well, as a general rule, don't underline text. It looks ugly. A better way is to use bold, which makes it stand out on the screen, or, if the words are not in a phrase, put them in a slightly bigger font size.

TEXT MISTAKES TO AVOID

Most people know that you shouldn't use capital letters in written communications, because it's the equivalent of SHOUTING, but we still occasionally see slides full of upper case text. There's nothing wrong with using capitals now and again for headings, but you *must* avoid them for the body copy, they really do annoy people intensely. And it's best to avoid italic type for your bullet points, because this reduces the legibility of the words.

Think carefully about using coloured text, even if it's your specified corporate shade. Black always looks crisp, gives a positive impression and is easy to read, even when the image is weak on the screen because of insufficient power in the projector or too much ambient light in the room. Text in red, yellow or green is best avoided because it looks cheap and tacky. Should you decide to ignore our advice and put your bullet points in a vivid colour, make sure it contrasts well with the background.

It's also essential you check for spelling mistakes. Once a slide is blown up large on a screen it's hard to miss errors, which make you look either careless or clueless.

Finally, make the words look attractive on the screen. Don't crush them up against the edge of the slide, space the lines so it looks as though some thought has gone into the preparation.

ANIMATION AND SOUND EFFECTS

It often aids comprehension to reveal one bullet at a time, building up a slide with a series of clicks. This prevents the audience jumping ahead. If you do plan to 'reveal' bullets in this way, be consistent in your method of reveal. Don't have some points whizzing in from the side, some from above and some from below. It doesn't make your presentation more interesting, if anything it draws attention to your lack of imagination. And please, please, please, don't be tempted by all the sound effects. You're not four years old!

David Slater, in the US *Sales and Marketing Management* magazine, speaks for many people when he says, 'There's a strong, growing intolerance for PowerPoint presentations with the old twelve-point font, the cheesy transitions, the car screech as a bullet comes across the street. You're really viewed negatively if you use that stuff.'

PICTURES, GRAPHS, CHARTS AND DIAGRAMS

Whenever you can, use visuals such as diagrams, illustrations, flow charts, graphs and photographs. They're a much more effective way of getting your message across and are much more engaging than words. Put up a picture of your new product or factory and then tell the audience about them rather than listing all the details as bullet points, which is immensely dull.

Make sure images are of sufficiently high quality, not low-resolution grabbed from your intranet or the web that pixellate when you blow them up. Many people consider clip art tacky and 'old hat', so it's best to avoid it unless you really have no choice. Whenever possible use photographs and drawings you've had commissioned or charts instead.

Diagrams are great for explaining processes, such as the steps of a sales procedure. Charts are useful for illustrating quantitative data in a way that's quick and easy to understand, such as pie charts or histograms.

Insight

Slides that are simply a full-screen picture with no words at all have great impact – and are most likely to stay in your audience's memory, advises Amanda. This is especially true when the picture relates to one of the key messages you want to get across. But avoid including images for the sake of it. They must be relevant or you'll irritate your audience.

VIDEO CLIPS

Relevant video clips can really enhance a presentation, because they give a welcome change of pace. But keep them short. Your audience's attention can easily drift if they're more than five minutes long. Your company may pay for these to be produced professionally. It's also relatively easy to capture action using a digital camcorder and edit the recording on your PC. The resulting file can be embedded in PowerPoint in seconds and can be set to start automatically when you come to the appropriate slide.

The art of good visual aids

When visual aids are used well they definitely help get the message across. When they're used badly they become a visual *hindrance* to effective communication. The art lies in planning your presentation from the perspective of your audience. Your aim should be 'Life' not 'Death by PowerPoint'.

TEN KEY POINTS TO REMEMBER

1 *Visual aids can make a good presentation better – they can't make a bad presentation good.*

2 *It's possible to give a compelling presentation without visual aids; many people absorb information better when they have something to look at or touch.*

3 *There are a number of other options for visual aids apart from PowerPoint including whiteboards, flipcharts, props and handouts.*

4 *Create the structure of your presentation first and then plan your visual aids around it.*

5 *Plan the overall look and style of your slides – many companies issue guidelines on company branding that includes a template for you to follow.*

6 *If you don't have company guidelines choose a background that isn't too distracting. A white background with slim graphics at the top, bottom or edges works well.*

7 *You need two distinct documents: your PowerPoint presentation – with as few words as possible – and your leave-behind which contains details, information and data.*

8 *Follow the 6 × 6 rule. Aim to use no more than 6 words per line and 6 lines per slide.*

9 *Stick to one, possibly two, sans serif fonts such as Verdana, Gill Sans or Arial.*

10 *Avoid cheesy transitions with sound effects and use pictures, graphs, charts, diagrams and video clips where relevant to make your presentation more engaging.*

11

Rehearsing and timing

In this chapter you will learn:
- *why rehearsal and timing are vital to success*
- *how to rehearse effectively*
- *about the value of feedback and continual improvement.*

Rehearsal is vital to success

Picture the scene. You're five minutes into your presentation and you realize you don't know how to go from one point to another. A slide comes up and you can't think where it fits in. Your mind suddenly goes blank. It's a nightmare scenario, and it gradually dawns on you that you haven't rehearsed sufficiently. But it doesn't have to be that way. You can make sure all the effort you've put into preparation pays off. You can make certain you deliver your core messages and bring your ideas to life with plenty of flavour. All you need to do is make time to practise.

Why people don't rehearse

Everyone knows it's important to rehearse. Yet when we ask on courses how many people actually do, it's rare for more than a couple of hands to go up. The rest of the group just looks sheepish. Most people realize they should practise, but the majority don't.

Yes, we know you're too busy. Yes, we know it can be tedious. Yes, we know. But rehearsal's not optional. It's a crucial part of the process. If you don't practise it's like failing to spell-check a report before sending it. You're setting things up to fail.

> ### Insight
>
> When I (Steve) am tight for time, and barely have a moment to spare to rehearse for an important presentation, I focus on three areas. I always make sure I know what I'm going to say first – the first two to three sentences pretty much word for word – so I get off to a good start. Then, because a chain is only as strong as its weakest link, I work on the areas I'm least confident about. That's where the presentation can easily go off the rails. And, third, I make sure I am able to deliver my key message/s with maximum impact, to ensure I achieve what I set out to do.

Factors that affect rehearsal time

How much time should you allow for rehearsal? It depends on a number of factors, including how long you'll be speaking for, how familiar you are with the subject matter, and how important the presentation is.

If you're an experienced presenter and are familiar with the subject, you obviously won't need as much practice time as a novice who is new to the material. But if there's a lot riding on the outcome, and you don't feel 100 per cent prepared, you'll want to spend time making sure your presentation is as good as it can be.

When people deliver the same thing several times they're less likely to bother with rehearsing. This is understandable but potentially dangerous. It's easy to become blasé and you can end up going through the motions. What you're aiming for is to appear fresh, as if you're saying it for the first time.

Possible ways of rehearsing

There are a number of ways to practise. Many people rehearse mentally. They think it through step by step and say the words to themselves. This is a vital part of the process. It helps you remember your material and make sure it's in the right sequence. One major advantage is that you can do this any time and any place you happen to be. But there are disadvantages. You can't check the timing and you can't practise gestures. Nor can you get a real sense of how well you're doing or feedback of any kind.

Another way of rehearsing is to do it for real, taking as long as you actually will when delivering the presentation. The downside of this approach is that it's time consuming. But the advantages easily outweigh the negatives. Running through your presentation in this way allows you to get as close as possible to what it will really be like. If you're using visual aids on the day, practise with them. The more familiar you are with the order of your slides, or how to draw a diagram on a whiteboard, the better you'll do on the day. You can check timing, flow, gestures, pausing, where you place emphasis on words and so on.

There may be some parts of your presentation you know well already, and it makes no sense to spend much time on them. One option is to concentrate on the bits that you feel least confident or knowledgeable about.

It's a good idea, in particular, to make sure you know what you're doing with the first two minutes. That's the part many people find most scary – once they get going they're fine. Another bonus of breaking your presentation down into chunks is that you can try out sections while driving or walking the dog, which makes good use of spare time. Once again, there are downsides. It's difficult to check how long it will take to complete the whole thing and you may end up having to 'wing it' with any parts you neglect.

It's often recommended that people rehearse in front of a mirror. Some find it helpful, others find it puts them off. A better solution is to use a video camera to film yourself. One of the disadvantages of the methods we've discussed is that none of them involve an audience. If you're planning a complete run through, why not enlist the help of a family member, colleague or friend? That way you get a real reaction. You can also practise eye contact. This can sometimes be a challenge to arrange when you're busy and for others to find time to assist. Bert Decker, author of *You've Got to be Believed to be Heard*, gets round this problem in a novel way. He recommends you practise with a paper audience, by drawing faces on sticky notes. While you won't get a response, it does feel more like there's a group in front of you. Another option is to cut pictures of people out of magazines.

A workable schedule for rehearsing

If you weren't so busy spinning plates you'd be able to take as much time to practise as you want. As well as working up individual sections, you'd have two full 'dress rehearsals'. But when you're struggling to get everything done already you'll have to settle for the minimum. What we're proposing here is that you create a workable schedule with, ideally, at least one complete run-through.

Timing your presentation

As you rehearse, check how long it takes. There's a difference between practice and delivery speed. More often than not when the adrenalin kicks in you'll speak faster than normal, though some people slow down because they're making eye contact and waiting for reactions. If you're working from a script, one double-spaced A4 page of 14 point type is about two minutes in duration when spoken. Ten pages are around 20 minutes.

Remember to allow time for comments or questions, especially if you plan to answer them as you go along. Three or four questions during a presentation can easily add five minutes to the overall time. It's useful when timing your presentation to have a 'Plan B' for what you would leave out if your time is suddenly cut at the last minute.

Rehearsing for team presentations

Getting people together to practise a team presentation can be a challenge when diaries are full, especially when it needs to be delivered at short notice. Ideally you want everyone together to rehearse. If that's not possible, make sure the missing people are briefed thoroughly. You need to plan the introduction, decide who does what, and agree on signals that indicate who goes next.

Make time to run through the whole presentation from start to end. That means people need to learn their parts before they arrive. Check you know where the transitions are and how they will work. It only needs something simple such as a gesture to show who the next speaker will be, followed by, 'Now Daniel will talk to you about ...' or 'Now I'll hand over to Raj who will cover the implications from the IT perspective.' There's nothing worse than fumbling around and looking anxiously at each other in a vain attempt to encourage someone to speak. You must also agree who will cover what. People all too often complain afterwards that someone else has stolen their thunder.

The value of feedback

If you're working as part of a team, you have a golden opportunity to get feedback on your presentation. Because everyone involved has a vested interest in getting it right, you can help each other improve. It's useful to invite an independent observer along if possible. Sometimes we're not the best judge of our own performance when we rehearse. It's all too easy to get so close to the material that you can't discern what needs to be changed to make it as good as it can be. Other people are more likely to uncover things that are in your blind spot. They're often, for instance, in a better position to comment on how effective the transitions are between one speaker and the next.

Objective feedback can be extremely valuable in any rehearsal situation, whether or not you're working as a team. It needs to be honest, specific and constructive if it's to be of any value. You need to be open to it and willing to adapt your approach. Choose someone who not only knows the subject but also has lots of experience in presenting. Invite them to tell you in detail what they think of both the content and your delivery style so you can decide on what changes to make.

Another option is to ask a colleague to observe the first rehearsal while assessing content and then move on to delivery style once this has been refined. Think of each practice run as an experiment. If your voice is a little flat, play around with emphasizing key words and adding pauses to create some variety. If you move around rather a lot concentrate on keeping still next time you present. Ask yourself and your colleague, 'How could I have done that better?'

It's not always easy to find someone with the time to watch you deliver your presentation several times – if at all. An alternative is to get hold of a video camera and record your performance. You'll get the benefit of both seeing and hearing what you're like from the audience's perspective. Some people hate the idea of playing back their film. We strongly recommend you give it a go. You may be surprised at how much better you are at presenting than you think. Once you realize you look and sound good it will increase your confidence no end. If you tend to be self-critical set yourself the task of watching the tape at least once to look for what went well. This will help you come up with a balanced view.

Rehearsing leads to confident delivery

If you want to do a good job, whether or not there's a lot riding
on the outcome, you can't afford to skip rehearsals. When you
make it important, you reap the benefits that come with feeling
well prepared and confident. If you're able to enlist people to help
by providing you with effective feedback, you're more likely to
achieve great results.

TEN KEY POINTS TO REMEMBER

1 *Rehearsal is the key to successful presenting.*

2 *People often don't rehearse because they're too busy and set themselves up to fail.*

3 *The amount of time you spend on rehearsal will depend on how familiar you are with the subject matter, how experienced you are in presenting and how important the presentation is.*

4 *Rehearsing mentally is convenient and time-saving. The disadvantages are you can't check the timing, you can't practise gestures or get a real sense of how you're doing.*

5 *It's a good idea to rehearse the first couple of minutes because that's when you're most likely to feel nervous.*

6 *To be successful you need a workable schedule with at least one complete run through.*

7 *Time your presentation when you rehearse and be aware you're likely to speak faster when you deliver it for real.*

8 *When presenting as a team get everyone together at least once for a rehearsal. Plan the introduction, decide who does what and agree on how you'll transition from one person to the next.*

9 *Objective, honest, specific and constructive feedback is extremely valuable during a rehearsal.*

10 *When you make rehearsal important you feel well prepared and confident.*

12

Dealing with nerves and anxiety

In this chapter you will learn:
- *how to cope with nerves*
- *how changing your thinking process increases confidence*
- *why preparation and being yourself are important*
- *how to channel nervous energy so it works for you*
- *how to relieve tension, relax and visualize success.*

The number one fear

There are two types of speakers: those that are nervous and those that are liars.

Mark Twain

'Sometimes it's the anticipation that gets to me,' says Lucy. 'My brain starts racing as I'm waiting to speak. I think my mind will go blank and everyone will stare at me. It happened once. It was as if I'd forgotten how to speak. I ended up reading from my notes. I didn't dare look anyone in the eye. When it was over I made a dash for my seat. My stomach feels queasy at the thought of it.' Lucy wishes fervently she hadn't agreed to do this. 'What if I make a fool of myself and say something stupid.' She gets up and moves to the front of the room. All eyes are on her as she starts to speak.

The principal reason many people come on the courses we run is to feel more confident when speaking in public. Some get slightly nervous – the proverbial 'butterflies' in the stomach. Others have full-blown panic attacks – they really can't go on. Most fall somewhere in between.

If you get anxious at the thought of giving presentations, you can take comfort in the knowledge you're not alone. If anything, you're normal. Countless surveys and studies show the number one fear in many parts of the world to be public speaking. It's not unusual for glossophobia, as it's technically known, to be placed ahead of death. At a funeral, as the comedian Jerry Seinfeld famously observed, most people would rather be in the casket than reading the eulogy.

The good news is that something can be done about it. You don't have to suffer from anxiety. It can be cured. You can learn to feel comfortable when presenting – you can even get to the stage where you start to enjoy it!

In this chapter we'll consider how we make ourselves anxious by the way we think about speaking in public, and we'll give you some practical techniques that will enable you to overcome your fears, so you can present with confidence.

Assessing your confidence level

To find out how confident or anxious you are when speaking in public, and discover which parts of this chapter will benefit you most, complete our Presentation Stress Inventory (PSI). Allocate one point for each stress symptom you experience. If you've never presented before skip this list and read the rest of the chapter to make sure you get off to a confident start.

1 *I avoid presenting whenever possible.*
2 *I lie awake the night before thinking about my presentation.*
3 *I worry about sounding foolish or saying something stupid.*
4 *I find myself pacing up and down or fidgeting in my seat before I'm due to speak.*

5 *I often feel unprepared.*
6 *My mind goes blank and I can't recall what I intended to say.*
7 *My face and neck flush.*
8 *My mouth goes dry when I speak.*
9 *I start to breathe quickly.*
10 *My hands shake and/or my palms sweat.*
11 *My knees wobble like jelly.*
12 *My stomach feels queasy.*
13 *I can't bring myself to look at anyone directly.*
14 *My voice sounds high-pitched or even squeaky.*
15 *My lips don't work properly and I stumble over words.*
16 *I open my mouth and no sound comes out.*
17 *I think I'll miss something out or say things in the wrong order.*
18 *I'm convinced the audience can tell I'm nervous.*
19 *I tell myself I'm no good at presenting and want the ground to swallow me up.*
20 *I experience some of these symptoms in everyday situations as well.*

HOW DID YOU DO?

If you ticked fewer than three items you rarely get nervous. That means you're probably experienced and have a reasonably high level of expertise. Either that or you're slightly reckless and throw yourself into presenting without worrying too much about the consequences.

A score between four and eight suggests you've learnt to channel nervous energy so it works to your advantage. You may only feel anxious on certain occasions, perhaps when speaking to a large audience at a conference, when presenting to your peers or bosses, or when asked to step in for someone at the last moment. Reading this chapter will help you consolidate your understanding of how to handle situations like this successfully.

If you ticked 9 to 13 items it's not unusual for you to feel anxious when you present. Take note of the section on how thoughts affect your confidence level. Try the stress busting and serenity skills exercises later in this chapter to relieve the tension in your body and learn how to reprogramme your mind. People are often most nervous at the beginning of their presentation. Learn your opening statement by heart. When you get off to a flying start the rest is likely to fall into place. Try some of the techniques in this chapter to help you feel even more confident.

A score between 14 and 17 means your nerves are definitely a problem. They are almost certainly getting in the way of you presenting effectively. It may be that you're new to speaking in public or you may be someone who doesn't like being the centre of attention. What you need to do is prepare thoroughly, apply the techniques in this book, and get lots of practice. We also suggest you consider attending a presentation skills training course that uses video recordings and freeze-frame coaching. While seeing and hearing yourself on screen can be daunting initially, you'll probably discover you're better than you think you are, and this will build your confidence.

If your score is around the 18 to 20 mark you may be suffering from glossophobia – a fear or phobia of public speaking. This may have arisen as a result of a traumatic, or even trivial, past event you've unconsciously associated with speaking in public. If you said yes to question one, it may have built up over a period of time. A yes for question 20 suggests you could benefit from sessions with someone who deals with deep-rooted confidence issues.

The role of the brain

Why do we get nervous or fearful? It's all down to the way the brain works. We are biologically wired to respond to danger. It's part of our survival mechanism and our success as a species. When we perceive something as threatening, the 'reptilian' part of our brain prepares the body instantly for 'fight' or 'flight' – either to face the danger or run away from it. The powerful hormones adrenaline and cortisol surge into the blood, raising our heart rate, providing a burst of energy, reducing blood flow to the skin, and making us breathe faster.

Anyone who's ever got anxious when standing up to speak will recognize these symptoms. It feels like you've just drunk five cups of coffee. As you start your presentation your heart rate can jump to 180 beats a minute, as if you'd just run a 400 metre race flat out. Here's the problem: the 'flight or fight' response was never developed with public speaking in mind. Its purpose was to enable us to wrestle a sabre-toothed tiger to the ground or run away from it before it could eat us. How this response deals with the challenges of talking to a group of customers or presenting to a conference is out of proportion. It's a prehistoric system that's failed to develop to meet the needs of a PowerPoint age.

But what about the cerebral cortex, the most advanced part of our brain? Surely that can tell we're not in mortal danger and over-ride the reptilian brain? Well, you might have thought so. But most of the time the fight or flight mechanism is too quick. Ever vigilant, taking no chances, it fires off its chemical messengers before the conscious brain is even aware it's happening, and by then we've got sweaty palms, lungs fit to burst and a heart that's racing.

If the reptilian brain acts immediately and automatically, why is it that some people don't get anxious when doing a presentation? The answer to that important question is simple but profound: because they don't perceive it as being threatening.

How we respond to various external stimuli depends on what goes on in our brain. If we consider something to be dangerous we'll react accordingly. Speaking in public, though, is not inherently threatening. Those who fear it have usually learnt to fear it, or some aspect of it.

Some are worried about rejection, about people in the audience thinking they're stupid, boring, incompetent. They fear being evaluated, judged negatively, tested. Others are afraid of failing, of getting it wrong, of making mistakes. They would hate to be thought of as unprofessional, sloppy, or not being prepared. People get anxious for various reasons, but these are the two most common.

FEAR OF REJECTION/BEING THE CENTRE OF ATTENTION

Both have a tendency to show up in other areas as well. If, for instance, you have a fear of rejection, you may dislike being the centre of attention, and get nervous when the spotlight falls on you. For that reason you may be a reluctant presenter, and only speak in public when you have to. Such 'generalized anxiety' across a range of social situations – you may hold back in meetings too – is often the result of experiences in childhood. It's not unusual for people who dislike presenting to relate tales of having had to read something out in class when they were younger and everyone laughing at them. As a result they will do anything to avoid repeating the pain.

FEAR OF FAILURE/GETTING IT WRONG

Kalib taps his notes on the desk before placing them neatly on the table. He has spent weeks poring over his PowerPoint presentation. He likes things to be accurate. His biggest fear is missing something out or making a mistake. He gets anxious about delivering presentations and hasn't had much sleep over the last few nights. As he starts to speak, he looks at the screen and then proceeds to read each slide carefully – point by point. Twenty minutes later, he returns to his seat relieved the whole thing is over.

Kalib's story may seem a little extreme but it's not unusual for us to see people present this way. Wanting to present perfectly adds enormously to your stress levels. If you worry about making mistakes when presenting it's likely you'll feel anxious in other situations, such as when handing in a report or completing a spreadsheet. As a result, you tend to be slow and methodical, to minimize the chances of anything going wrong.

Being nervous in different situations

Of course, people have different levels of confidence in different situations. You may be comfortable speaking informally at a team meeting and only feel anxious when asked to speak to 200 people you don't know at a conference. Perhaps you only worry when senior or influential people are in the audience. You might be fine with external presentations but struggle when delivering internally. We all have different 'rules' about when to get nervous.

Social Styles and anxiety

In Chapter 5 we introduced the concept of Social Styles and four types of behaviour – Drivers, Expressives, Analyticals and Amiables. Each type experiences and handles anxiety in a different way. Which of the following reflects your nervousness profile?

Analyticals tend to get anxious the moment they know they have a presentation to give, and things get worse as the time approaches. They spend as much time as possible preparing because they want everything to be 100 per cent accurate. They worry they might miss something or make a mistake. They remain nervous all the way through the presentation, and only relax when it's over.

Some **Amiables**, but not all, experience anxiety in a range of social situations, particularly when meeting people for the first time or interacting with others who are senior to them/of a higher status. It can often affect their ability to speak up in meetings, as well as when giving presentations, which is when they feel most exposed. Many Amiables are concerned about what others think of them. Their biggest fear is looking stupid, and they take criticism personally.

Many **Expressives** have a tendency to 'wing it'. They value spontaneity and don't like too much structure – it can feel like a straightjacket to them. Because they can think on their feet, and have the gift of the gab, they often get away with it. They like to be able to improvise during a presentation. Expressives rarely get nervous at the beginning of a presentation, if anything they're bouncy and upbeat. But sometimes, if they haven't prepared or planned well enough, they get part of the way through and start to lose their way, repeating things and rambling and it's at that moment the nerves start to show.

Drivers often display lots of self-belief and self-confidence, and are the style least likely to get nervous when they feel they know what they're talking about. They generally rely on their own evaluation of how well they've done, and don't worry too much about what others think of them. However, their belief and confidence in themselves is not always justified but if it all goes wrong they may blame circumstances or others, rather than taking responsibility themselves.

Why nerves are a problem

Why are nerves such a problem? Because of the negative effect they can have on your presentation. When you get anxious a number of things happen, some of them psychological, some of them physical.

The big psychological issue many people have is that their mind goes blank. They stand up ready to speak and they have no idea what they were planning to say. There may be an internal running commentary telling them constantly how they could have done things so much better which dents their confidence.

On the physical side, all that restless, nervous energy flooding the body can find expression in a range of distracting, irritating mannerisms, such as:

- *stepping backwards and forwards*
- *endlessly twiddling a ring*
- *avoiding eye contact/looking down*
- *using fillers such as 'um' and 'er'*
- *gripping a lectern so tight the hands turn white*
- *fiddling with a pen or other object*
- *touching the face or hair.*

Nerves can affect the voice too. The muscles in the throat and neck will sometimes tighten and constrict. This affects the vocal chords and can result in a squeaky, high-pitched tone. Occasionally the voice dries up altogether. Psychologists call this 'emotional leakage', and it's a problem because it undermines the credibility of your presentation and the impact you have. When you 'um' and 'er', shuffle back and forth, or show in other ways that you're nervous, it gives the impression that you're unsure of yourself. These tell-tale signs can make the audience doubt you, on the basis that 'if you're not confident in what you're saying, why should I be?'

Research shows that whenever there's an inconsistency between the silent messages your body sends out and the content of your presentation, it's the silent messages that people will believe – and you will struggle to get your message across convincingly and compellingly if you appear nervous.

One suggestion of nervousness on its own can raise doubt in the mind of your audience, but several together can destroy any chance of them believing you, trusting you and acting on what you say. So you need to make sure you minimize, and ideally eliminate, any non-verbal signals that suggest you are uncomfortable.

Feeling confident

It's lack of faith that makes people afraid of meeting challenges, and I believe in myself.

Muhammad Ali

Think of something you're good at, something you like doing. Maybe skiing, or singing, or cooking, or dancing, or DIY, or knitting, or playing a musical instrument. Perhaps you've done it many times, and done it successfully. How do you feel about it? You probably enjoy it. Perhaps you look forward to doing it. Almost certainly you get a feeling of confidence when you think about it. You believe, you know, you can do it.

But when you think about presenting, how do you feel? You probably don't look forward to it. You almost certainly don't enjoy it. And you don't feel confident because you believe you don't speak well in public. Maybe you even know you can't do it.

That's where nerves, anxiety and fear come from – having to do something you know you can't do or believe you can't. It's true of pretty much everything – sitting exams, abseiling down a cliff, taking a driving test …

It's a simple but extremely important sequence: T → F → A

146

The thoughts (T) we have lead to the feelings (F) we experience which lead to the actions (A) we take. When we change our thoughts, our feelings automatically change and so do the actions that follow.

The solution to being afraid of presenting is, therefore, obvious. You need to develop confidence in your ability to speak successfully in public. Once you have that confidence, that belief in yourself, the worst of the nerves will evaporate. They will never disappear completely, nor would you want them to. If you ever get to the point where you don't feel any butterflies, you're in danger of losing your edge and becoming complacent.

Antidotes to feeling anxious

How do you develop that confidence? There are several different ways, which we discuss in detail below. The most powerful involve changing fearful beliefs into empowering beliefs, and these can transform the way you think about presenting in an instant. Others concern building up the skills of speaking in public, because as you become more competent so you grow in confidence.

PREPARATION IS INOCULATION

One of the most effective routes to feeling more confident is effective preparation. Emotions are often messages we send to ourselves about things we need to attend to, and one of the reasons we get anxious is because we haven't put enough time and effort into planning our presentation. The more familiar you are with your material the more comfortable you will be when you stand up and speak. So make sure you know the sequence of your slides. That way you won't get any surprises on the day. Practise your transitions from one point to another, and rehearse the parts you don't know very well. Every minute you invest in preparation will pay dividends in terms of confidence when it comes to delivery. When you know your stuff you start to relax. Confidence and good preparation go hand in hand.

PRACTISE, PRACTISE, PRACTISE

One of the simplest but most effective ways of increasing your confidence and banishing anxiety is to practise, practise, practise. The more presentations you give, the more comfortable you'll become. You'll learn skills as you go along that will enable you to handle different situations successfully. Of course you'll feel nervous initially, and have some challenges along the way. But if you follow the advice in the title of the famous book by Susan Jeffers, *Feel the Fear and Do It Anyway*, you'll quickly develop the ability to speak in public without nerves being an issue. One of the reasons so many people suffer from glossophobia is that they never face their fear, they run away from it and avoid giving presentations unless they absolutely have to. But if you take every opportunity you'll find practise improves your confidence enormously.

BEING REAL

One of the reasons some people get nervous when presenting is that they're worried about how they'll be perceived and as a result they put on a bit of an act. Instead of communicating what they know in a relaxed manner – as they would if someone asked them about the subject of their presentation at the water cooler – they give a 'performance' which comes across as forced and formal.

The problem with this approach is that you're always afraid of your 'mask' slipping, of getting found out. You can only suffer from stage fright if you put yourself on a stage, and that's what a lot of people do when speaking in public. But when you take a more conversational approach to presenting, focused around communication rather than trying to create an impression, you come across as genuine and authentic. We've developed the Matrix of Authentic Presenting (MAP) to demonstrate how this works and how it relates to the skill level of the presenter.

The vertical axis indicates how skilled you are at public speaking. It relates to things such as voice, body language, content, structure,

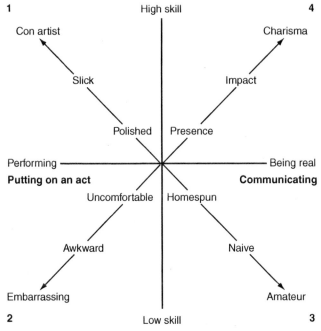

Figure 12.1 The Matrix of Authentic Presenting (MAP).

and how engaging and easy to understand your presentation is. Understanding and applying these areas is essential for success.

The horizontal axis is about whether you are performing (left-hand side) or being yourself (right-hand-side). Sometimes when people get up to present they undergo a personality change. Their desire to be 'professional' stops them from being themself and communicating well.

Quadrant 1 A presenter who is highly skilled and puts on a performance
Speakers in this quadrant have honed their skills in presenting – they're articulate, use gestures well and structure their content in a logical way. But skills on their own aren't enough to convince an audience. People want to trust the person they're listening to. Because the Quadrant 1 speaker puts on a performance, the

audience doesn't experience them as genuine. A Quadrant 1 presenter is perceived by the audience as polished, slick and, at the extreme, lacking in sincerity and untrustworthy.

Quadrant 2 A presenter who lacks skill and puts on a performance

Presenters in Quadrant 2 also put on an act – often because they think it's the professional way to present. But it comes across to those watching that they're playing a role. The Quadrant 2 presenter is not only trying too hard but also lacks skill. They may have distracting mannerisms, such as nervous fiddling, or they may simply lack impact. This kind of presenter is uncomfortable to watch, appears awkward and can sometimes even be embarrassing.

Quadrant 3 A presenter who lacks skill but is comfortable being real

Even though they're lacking in skills, Quadrant 3 presenters often get a good reception because they're real. People will usually forgive a few distracting mannerisms if they warm to the person who's speaking. Because this type of speaker comes across as sincere the audience is more likely to trust the message. Quadrant 3 presenters come across as homespun, possibly amateur, but they often lack impact.

Quadrant 4 A highly skilled presenter who is comfortable being real

You should aspire to be a Quadrant 4 presenter because the combination of high skill and being real in front of an audience is extremely powerful. Such presenters are able to communicate their messages clearly and, because they're comfortable being themselves, they also come across with passion and conviction. They have bags of impact, presence and, when highly developed, even charisma.

The best way to determine where *you* are on the Matrix is to get some feedback. You can record your presentation and play it back or ask someone you trust to be honest and encouraging to tell you how you come across.

You'll never do a perfect presentation

As we mentioned earlier, one of the reasons many people get nervous is because they feel their presentation has to be perfect, that they will have failed if they make even one mistake. This is unrealistic. It sets the bar unachievably high. Everyone makes mistakes, it's part and parcel of being a human being. You'll miss things out. Your mind will go blank for a moment. You'll deviate from your planned structure. Your remote slide changer will stop working. You'll say you have four points to make and only be able to remember three of them.

Presentations never, ever turn out exactly as you planned them. When you go to see a band live you don't expect them to play as well as they did on the original recording. There will always be slips of one kind or another. It's the nature of a live performance. You can't possibly control everything.

And so what if you do make a mistake? Does it really matter that much? Some people worry that unless their presentation is 100 per cent the audience will think they're incompetent and unprofessional. This simply isn't true. And taking that perspective sets things up to fail. As soon as you make a mistake you start to panic. It's normal to slip up a few times when presenting, it's no big deal. And if you're using PowerPoint, you're unlikely to go too far off track. If you do miss something important out, you can always include it when it comes into your mind: 'I'd just to like to add something to the point I made earlier ...'. As long as you achieve your purpose, and communicate your key messages, you can count your presentation a success.

The audience is on your side

Something else to consider if you're afraid of making a mistake or looking stupid is that most of the time the audience is on your side.

They want you to do well. Even if they disagree with the points you're making, they're understanding if things don't work out exactly as planned. They often admire you for having the courage to stand up and speak because most people are like you, they get nervous when having to present. They won't mind if you pause for a moment to gather your thoughts when your mind's gone blank. In fact, unless you draw attention to it, they probably won't even know.

THEY DIDN'T KNOW WHAT YOU WERE GOING TO SAY

And that's a really important point. Unless you regularly present to conventions of mind-readers and gatherings of clairvoyants, your audience doesn't know what it was you were going to say. So if you go 'off-piste' they won't notice. If you think of your structure as simply a starting point for spontaneous elaboration, rather than as a straightjacket you have to follow no matter what, you'll free yourself from the tyranny of having to get it right.

The power of visualization

The discussions we've had so far have been about changing your fearful beliefs into empowering ones by disputing and challenging some of the thoughts you have about what you must achieve for the presentation to be a success (it's normal to make some mistakes); how you should be when presenting (real); and what the audience thinks (they're on your side).

You can also change your beliefs and the way you think by using the kind of visualization techniques that help elite athletes to achieve peak, world-beating performances. There are many ways of doing this, but at its simplest visualization is a kind of creative daydreaming in which you see yourself behaving exactly as you would like in a specific situation. One powerful NLP (Neuro-Linguistic Programming) technique is called New Behaviour Generator. It's much like being a director of a film where you play the lead role. All you need to do is follow these four simple steps:

1 *Find a quiet place where you won't be disturbed.*
2 *Picture yourself at a time in the future when you're about to present. Notice your facial expression and posture. Adjust the image until you're happy this future you looks confident.*
3 *Let the film run and observe how strong and positive you look. Hear the sound of your voice and become aware of the response of the audience. They're leaning forward and interested in what you have to say. Fast forward to the end of the presentation. Perhaps there's a round of applause. Adjust the film as many times as you want until you're entirely happy with it.*
4 *Now step into the film and experience the 'movie' again, this time through your own eyes. Feel your confidence grow stronger. Become aware of the positive response from the audience. Bask in the knowledge you've done a great job.*

Repeat this visualization several times and you will start to feel more confident about presenting. That's because the mind can't tell the difference between something that's remembered and something vividly imagined. And when you actually stand up to speak you'll behave as if you have really had the experience of doing so successfully. If you would like to learn more about using the power of NLP, check out our best-selling book *Teach Yourself NLP*.

Positive self-talk/affirmations

If you have an internal running commentary that points out your shortcomings, as many people do, you're bound to feel nervous. Your internal critic can easily be on your case day and night – even during a presentation, which is disruptive to your flow to say the least. Negative self-talk sometimes spirals out of control, and makes it impossible to think rationally about how you're really doing. One approach, also drawn from NLP, is to change the location, volume or tonality of your internal voice, so that it doesn't bother you so much. It's also possible to alter the content of what it says, so it becomes a champion – 'Go on. You can do it!' – rather than a critic.

You can use affirmation in the same way. Regularly repeating to yourself comments such as 'I'm an interesting and engaging presenter' or 'I am someone who speaks clearly and engagingly' will help reprogramme the mind, and over time you will come to believe them. This then works as a self-fulfilling prophecy. When you believe you're a good presenter, you will start behaving like one.

Acting as if

Another great technique – yes, it's from NLP as well – is 'Acting As If'. When you act as if you're confident, or as if you're an accomplished presenter, you will unconsciously take on the characteristics and mannerisms of someone who can do it well. Another way of achieving the same thing is to pretend you're a particular person that you know who doesn't get anxious when presenting.

Insight

We all get nervous from time to time – even your authors! Something we find useful when stress levels get higher than normal is to remember presentations in the past that went really well. We 'float back' into the memory and experience the feelings we had as we spoke and the positive feelings we had afterwards. This enables us to get into a more resourceful state, which in turn makes us feel more comfortable about the presentation to come.

Relaxation and Serenity Skills techniques

Another way of dealing with nerves is to intervene directly using your body. This works because the mind and the body are inextricably linked. When you change one, you change the other. Doing relaxation, breathing and visualization exercises can help to calm your anxieties. So if you're wondering how to deal with shaking hands, jelly knees, flushing, a dry mouth, sweating or a sudden desire to visit the toilet, the Relaxation and Serenity Skills exercises below are for you.

Exercises

Stand up straight

Stand up straight, with your feet shoulder width apart, stomach and bottom in, and head up so you look confident. Your unconscious mind associates this posture with feeling confident and responds accordingly. When you adopt this stance, imagine shifting your attention and energy away from your head, through your body, down to your feet, and into the earth. This helps you feel grounded.

Shaking out the stress

Anxiety expresses itself in the body. We get butterflies in our tummy. There's tightness in the jaw. We have jelly knees. Shoulders get tense. In many people this tension builds up as the presentation gets closer.

One way of letting go of physical stress is to shake it out, starting with your arms and hands. Let them go limp and then shake them. Imagine the anxiety falling out from the ends of your fingers. Circle your arms. Rotate your shoulders forward several times, then repeat the motion rolling backwards. Shake out your feet and legs and wiggle your hips. Buttocks can hold a lot of tension. Squeeze the cheeks of your bottom tightly together then let go. Repeat until your muscles feel tension-free.

One of the areas affected by stress is the neck. Roll your head to the right, back, to your left, forward and then go round again. Once you've repeated this twice more, repeat
(Contd)

the move in the other direction. Open your mouth and eyes wide. Then close them tightly and you'll relax your facial muscles. Yawning helps too. It relaxes your neck, throat and mouth. Open your mouth as wide as you can when you yawn and then let all that tension out. Finally, clean your teeth with your tongue. This really loosens the jaw.

Breathe deeply

The only problem with shaking out the stress from the body is that you can't do it when other people are in the room. You need to find a quiet spot by yourself. But one thing you can do when you're around others is control your breathing. This works because it's physiologically impossible to breathe deeply and be nervous at the same time. Any kind of controlled, focused inhalation will confer benefit, but the following pattern derived from yoga is especially effective.

The four-fold breath

Relax and exhale to the count of four. Hold the breath out for a count of four. Inhale to the count of four. Hold the breath in for the count of four. Repeat the cycle and continue for at least three minutes. Count at an even speed that is comfortable to your breathing.

Experience leads to confidence

Most people are nervous the first time they present. But as they gain experience the anxiety diminishes. Using the concepts and techniques in this chapter will help you through the early stages. If you seek opportunities to practise you'll soon develop a feeling of ease, and you may even, dare we say, ultimately start to enjoy it.

TEN KEY POINTS TO REMEMBER

1 *If you get anxious at the thought of giving a presentation, you're not alone.*

2 *The fight or flight mechanism of the reptilian brain kicks in too fast for the cerebral cortex to let your body know you're not going to die when you present.*

3 *People sometimes fear rejection, being the centre of attention, fear of failure or getting it wrong.*

4 *Analyticals tend to get anxious because they worry about making a mistake. Amiables are concerned about what others think of them and fear rejection or looking stupid. Expressives tend to 'wing it' and can show nerves when they lose their way mid-flow through poor preparation. Drivers display lots of confidence and if it all goes wrong blame circumstances or others rather than taking responsibility themselves.*

5 *Nerves are revealed through distracting mannerisms such as fiddling with rings or pens, stepping backwards and forwards, avoiding eye contact and using fillers like 'um' and 'er'.*

6 *The thoughts (T) we have lead to feelings (F) we experience which lead to actions (A) we take.*

7 *When people get nervous they often put on an act instead of being themselves and communicating in a relaxed way. The Matrix of Authentic Presenting demonstrates how the degree to which someone performs vs. being real works in relation to the skill level of the presenter.*

8 *Two key thoughts to keep in mind are:*
   ▷ *there's no such thing as a perfect presentation*
   ▷ *the audience is on your side.*

9 *Doing relaxation, breathing and visualization exercises helps to calm your nerves because mind and body are inextricably linked.*

10 *For most people anxiety diminishes as they gain experience. The more you present, the more confident you feel.*

13

Final preparation

In this chapter you will learn:
- *how to prepare effectively*
- *about different room layouts*
- *how to manage the logistics – equipment, room layout, lighting, etc.*
- *about the importance of clothes and what to wear.*

The importance of final preparation

So it's the big day. Or is it? Not all presentations are set piece speeches to 1,000 people at a conference about the state of the industry or pitches to the Board for a multi-million pound investment. Many of the presentations you give will be mundane, everyday affairs – the regular weekly/monthly update, the finance report, a 'milestones' or 'lessons learnt' meeting. Some, though, will be more challenging: a visit to or from a client or supplier, running a training session, taking part in a high-profile seminar, or even jetting off to another country to share your expertise.

Whatever the situation, you can't afford to fall at the last hurdle and that means doing your final preparation. Things you need to consider include equipment, logistics, room layout, what to wear, lighting, and travel arrangements.

Preparing for everyday presentations

Even if you're only giving a ten-minute debrief in your office, you need to make sure everything's in place. When you're presenting on your 'home turf', things are largely under your control but that can make you complacent. Make sure you take a moment to get everything ready ahead of time, rather than rushing around when the others have arrived. If you're using PowerPoint have the projector ready along with any props or paperwork you might need. If the presentation is in a colleague's office, you may not be able to get access before the start of the session. The best you can do most of the time is to be sufficiently well-organized that you can set up inside a minute once you get in.

Many businesses now have open plan offices, so you and your colleagues may not have your own space. That means you'll most likely be presenting in a meeting room and there will be more to think about. It's ideal, but not always possible, to get in before you're scheduled to begin. The room may already be in use, and you may not have access until the last minute. Once again, you need to be ready to set up quickly.

It goes without saying that you need enough space for the number of people, but you may have to make the best of what's available. If it's a tight fit, consider removing some furniture. That may be easier said than done. Many meeting rooms have one large 'boardroom' table that seats a dozen people, and you'll have no alternative but to work around it. If only a handful of people are attending your presentation, get the group focused by positioning everyone at one end of the table.

When booking a meeting room in advance it's a good idea to confirm arrangements for the layout and equipment beforehand too. In bigger companies there's often a support team that organizes logistics, such as setting up rooms. When you specify your needs clearly you're more likely to get what you want.

If there's a choice of rooms, go for one in which the layout is most appropriate for your needs. Boardroom or Circle style are best for most everyday small-group presentations. Think also about possible distractions, such as windows where there's a lot of activity going on outside, noisy traffic or even beautiful scenery.

EQUIPMENT LOGISTICS

One of the things you'll need to sort out, if you're using slides, is how to project them. Sometimes that's straightforward. An increasing number of meeting rooms have ceiling-mounted projectors, so all you have to do is plug in your laptop using the cable provided. Select 'computer' on the remote control and you get a picture on the screen that's focused and square to the screen. You're probably also on your company network, which makes it easy to access the file.

Sometimes, though, you need to set things up yourself. You go into the room and the projector's on the table, or you bring it with you. While it only takes a couple of minutes to get everything organized, you need to allow sufficient time. Most readers will be familiar with setting up for PowerPoint, but you might find the following checklist useful:

▶ *Place the projector on a flat surface the correct distance from the screen for the image size you want. You may need to move it back and forth if there's no zoom control.*
▶ *Connect your computer and use the special function key to display the image on the monitor and screen. Which key it is depends on the make of your computer.*
▶ *Adjust the focus control on the projector to give the sharpest picture possible.*
▶ *If the image isn't square use the 'keystoning' control. You may also need to raise or lower the legs of the projector to alter the height or change its angle in relation to the screen.*

While it's great to have a room with plenty of natural light, because it creates a bright and airy environment, it can be problematic if it stops people seeing the screen clearly. Drawing blinds and switching off any room lights will obviously improve visibility. As a final check, go to the back of the room and make sure the slides can be seen easily.

FLIPCHARTS AND WHITEBOARDS

If you're using a flipchart make sure you've got plenty of paper
on the pad. Discard any used sheets, it doesn't give a positive
impression when you turn the page and there's writing on it
already. You'll usually find some pens in the room but they're often
of variable quality so check they're okay before you start.

Whiteboards need to be cleaned thoroughly ahead of time. When
you walk in the room they'll often be covered with all manner of
scribbles in a multitude of colours from previous users. Make sure
you have the correct whiteboard pens with sufficient ink, and a
board eraser to hand in case you need to make any changes.

More often than not you'll create your flipcharts or whiteboard
diagram as you go along. But consider preparing any complex
diagrams ahead of time, to avoid the pace dropping while you
write them up.

Six popular room layouts

Boardroom style

Boardroom style (see Figure 13.1) is frequently used for company
meetings. It's a good choice when people need to make notes.
Depending on the dimensions of the room and size of the table,
it's ideal for 12 to 15 people. The speaker usually stands at one end.
In some instances, you may opt to deliver a seated presentation
instead.

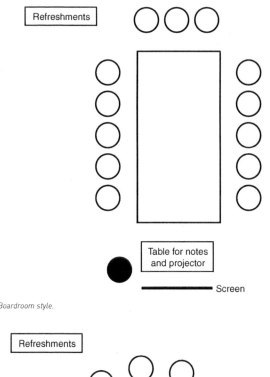

Figure 13.1 Boardroom style.

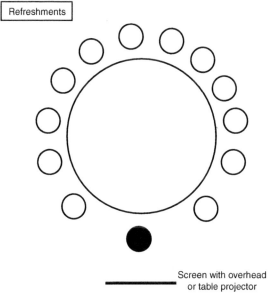

Figure 13.2 Circle style.

Circle style

Circle style (see Figure 13.2) is similar to the boardroom with a round table instead of one that's rectangular. This is a good arrangement for encouraging open discussion. Because there's no clear head of the table, it promotes democracy. Each speaker can deliver their presentation standing or seated at the table. Smaller versions of both the Boardroom and Circle style are ideal for very small groups.

Cabaret style

Cabaret style (see Figures 13.3 and 13.4) is frequently used with larger audiences and at formal dinners. Tables can be round or rectangular and usually seat from three to eight people. Chairs are arranged so it's easy for everyone to see the speaker. For large events the speaker is sometimes on a stage so people can see clearly. Having space between the tables allows you to circulate to encourage engagement and interaction.

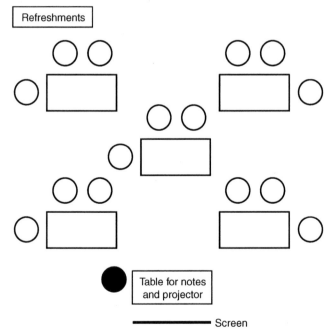

Figure 13.3 Cabaret style.

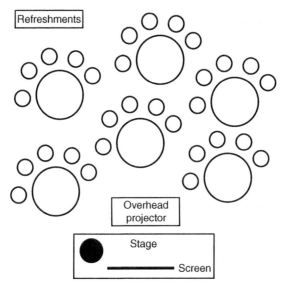

Figure 13.4 Cabaret style with round tables.

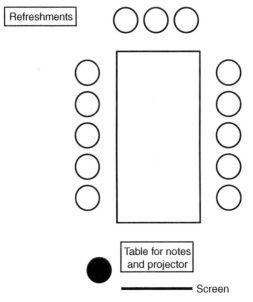

Figure 13.5 Horseshoe style.

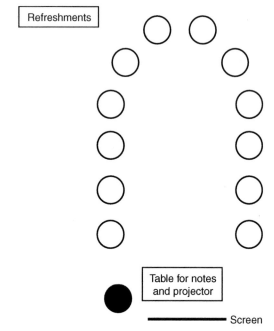

Refreshments

Table for notes and projector

Screen

Figure 13.6 Horseshoe style without table.

Horseshoe or U-shaped style

The horseshoe or U-shaped style (see Figures 13.5 and 13.6) is ideal for training sessions. As Figure 13.6 shows, it can be adapted to create a more intimate environment by removing the desks. This allows the speaker to walk through the centre and participants can easily discuss things with each other. This layout is great for getting people to open up but not so good if they need to make notes. It is ideal for between five and 12 people.

Classroom style

The classroom style (see Figures 13.7 and 13.8) is commonly used for seminars but it can evoke negative memories in some minds of being back at school. There are two versions – one with and one without tables. Opt for tables if participants need to jot things down. Sometimes tables are placed at angles rather than in rows to make it easier for everyone to see.

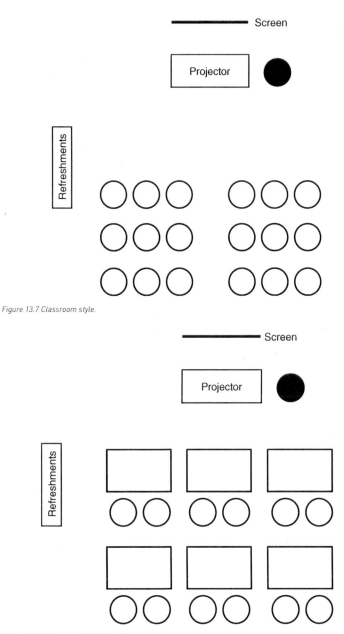

Figure 13.7 Classroom style.

Figure 13.8 Classroom style with tables.

Theatre style

Theatre style (see Figure 13.9) is usually reserved for the big occasion and very large audiences. Some auditoriums have sloped floors, which means the seats towards the back are raised to allow everyone a clear view. In this type of layout, there's often a stage at the front for the speaker.

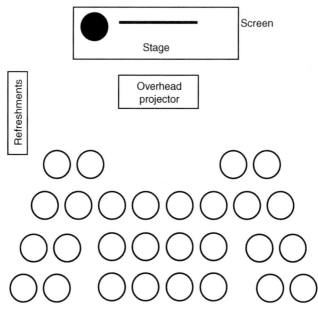

Figure 13.9 Theatre style.

Insight

Sometimes the best laid plans don't work out as you hope. I (Amanda) once requested a cabaret-style layout and on the day walked into a large theatre-style room with a stage and lectern. The organizer said, 'Sorry, there was a mix-up with room bookings and this is all we have left.' Presenters need to be flexible and able to think on their feet. Even in these circumstances you can shift chairs out of the way and create the layout and atmosphere you want. Sometimes you have no choice other than to work with what you're given. The key is to arrive early and take it in your stride.

Bigger occasions on your own turf

Sometimes, though, presentations are more of a challenge. Perhaps you have to put forward a proposal to the senior team, speak to clients or suppliers, or have a bigger audience. In these situations there's even more to think about.

It could, for instance, be the first time you've presented in the Boardroom or Executive Suite and you're not familiar with the room. If so, it's a good idea to go to see it beforehand if you can. It's not until you look at the space and the way the furniture is laid out that you get a real sense of how you want things to be. You may prefer to have a particular layout to suit the purpose of your presentation and the number of people attending. (See above for advice on room layout options.)

As the occasion grows in importance, so the need to check your equipment ahead of time increases, especially when you're presenting in an unfamiliar room. When standing up in front of a larger group it's a good idea to use a remote mouse, which gives you the freedom to move away from the keyboard.

When it's your responsibility to set things up, and there are more people attending, make sure any cables are taped down or covered with rubber matting strips. Other things to think about include the temperature in the room (if it's too warm you risk them falling asleep, if it's too cold, they'll be distracted), refreshments and breaks (if it's a longer presentation) and whether you need to provide handouts, notepaper or pens.

WHAT TO WEAR FOR HIGH-PROFILE OCCASIONS

With everyday presentations you don't need to worry too much about how you dress, though it's still a good idea to make sure your impact is positive. But when the stakes are high you need to go up a gear and look your best. First impressions count. Obvious things you can do include: have your suit dry cleaned if it's looking a bit tired, give your shoes a polish, and make sure your shirt or blouse look fresh. If you know you look good in a particular outfit, you're more likely to feel confident.

> ## Insight
>
> I (Amanda) have some outfits I feel really good in and wear for special occasions. For a presentation to 90 people in a hot, humid room in India I wore a favourite red jacket that makes me feel great. Needless to say, the jacket came off pretty quickly once the event was over!

Presenting off-site

Not all presentations take place on familiar territory. Sometimes you'll go to another company location, visit a client or supplier, or attend an 'off-site' at a hotel or conference centre. Make sure you arrive with plenty of time to spare. You're unlikely to have access to the room straightaway but there's nothing worse than dashing in at the last minute breathless, sweaty and flustered. This obviously won't create a positive impression.

At times the set-up will be far from ideal but you'll have to make it work. You're unlikely to have much if any control over where you present or the layout of the room. More likely than not there will be a projector but it's just as well to check ahead of time. If there's any doubt in your mind, and it's an important presentation, take one with you as back up. You need to be ready to plug in your laptop and get started as quickly as possible. Clients will judge you on how efficiently you manage the whole process. Most projectors work in the same way so it shouldn't be a problem.

If you're presenting off-site and a room has been booked for you, arrange to go to see it beforehand whenever possible. Some hotel and conference rooms are less than ideal as they have pillars or columns you have to work around – forewarned is forearmed. One hotel room in Edinburgh where we presented had a low-beamed ceiling and a huge ornate fireplace. While it looked fantastic, it was hard to find somewhere suitable for the projector and screen, and taller delegates had to duck their heads when they walked across the room.

Someone at the venue will be responsible for setting up the room to meet your specification, assuming you're the only speaker. If you're one of many and don't have direct control contact the organizers and ask them how the room will be arranged and what equipment will be available. At some venues, there will be audio-visual (AV) support available. It's a good idea to make a note of the AV technician's number – it can be a life-saver should you need help on the day.

CLOTHES CREATE AN IMPRESSION

You need to give a bit more thought to what you wear for external presentations. Choose clothes to match the occasion, taking account of what the audience will be wearing. It doesn't make sense wearing the same things when presenting to a city law firm as to a group of shop workers. If everyone will be in jeans go one step higher and aim for 'smart casual'. If the audience will be in suits, wear your best one. To dress with authority put on sober, dark colours. To tone things down and create a more informal feel, leave your jacket undone.

When the spotlight's on you – the big event

When the spotlight's on you at a big event, such as a seminar, keynote speech or conference, make sure you get plenty of sleep the night before so you wake up fresh. Even if your slot isn't until later in the day you need to make sure you're bright and ready to give your best. Some presenters start their day with physical exercise – a swim or workout can help to get your energy up and eliminate any tension. Others do a vocal warm-up in the shower – the acoustics in bathrooms are great for practising your opening lines. As you wash your hair, give your scalp a massage to increase the blood flow to your brain. If you're feeling nervous start using some of the relaxation exercises from Chapter 12.

When you've got some distance to travel, or are presenting overseas, it makes sense to go the night before. Battling with traffic or dealing with train or airline delays can send your stress levels soaring, the last thing you want before a major presentation. If you're going abroad remember to take some travel plug adapters with you. We've lost count of the number of times we've ended up racing around at the airport trying to find some. It really helps to have maps, directions, travel tickets and hotel details printed out in advance.

HANDLING THE LOGISTICS FOR BIG EVENTS

Find out about the layout and equipment well in advance, so you know what to expect. If you're able to see the venue as well, even if it's just an hour or two beforehand, it helps enormously with larger groups where you need to plan how to work the room. If it's in use already you may only be able to take a quick peak. If there's a stage, practise walking across it, and up and down any steps, to get a feel for what it will be like.

If there are tables, check how much space there is for you to walk between them, should you want to. If the layout is theatre style, this won't be an option. Sit at various places in the room, including the back, to get an audience perspective. If it's not possible for you to visit the room ahead of time, try to see a scale drawing so you get a sense of what it's like.

EQUIPMENT AT BIG EVENTS

When you're one of several speakers at a conference the organizer will sometimes ask you to send a copy of your slides in advance – so that everything can be set up ahead of time. As a precaution we recommend you have a back-up with you in case something goes awry, both on a laptop and on a USB drive or CD/DVD.

If you're using music or video clips as part of your presentation make sure the sound system is effective. Most large venues have sophisticated audio facilities so it shouldn't be a problem but it's vital you check. You may need to adjust the volume up or down as you go along. Those using a lot of video clips and music should consider hiring a technical AV assistant to manage the whole thing. They advance slides, start videos, adjust the volume, where you're using sound, and even dim the lights. You'll need to provide them with a detailed list of what happens when and include some written cues for them to follow. If you don't have this luxury, make sure you know how to adjust everything and ask someone to manage the lighting when necessary.

USING A LECTERN AND MICROPHONE

At seminars and conferences some people prefer to use a lectern that's set up with a microphone. It certainly provides a handy place to rest your notes, but it's also a barrier between you and your audience. We recommend you switch to a lapel microphone instead because it gives you the freedom to move around. It's a good idea to get someone to check the volume on microphones as they usually need adjusting for each person's voice. You can leave your notes on the lectern and return to them as needed. If you're worried about changing slides, simply use a remote mouse.

USING A TELEPROMPTER/AUTOCUE

If you're using a teleprompter/autocue you'll need a lectern. You can move around if you arrange for additional prompt screens to be positioned to give you greater flexibility – but this is not the norm. Generally you'll stand in one place, with transparent plastic screens at 45 degrees on both sides of you. If you decide to use a teleprompter/autocue, make sure you're familiar with how it works. It takes practice to be able to read the words as they're scrolled up by an operator without it being obvious you're doing so.

WHAT TO WEAR FOR BIG EVENTS

Obviously you'll want to look your best for a big event. Try a few things on and walk as far away from a full-length mirror as the first row of your audience will be. This gives you an idea of what they'll make of your appearance. If you're presenting on stage consider how your clothes will stand out from the background. If you're not sure, take two outfits with you just in case – one dark and one lighter.

If you're a man, you can't go wrong with a good quality dark suit. Black and deep blue are safe bets because people associate them with being professional. Make sure your suit is a comfortable fit. Check zips and buttons of trousers are done up. Remove pens, wallet, glasses, mobile phones, and loose change from jacket and trouser pockets. They create a nasty bulge and spoil the effect. Go for a crisp, clean shirt with a suitable tie and polish your shoes well.

If you're a woman, dark, solid colours and tailoring will give you an air of authority. Trousers and long to mid-calf length skirts work well. Take care with plunging neck lines and very short skirts which create a certain perception in some people's eyes. Choose colours that suit your hair and skin tone. Patterns can be hard to look at for long periods and the same is true of shiny fabric that reflects the light. Subtle patterns such as pin stripes work well. Accessories should match your outfit. If you plan to wear jewellery, keep it subtle, otherwise the audience may be glued to your 'over the top' earrings rather than listening to you. High heels can add sophistication unless they're very high, when they can look tarty. Flat shoes are better for longer sessions where comfort is important.

Ready for action

Once all the preparation is complete, no matter what sort of presentation you're delivering, you're ready for action. All that's needed is for the audience to take their seats. You'll be secure in the knowledge that everything will run like clockwork.

TEN KEY POINTS TO REMEMBER

1 *In your final preparation consider the following: equipment, logistics, room layout, clothing, lighting and travel arrangements.*

2 *When you present on your 'home turf' it's often, and not always, easier to set up the logistics and check equipment in advance.*

3 *Make sure you're familiar with the equipment in the room you're using. This allows you to set up quickly. Check that the slides can be clearly seen and adjust the lighting if necessary.*

4 *There are six popular room layouts; boardroom style (good for making notes), circle style (encourages open discussion), cabaret style (frequently used for larger events), horseshoe or U-shaped style (ideal for training sessions), classroom style (often used for seminars), and theatre style (reserved for big occasions).*

5 *For big occasions on your own turf check your equipment ahead of time and make sure you dress well and appropriately.*

6 *When you present off-site allow plenty of time to get there and set up.*

7 *If you've got a distance to travel, or are presenting overseas, it's best to go the night before.*

8 *For large events find out about the room layout and equipment well in advance. If there's a stage practise walking on it and get a feel for the steps if they have them.*

9 *We recommend you opt for lapel microphones because they give you the freedom to move around.*

10 *A safe bet for men at big events is a good quality dark suit. If you're a woman dark solid colours give you an air of authority.*

14

Engaging your audience

In this chapter you will learn:
- *how to make a positive first impression*
- *how to connect with your audience*
- *why eye contact is crucial*
- *how to read your audience and adapt to meet their needs.*

Impressions, awareness and flexibility

How often, when sitting in an audience, have you made up your mind within a few seconds whether or not a presentation is going to be good? If you know the speaker already, you have an idea of what to expect. If you don't, you may have heard about them. If not, the impression they make at the start is crucial because it shapes your view. Good presenters know the importance of a great beginning. They're also acutely aware of the need to pay attention to their audience's reaction as they go along. Being aware of subtle shifts in behaviour tells them when to adapt their approach. They're flexible enough to be able to make changes when the need arises.

Getting off to a good start

A good speech is a one-on-one conversation with each audience member.

Ralph Archibold

You have to connect with your audience quickly, once the preparation is complete, to be certain of getting off to a good start. This process begins before your presentation. One of the best ways of starting well is to greet people warmly as they arrive. If you have one or two colleagues arriving for a meeting and you know them well you will naturally share a bit of small talk about what's been happening in the office, find out about their latest holiday or how the kids are doing at school.

If you don't know them well, the small talk may be more about company issues.

If you've never met them before it's a good idea to break the ice by finding something to say that they can relate to. You can mention a mutual contact or tell them about an organization you belong to that may be of interest to them. All of this can take place while you're waiting for other people to arrive, usually over a coffee. This may sound obvious but it's all too easy to get off to a bad start. If you rush in at the last minute, start shuffling papers and have a grim look on your face, they won't warm to you in the same way. From then on, it will be an uphill climb.

With large groups you may have a chance to mingle beforehand. Shake as many people by the hand as you can because it creates an individual connection. Personal contact also helps break down barriers and settles your nerves. If you're able to recall some names, find a reason to refer to them during your presentation. This personal touch will usually impress an audience.

First impressions

Once you've created a connection the task from then on is to keep people engaged throughout. The first opportunity you have to do this comes in the impression you make within the first 10 to 30 seconds. The way you walk, stand, smile and your overall demeanor provide vital clues that allow them to make a rapid decision about you. Human beings have finely tuned survival instincts that equip them with the ability to work out who is friend or foe almost instantly. If people like you, they continue to look for evidence to support that initial reaction and vice versa.

This is just as important for presenting around a table to one or two people as it is when speaking to a large group. You can't afford to ignore the range of things that influence their views, including your energy level, attitude and overall manner. You need to come across as honest, warm and vibrant with a mix of authority and approachability. In most presentations, you need to take your message seriously and at the same time be able to lighten things by being playful. There are a few situations where a light-hearted approach may be viewed as flippant, such as announcing redundancies or passing on other bad news.

Insight

The big challenge when it comes to creating a positive first impression, writes Steve, is that at the beginning of a presentation you're likely to be nervous, and your attention tends to be inward, because you're focusing on remembering your opening remarks. That's why it's a good idea to know your first three sentences off by heart, so you can shift your focus to the room and the audience, which allows you to make a great first impression.

Building rapport with a group

15 per cent of your financial success comes from your skills and knowledge, while 85 per cent comes from your ability to connect with other people and engender trust and respect.

Nicholas Boothman, *How to Connect in Business*

Building rapport with a group is a skill that many people develop naturally through everyday life experience. To be successful as a presenter you need to be able to take your skills in connecting with others to a higher level. This process begins with being consciously aware of how your behaviour takes you closer to or farther away from your goal. Observe what works and what gets in the way. Obviously you need to do more of the former and less of the latter. By putting your approach under a microscope you'll gradually find out what works in different situations with a variety of people.

CONNECTING WITH PEOPLE YOU KNOW ALREADY

When you're presenting to small groups of people you know well, building rapport is relatively easy. Before getting down to business you can reconnect through small talk – catching up on news and a bit of office banter if it's an internal presentation.

If you're presenting to a client you've met before you may spend a few minutes chatting about a common interest, the results of a football match or some other current news story.

Obviously if you're dealing with 'Driver' behavioural types you need to keep this to the minimum or they'll switch off, especially if they're tight on time.

When you know your audience and get on with them reasonably well you'll naturally mirror their body language and voice tone. If you're presenting to someone you don't gel with, this is less likely to happen. To win them over, deliberately match their behaviour. This doesn't mean creating an exact copy. If you mimic them you'll annoy them. It has to be subtle. If you want to learn more about this we suggest you read *Teach Yourself NLP*.

CONNECTING WITH PEOPLE YOU DON'T KNOW

When you're presenting to people you don't know it's relatively easy to make small talk over drinks before you start to speak. If you work for the same company the simplest starting point is to talk about some company initiative that affects their department or ask them about their role. If they work for another organization ask them about their journey, talk about the weather, or some current news event. Once you've broken the ice ask about their business too.

A good strong opening helps to establish your credibility. Smile as you step up to speak. Use eye contact to connect with them and be yourself – audiences warm to presenters they trust. Make them feel like they know you. This is easier than it sounds. If you think of them as old friends you haven't met for a while, that will come across in your voice.

CONNECTING WITH GROUPS

Many new presenters are skilled at building rapport one on one and want to know how to manage this process with more than one person at a time. You need to pay attention to the general behaviour of the group. For a meeting first thing on Monday morning, though, you may come across a general 'laid back' feel, as if everyone is still in weekend mode. You also need to have a weather eye out for people who are behaving differently from the norm. Even with a small group of two to three people you'll notice differences in behavioural styles, with the Expressives often the most animated and lively.

CONNECTING WITH LARGE GROUPS

Don't be tempted to hide behind a lectern or desk as you're less likely to make an instant connection. Furniture of any type creates a barrier between you and your audience. We're not saying you should never use a lectern, but where you can do without one it allows you to get closer to your audience. If you're using PowerPoint, opt for a remote mouse. This gives you the freedom to move around rather than being slavishly stuck next to your laptop.

With larger groups you need to connect with their energy. If the room is buzzing with chatter and laughter, start with something upbeat. If the mood is sombre, begin on a serious note. If you've done your homework, you should be able to predict how they'll react unless something happens immediately beforehand to shift their mood. If it does you need to be able to adapt your approach at the last minute. There's more on how to match energy in Chapter 20.

In your opening, include a reference to something you have in common with the audience. Talk about the occasion and how people may be feeling. Congratulate them on a recent achievement or commiserate over a collective problem they face. If you work in the same industry or share the same background let them know. Your aim is to create a bond between you and the group. Another simple way to build rapport is to let them know you're happy to be there.

ACKNOWLEDGE THEIR EXPERTISE

Acknowledge your audience's previous experience and expertise. If they're more qualified than you, or are experts in their field, don't let on if you're overawed by them. They've come to hear what you have to say so believe in yourself and think of them as equals. Let them make up their own minds about the points you want to make. Most people trust their opinion first and foremost.

Making eye contact

Your message goes where your voice goes, and your voice goes where your eyes send it.

Francis Xavier Muldoon

Eye contact creates an emotional bond between you and your audience. It signifies trust and confidence. One of the best ways to achieve rapport and engage people quickly and easily is to look at them. Distribute your attention around the room evenly. In a seated presentation or with small groups make sure you don't miss the people sitting immediately to your left or right. With large audiences, you need to make it obvious that you're shifting your gaze by moving your head too. Some presenters follow a 'W' shape, starting at the rear left moving to the front, out to the centre back, return to the front and ending at the right back. Repeat this throughout the presentation. Others pick out small groups in different areas of the room. They shift their gaze from one group to another. Aim to give the impression you're talking to each person personally.

HOW LONG IS LONG ENOUGH?

When you fix your eyes on someone for more than a couple of seconds they'll often nod or smile at you. Some presenters look at each individual for one or two seconds and then move on. This will either make you appear nervous or look like you're going through the motions. If you know you tend to flit from one person to another, look at the colour of their eyes. This will force you to linger a little longer. Around two or three seconds is a reasonable length of time. If you fix your eyes on someone for too long it starts to feel either too intimate or intimidating.

EYE CONTACT AND AUTOCUE

If you're using an autocue it will appear as though you're making eye contact with your audience. Look away from the screens from time to time and look through the plastic screens for a natural effect.

BUT I DON'T WANT TO LOOK AT THEM!

The idea of looking people in the eye may seem terrifying, but when you think of them as human beings the fear disperses as you forge a connection with them. If you don't look at your audience they'll think you're uncomfortable or assume you're a bit shifty.

There are all sorts of strategies offered to help people deal with nerves, such as 'look over their heads' or 'imagine everyone is naked'. We don't advise you follow either of these tactics because the whole point is to make a connection. That means actually looking at people. Sometimes, if you're feeling anxious, it's tempting to focus on someone you know, the person who appears most friendly, to gaze into space or at the floor for long periods. Avoid looking at one important or senior person too. The other people present will feel neglected. Be aware that they often play a key influencing role too, so this strategy can backfire.

Dialogue vs. monologue

Your aim when presenting is to communicate with your audience. If you simply talk at them you may as well send them a document to read. A monologue requires no response from people and is likely to send them to sleep. Don't read each point on your slides word for word. People find this patronizing.

Dialogue implies the audience is engaged and taking an active part in proceedings. Add value to slides by bringing them to life and emphasizing important issues.

Keep connected when using PowerPoint

When participants on our presentation skills courses see themselves on video they're often amazed at how much time they spend with their back to the audience talking to the screen, their notes and laptop. This loss of eye contact prevents them from maintaining that vital connection with the group.

To avoid this problem simply look at the screen briefly, just long enough to remind yourself what's there, and then turn to face them. Only speak once you're looking at the audience. When you do this, you'll put more pauses in your presentation. Don't worry about it appearing stilted because it doesn't seem that way to the group. The same process applies to notes and scripts. Glance at them without speaking. Look at your audience and speak.

The temptation to stare at your laptop when you're using slides can be almost irresistible for some presenters. When you look at the screen, you share the experience with the audience. When you look at a laptop, they can't join in. Our advice is to close the lid slightly or set the display for screen only.

There will be times when you want to have the audience's attention solely on you. You can black out the screen by pressing the 'B' key on your keyboard and press 'B' again for the image to re-appear. The 'W' key works in a similar way, except the screen changes to white instead of black. You can move quickly to a particular slide by selecting a numerical key that relates to the slide number and then pressing enter.

Don't show any slide until you're ready to talk about it. If it's complicated, introduce it first. Then show it and let the audience look at it in silence. This gives them time to take it in. If necessary, you can then point out something important you want to emphasize. Don't leave slides up when the information is no longer relevant. If this means the next slide would appear too soon, use the 'B' key.

DON'T BLOCK THE SCREEN

One of the most common traps inexperienced presenters fall into is to stand or walk between the projector and the slide. The image then falls on them rather than the screen. This is irritating and distracting for the audience. Instead, stand to one side. Gesture towards them and point to draw attention to the things you want to emphasize.

LAPTOP PRESENTATIONS TO SMALL GROUPS

Sometimes you may need to present sitting at a table to one or two people with a laptop. Make sure you position it carefully so everyone can see clearly. If the angle isn't right, the light can shine on the screen making it difficult to see properly. The same rule applies in this situation as before. Look at your audience whenever

184

possible. Guide them to look at the screen when you want to highlight a point. When you want their full attention use the 'B' key so they are not distracted.

Expect success

Expect to be successful, believe in yourself, and believe that what you have to say is important. If you have a positive attitude so will they. If you're warm and friendly, they'll like you and want to pay attention. Aim to create an emotional bond with your audience through the language you use. Love your audience. Show them you care and are there just for them. Be yourself, make eye contact, and act as if you're speaking to friends.

Reading your audience

Once you've got off to a flying start you need to maintain the momentum and that means reading your audience. Observe them closely so you know how they're reacting to your presentation. If they seem fired up to listen, keep doing what you're doing. If it only seems okay, challenge yourself to find a way to make sure what you're doing is more than mediocre. If you know it's not working, take action. If you don't, you'll plough on regardless and wonder afterwards why you didn't achieve your purpose.

BE AWARE AND STAY AWARE

Being aware of what's going on is crucial. Presenters vary in how much they take in. Some have finely tuned observational skills and pick up on every nuance. Others seem so focused on what they have to say that they wouldn't notice if the audience were all snoring away. It's vital you keep your antennae up throughout. That means looking for signs of boredom or tiredness such as people shifting in their seats or closing their eyes. Look out for other reactions too such as facial expressions that indicate disagreement, confusion, agreement, pleasure and so on.

We attended a conference where there were several workshops running at once. We wanted to see a certain well-known expert speak (who shall remain nameless) and opted for his session. It wasn't long before we realized we'd made the wrong choice. Not only was it dull but the speaker didn't seem to notice when the first few people voted with their feet and headed for another seminar. After a while, more followed suit. The speaker continued without adapting his approach at all. He had a plan in mind and he was going to follow it. We're not sure what happened then because we were among the next 15 people to leave the room.

USE YOUR SENSES

The first crucial step is to focus your attention on the audience. Use all of your senses to keep alert to how they're feeling and reacting. Check energy levels at the start and then you can compare that with what you see at various stages throughout your presentation. With large audiences, simply pick one or two people out and use them as your benchmark. Take in as many details as you can, including facial expressions. Become a people watcher.

One of the reasons eye contact is so important is that it allows you to look for the small signals that tell you to adapt your approach. These are often subtle changes of skin colour, facial muscle movement and/or breathing that provide clues to people's inner states. It's one thing to observe what you notice with your senses: what you see, hear, feel, taste and smell. It's quite another to place an interpretation on that information and draw a conclusion of some kind. You may be right and you may be wrong.

Do they appear bored, confused, interested or excited? Are they making notes and listening attentively? Are they nodding in agreement or nodding off through boredom? If they're nodding and leaning forward, they're probably engaged. Or are they checking their mobile phone or looking at their watch? Are they laughing? Be careful not to jump to conclusions. It could be that your zip is undone or that they've seen the funny side of a comment you've made.

What you're looking for is clusters of signs that tell you it's time to change the energy, cut short a particular topic or clarify a point because some people look confused. If they're fidgeting you may guess they're not engaged. Shaking of heads may indicate disagreement. Look for patterns of behaviour. Arms crossed means different things. The person might be cold. They may sit that way habitually or their closed body language could be telling you they're unhappy with what you've said. You can obviously get non-verbal feedback as you go along simply by looking for it. You can also ask for it. If you're unsure about the signals you're picking up, ask questions to gauge the reaction.

LOOKING FOR SIGNALS IN LARGE GROUPS

When you have a large audience it can be difficult to see people's faces or reactions clearly. In these situations you need to pick up on the general feel you get from the audience as a collective unit. You'll notice whether or not most people are looking at you, making notes or not, and so on. The people towards the front can provide a barometer for how the rest of the group is doing.

USING PERIPHERAL VISION

Some experienced presenters learn how to use their peripheral or side vision to help them extend their awareness of the audience when presenting to large groups. Studies have shown that presenters who expand the field of their peripheral vision are better able to maintain rapport with their audiences. This makes sense in that the broader your vision the more you can notice about your audience's reactions. Nerve cells (called rods), which are located largely outside the macula (the centre) of the retina, are responsible for our ability to see objects and movement outside of our direct line of vision. Because peripheral vision is good at detecting motion (a feature of rod cells) it allows presenters to see how each person responds simultaneously.

So how can you expand your peripheral vision? A simple way to do this is to choose a focal point on the far wall from where you're standing. The longer you look at it the more aware you become of how your peripheral vision is expanding. If you continue for half a minute or more you will have greater visual awareness of what is going on around you. When you're getting used to this it's a good idea to test it first so you know how it works. Hold your arm out to one side and slightly behind you. Move your fingers. You will become aware of the movement without seeing your fingers clearly. It's easy to incorporate this as part of your routine when you first step up to speak.

Reasons why people switch off

In Chapter 6 we said there needs to be something interesting happening at regular intervals if you're to keep the audience engaged and the attention level high. If not, people will start to lose focus and switch off. Sometimes there are other contributory factors you need to take into account. The list below contains some of things you may encounter.

- ▶ **They don't want to be there** *More often than most presenters would like they are faced with some audience members who were told to attend. Some will be happy to be there and open to listening. At the other extreme there will be people who are determined not to like it, sit with their arms folded and seek every opportunity to find something wrong with it. If you've prepared well and make the benefits to them clear you will win most people over. If that doesn't work you may decide to suggest that the dissenters leave.*
- ▶ **They've heard some of your material before** *There will be times when your audience already knows some aspect of your*

presentation but you need to cover it anyway. It may be a regulatory requirement, it could be that they will find some parts useful, or simply that you've been asked to deliver a refresher. Most people won't mind hearing about things they know about providing you acknowledge this. If you're not sure you can always ask for a show of hands to check your assumption.

▶ **They're bored stiff before you start** *On the day you may find you are last on the list after a string of dull presentations. You then have the challenge of awakening people from an almost comatose state. In some ways this is an easy one to deal with because all you have to do is start with something that grabs their attention to be better than the rest.*

▶ **There are last-minute changes** *You may have researched your audience well and something happens the day before to change things. There could, for instance, be an announcement about a merger, internal re-organization or a new broom at the top taking over the team. You may need to adapt your presentation at short notice or simply make reference to the change and how this affects the people in your audience.*

▶ **Your strategy doesn't work** *Even the best laid plans don't always work. If what you had in mind doesn't hit the mark you need to think on your feet. Assess your audience's needs and be prepared to deal with issues and concerns they raise in the moment. If necessary, ask them what they want. The worst strategy you can adopt in this situation is to press on regardless. At best they will think you're not aware of their needs, at worst they may think you're a bit dim. Assuming you have the knowledge and skills to deliver it go ahead. If not, tell them and arrange for the right person to present at a later date.*

▶ **Your skills aren't quite up to scratch** *It takes time and practice to hone your skills. If there's an area you're still working on such as a monotone voice you may notice people start to zone out. Obviously, this provides you with a reminder to pause, add variety to your voice, and emphasize key points.*

STAYING POSITIVE

Don't beat yourself up if things don't go as smoothly as you hoped. It's important not to take a 'negative' reaction personally or allow it to sap your confidence. If you look on every piece of feedback as useful information to help you adapt your approach, you'll remain positive. Any seasoned speaker has lots of 'war stories' to tell. The more presentations you do the more experience you gain. Gradually you'll reach a position where you can take setbacks in your stride.

If what you're doing isn't working, do something different

Right from the beginning you need to be flexible and ready to adapt your approach. Once you've diagnosed a problem you have to take action. If you continue as you are, you'll continue to get the same result. The secret of success lies in doing something different if what you're doing isn't working.

We've identified a few of the most common behaviours you may come across and suggested ways to get your audience back on side.

MANAGING LOW ENERGY

If one person in the audience starts to drop off to sleep, ask a question of someone else by name in the group. Move closer to them.

They'll become aware of your physical presence and that can be enough to bring them back to the room. If not, ask them a question and use their name if you know it. It needs to be the second or third query. If you ask them the first time everyone will know why you're doing it and you may embarrass the person.

When the energy of the whole audience is low it can be difficult to get their attention back unless you take decisive action. Sometimes it is as simple as using a strong gesture to emphasize a point or changing your voice tone. Do something interactive that involves your audience. Get everyone on their feet completing some sort of activity, ask a question which involves them raising their hands to show whether or not they agree with your point. Mention people in the audience by name where you can. If you say, 'Bill was saying earlier that he's a big fan of the new branding material because ...', he will be engaged and other people will become alert in case their names are mentioned. If appropriate to the topic, ask for a volunteer to help you demonstrate some aspect of your presentation.

Insight

People feel what you feel, says Amanda. If your energy is low, their energy will soon become low. One thing I've learnt is you need to get a good night's sleep before a big presentation. If you notice your audience zoning out, you'll need to give your energy a turbo-charge or you could lose them completely.

DEALING WITH CONFUSION

If you're speaking at a meeting with a few people present you'll know what action to take because there are fewer people to observe. If one person looks puzzled, you can ask a question to uncover the problem. If everyone appears confused, you can acknowledge the behaviour you're witnessing by saying, 'You look a bit confused, I don't think I've made this clear. Let me put it another way.' If that doesn't do the trick, ask them what aspect is still unclear.

If you've been talking for a while on one topic and some people are looking bored, cut it short, emphasize the main point briefly in your recap and move on to something else. It can help to simply change the pace or move to a new position to add variety. If you need to continue with the same topic tell them what you're about to say is important. If you accentuate this with your voice tone too they're more likely to sit up and take notice.

When they're engaged

When an audience is engaged they're attentive, alert and relaxed. If the topic is light-hearted they laugh and are prepared to have fun. If it's serious they may be making notes, listening carefully or leaning forward. Questions can be an indication that people are interested and want to know more. Although they may not be in this state all the time you know when they're hooked. All you need to do is keep things that way.

Common mistakes

If you follow the advice we've given in the chapter so far you'll be successful. Even the best prepared presenters sometimes fall at the last hurdle because they do one small thing that reduces the impact they could have made on the audience. Here are some common pitfalls to avoid. Don't:

- ▶ **Admit you haven't had time to prepare fully** *They'll think you don't care enough or are after the sympathy vote.*
- ▶ **Apologize** *Presenters apologize for being late, equipment not working and a host of other things. Instead, act as if you have everything under control and you'll look and sound confident and competent.*

- ▶ **Appear hesitant** *Know your open and close off by heart and you'll feel secure and in charge of things. If your 20-minute slot is reduced to five minutes you can still do it based on your opening session because it contains everything you need.*
- ▶ **Suggest you're no good at public speaking** *They'll observe you even more closely for evidence that proves your point.*
- ▶ **Say you would rather be somewhere else** *Surprisingly a few presenters sometimes say this. If you don't want to be there don't let on. Nobody likes whingers.*
- ▶ **Tell them you've delivered your presentation before lots of times even if it's true** *They'll think you're just going through the motions.*
- ▶ **Get names wrong** *If you refer to your host, or someone well known to the audience by the incorrect name they'll think you haven't done your homework.*
- ▶ **Start with a joke** *We've mentioned this one before and it's so important it's worth saying it twice. If you don't get the joke just right for the audience it will bomb. Why take the risk?*
- ▶ **Introduce new material at the end** *This will just confuse people. If you forget to mention something during the presentation it's highly likely that only you will know. Leave it for another time or a follow-up document.*

TEN KEY POINTS TO REMEMBER

1 *Good presenters know the importance of a great opening and the need to pay attention to their audience's reaction.*

2 *You can start to connect with your audience before the presentation starts by chatting to them – or mingling with a large group – before you present.*

3 *The first 10 to 30 seconds is the time when you need to make a positive first impression.*

4 *Be aware of how your behaviour leads you closer – or farther from – your goal of building rapport with a group.*

5 *One of the best ways to achieve rapport is to maintain eye contact with people. With large audiences you need to make it obvious you're shifting your gaze by moving your head too.*

6 *To keep connected to your audience when using PowerPoint look at the screen briefly and then turn and look at them. Only speak when you're facing them.*

7 *You need to read your audience. Observe them closely so you know how they're reacting.*

8 *The secret of success lies in doing something different if what you're doing isn't working.*

9 *You'll know when your audience is engaged because they're attentive, make notes and ask questions.*

10 *Avoid common pitfalls such as admitting you haven't prepared, apologizing, appearing hesitant, saying you're not good at public speaking or would rather be somewhere else.*

15

···

Posture, body language and movement

In this chapter you will learn:
- *about the importance of posture, body language and movement*
- *how to stand, move and use gestures well*
- *about differences in body language for small, medium and large events*
- *how to adapt your non-verbal communication to suit your audience.*

Communicating your message

Have you ever had the experience of looking at someone, hearing them speak and doubting what they're saying because of their body language? It could be that they're talking about how open they are to new ideas with their arms folded across their chest. It might be that they're presenting an important message but there's no physical evidence of passion for the subject.

If you want to communicate well it's not enough to focus on the content of your presentation. Body language is an integral part of human communication and an essential component in getting your message across effectively. Your words and body language need to match if people are to believe and act upon what you have to say.

What are your 'silent messages' saying?

Wherever you are, whatever you're doing, you're always sending out 'silent messages' that reveal what you're thinking and feeling. Even if you were to sit or stand without saying a word you would be communicating – as much as if you were shouting at the top of your voice and waving your arms around. And when we're with other people they seek to make sense of these silent messages we radiate – every gesture, every expression, every movement gives them a sense of who we are and what's going on for us.

Much of the time this process happens unconsciously. We're not aware of the signals we're sending, and others are not aware they're receiving and decoding them. Nevertheless, body language is an important component of the way we communicate. And never more so than when we give a presentation, whether it's around a table at a meeting or standing in front of a large group. All eyes are on us. People are paying attention to us more closely than normal. We're under scrutiny. So we need to make sure our silent messages communicate what we want to communicate and not something that's inconsistent with what we're saying.

SEE YOURSELF ON VIDEO

That's why it's good to see yourself in action and the best way is to video yourself. That way you get a reality check on your presenting. Many people have video cameras these days, if not it's worth going on a course where you're filmed giving presentations. You'll probably be pleasantly surprised. Most people are better than they think they are. But you'll almost certainly identify some 'silent messages' you want to change. Maybe you move around too much. Your posture is weak. You gesture ineffectively. Or you look grumpy all the time. Once you're aware of what you do, you can take action to eliminate any behaviour that's problematic or introduce anything that's missing.

In this chapter our aim is to give you an idea what to look for and be aware of when reviewing your own body language. We'll start by looking at how best to stand, go on to consider when and how to move, then consider different kinds of gesture and conclude with facial expressions.

How to stand

The best way to stand at the start of your presentation is with your feet shoulder-width apart with your toes turned slightly outwards. This position not only feels grounded but also looks powerful to others. To ensure your weight is evenly distributed you need to find your centre of gravity. Do this by rocking gently backwards and forwards, moving the weight onto your toes and then your heels. Stop when you feel 'centred' and balanced. Then soften your knees slightly, to minimize any tension in your lower body (see Figure 15.1).

Figure 15.1 Good posture.

HOW NOT TO STAND

▶ *Don't place your feet too close together. With only one central point of contact with the ground you're less stable and more likely to sway.*

▶ *Avoid turning your toes inwards – it makes you less solid.*

▶ *Take care not to spread your feet too far apart. This 'straddle stance', seen in Holbein's famous portrait of Henry VIII, can give an impression of arrogance and 'trying too hard'.*

▶ *Don't place one foot in front of the other – you'll look less 'strong' and may end up putting your weight on one hip. This is a more relaxed stance, but it can suggest you're not taking things seriously enough.*

▶ *Avoid crossing your legs in a 'scissor stance' – it gives the impression that you have mixed feelings about giving the presentation.*

▶ *Be careful not to allow your foot to roll over onto its side or, worse, tip your shoe back on the heel. This can look rather 'girlie', especially if you're wearing stilettos.*

▶ *Don't allow your feet to face left or right. Keep them towards your audience. Your eyes will tend to follow your feet and it's better if you're not looking over your shoulder.*

Moving on purpose

So, you've got yourself into a strong, balanced, solid, centred stance. Do you stay there, in one place, or do you move? This is something we're often asked on courses. As with many aspects of presenting, the answer depends on the situation. If you stand as still as a statue when speaking to a conference of 1,000 people, you'll come across as static and lacking in energy. The bigger the occasion, and the larger the audience, the more you need to move. If you charge around a small room containing just four people you'll probably drive them crazy inside two minutes.

What's most important is that you move in a way that appears purposeful not random. Some presenters have lots of restless energy when standing, they continually shift from one foot to another. Others move from side to side or backwards and forwards. It looks like they're practising their 'salsa' moves. They appear uncomfortable and this undermines their impact. Other speakers rise up on their toes and then down again repeatedly. When taken to an extreme these behaviours becomes distracting and even irritating to watch.

So avoid shuffling just one or two steps back and forth or to the side. Make it clear that your movement is deliberate. Take at least three steps, stop, settle back into your balanced stance, and stay there for a while. If you're endlessly pacing the room or stage, you'll come across like a caged tiger that's trying to escape.

A good time to move is when you transition from one point to another – and you leave a longer pause. Walking across in silence, just a few seconds, can be a powerful way of signposting the fact that you're moving on. It also changes the energy slightly, and stimulates interest, as you will then start speaking from a different place. While you might sometimes want to talk while you walk, you'll generally have more impact if you say nothing as you relocate.

But it's all a matter of personal style. Management guru Tom Peters, for example, is constantly on the move, charging around the stage with a machine gun delivery that never stops. It's extremely powerful, but only works in bigger settings. Don't try it at your next departmental meeting! Generally, it's better to move across the stage rather than back and forth.

WHERE TO MOVE TO

When moving, always lead with the foot that's closer to where you're going, and step out smoothly and confidently. Avoid jerky, rushed movements that signal anxiety.

How much you move around will depend on the shape and size of the room. If there's barely any space for the audience and furniture you're likely to stay where you are. Sometimes you'll have the luxury of a bit more room, which means you can move around.

It's a good idea to decide before you start the presentation which places you plan to speak from – it avoids indecisiveness and uncertainty when you're up and running. Typically you'll want two, maybe three, different spots. Most speakers start their presentation at the front of their audience in a central position, or to one side when they're using PowerPoint. The options you have depend on how much space there is and the size of your audience. If you're using PowerPoint, you'll have more freedom if you use a remote control to change the slides. Without one you won't be able to stray far from the keyboard.

In small to medium-sized rooms your baseline position will probably be close to the screen as you may want to point things out. Where the other places are will be determined to a large degree by the layout of the room and the size of the audience. Make sure you're able to maintain eye contact at all times, and don't have to walk too far between the different locations. Be careful not to stand too close to people who are seated. It can feel like you're towering over them, especially if you're tall, and they may find it intimidating.

When presenting to medium-sized groups there are different issues to consider. The shape of the room and space available will affect your choice of where to stand. You may, of course, still opt for sitting down for an informal, relaxed feel.

When presenting to larger groups it's important to make sure everyone can see you. Sometimes you'll be on a stage, which makes that easy. Whatever the situation you need to plan how you'll move and make the most of the area available to you. If you're using a lectern to rest your script or notes on, be prepared to move out into open space when you can. Lecterns are not a barrier to hide behind – you'll increase the impact you have if you're brave enough to step away.

Insight

One of the things that irritates a lot of people is when presenters pace backwards and forwards like a tiger in a cage the moment they present in a room with a little bit more space than the average business meeting room.

While movement can be good, says Amanda, anything that becomes too repetitive can drive your audience to silently scream 'Please stand still!'

STEPPING UP TO SPEAK

When you are standing to present, you will generally need to step up to speak. This for some people is the most nerve-wracking moment of all. Suddenly all eyes are on you. And since your audience will be forming an opinion of you from the first moment they see you it's important you convey the right impression. If you stroll up as if you haven't a care in the world they may think you're not bothered. If you rush to get to your spot and start speaking immediately you'll come across as nervous.

Whatever you do, don't drag your feet as if you were heading for your execution. Walking purposefully with an even pace, not too fast and not too slow, will make you look confident and self-assured. Aim for a feeling of power and grace. A steady, deliberate stride gives you instant gravitas and authority without appearing arrogant.

Overall posture

Well that's the bottom half of the body sorted but what about the upper half? Well, it's all about posture. You need to stand tall, as if there's a piece of string attached to the top of your head pulling you up, with your shoulders pulled back and your stomach and bottom tucked in. When you stand like this you look and feel confident. This posture is also perfect for breathing well and projecting your voice. With your chest and ribcage open you can easily fill your lungs and get plenty of volume without having to shout.

COMMON POSTURE ERRORS

All too often, though, people slump when giving a presentation. Maybe because it feels too 'open' and exposed with the shoulders pulled right back, so they allow them to come forward and collapse inwards. Not only does this look like you're protecting yourself, it also restricts the flow of air in and out of the body – so the voice comes out soft and weak, further increasing the impression of submissiveness (see Figure 15.2).

Another problem regarding posture that sometimes occurs when presenters are nervous is that they turn sideways to the audience rather than facing them directly. 'Avoidance' orientations of this kind signal quite clearly that the person would rather be somewhere else.

Figure 15.2 Poor posture.

SEATED PRESENTATIONS

When you're presenting to small groups you'll sometimes be seated. This can be comforting to those who tend to get anxious because much of their body is concealed behind a table. But as a result they sometimes neglect their posture, which is every bit as important in this situation as when standing.

To create a positive impression, sit upright with your bottom at the back of the chair and your feet flat on floor, so your thighs make a 90 degree angle to your calves. Take care never to allow your bottom to slide forward or you'll find yourself leaning back. That can mean, in some people's eyes, laid back, as if you're not really bothered. And watch for any tendency to put more weight on one elbow over the other, so you end up leaning to one side.

You're aiming to achieve the same centred posture as when you're standing. Shoulders should be back, and head up with your chin parallel to the table. Rest your lower arms on the table making it easy for you to support your message with appropriate gestures. When you do this, you look and feel confident. This doesn't mean you have to sit in this way all the time, but it's a positive way to start.

Insight

Something we've noticed when people give seated presentations is a tendency to have the chair pushed back from the table – which results in the body leaning forward at an angle of 45 degrees and all the weight on the elbows. This makes it difficult to gesture effectively. The hands can't move freely. It's better to bring the chair closer to the table, and place the weight on the side of the hands. This allows them to gesture without constraint, resulting in a more conversational style.

Leaning postures

A halfway house can be to lean on a desk or the back of a chair, so you're higher than everyone else but not actually standing. This can also be interpreted as relaxed, perhaps even casual. It may be fine when chatting to your team or colleagues, but is perhaps inappropriate when presenting to clients, bosses or people you've never met before. We've also seen people stumble when a chair tips over and heard 'groaning' sounds as a table creaks under their weight, so take care in situations of this kind.

How to hold your head

The way you angle your head sends subtle signals that have a profound impact on the way you're perceived. While you'll obviously move it around as you're speaking, you should keep returning to a 'standard' position where the head is 'square', neither tipped to the front, back or one side. In particular you should avoid the following angles.

▶ **Looking down the nose** *If you're in the habit of tipping your head back you're in danger of coming across as superior. There's an implied arrogance in this posture because it suggests you're 'looking down your nose' at your audience.*
▶ **The Chin Tuck** *When you tip your head down you display a classic sign of vulnerability called the 'chin tuck'. It's a tell-tale posture that people use to protect themselves from being punched in one of their most exposed areas. While this is unlikely to happen in a business presentation, some people who experience presenting as dangerous unconsciously press their jaw into their neck in the same way that professional boxers do.*
▶ **The Head Cock** *Some presenters cock their head to one side. This makes them appear quizzical or uncertain like dogs trying to understand what their owner is saying. It can also come across as coquettish – Marilyn Monroe and Diana, Princess of Wales used to do it – and can be interpreted as submissive.*

Hands and arms – what a nightmare!

The biggest problem many presenters have, both experienced and newcomers, is knowing what to with their hands. It comes up time and time again on the courses we run. People worry endlessly about whether they're gesturing too much or too little, and where to put their hands when they're not gesturing. It's easily one of the biggest causes of anxiety when presenting. And really it's all rather simple. Using your hands when speaking is natural and normal. When people carry on a one-to-one conversation they gesture as a matter of course. In fact, it looks strange if they don't, as if they're not really interested in what they're talking about. The more passionate we are about something the more animated we are in our gestures.

It's the same when giving a presentation, which is essentially a conversation with several people. You need to gesture, because if you don't you come across as if you don't really care about the subject matter.

GESTURES NEED TO BE MEANINGFUL NOT ARBITRARY

But you need to get the balance right. While you don't want hands whizzing round like windmills in a gale you do want to demonstrate energy and enthusiasm. Too much gesturing, too little gesturing – both are bad practice when it comes to presenting.

What's most important is that you move your hands and arms in a meaningful way, so they match the content of your presentation. When gestures are motivated by what you want to get across they look natural and authentic. But when they're arbitrary, and don't seem to fit with your message, they can undermine the credibility of your presentation.

That doesn't necessarily mean your gestures should be planned: in fact, unless you're an experienced presenter, it's better to keep things spontaneous, or it can end up looking contrived. The secret is to prepare well, so you're not having to worry about whether you'll remember your material, then just allow the movement of your arms and hands to flow with what you're saying.

PERSONALITY MATTERS

It's important, though, to follow a few simple 'rules'. Gestures need to reflect your personality. Some people are naturally more expressive than others. If you're relatively quiet, rather introverted, it wouldn't ring true for you to use lots of large, fast gestures. Slower, more subtle movement will be more credible. Bubbly, extrovert personalities, on the other hand, find it hard to move slowly and can be tiring to watch if they keep that up for any length of time.

Problems can occur when a presenter strays too much outside his or her natural style. Gordon Brown, the ex-British Prime Minister, struggled with his body language in public, formal settings. His movements often seemed awkward and clumsy. It seemed to us that he was trying to gesture in the same animated way that Tony Blair, his predecessor, had done – but couldn't carry it off because his personality style was different. Don't be a bad imitation of someone else – just be yourself.

TYPES OF GESTURE

Gestures serve a number of purposes when you're presenting. They:

▶ **Add vitality and enthusiasm to your presentation** *They stop it from becoming static and passionless. Using your hands injects energy into what you're saying – the more you gesture the stronger your voice becomes. The two are inextricably linked.*

▶ **Act as visual aids** *You can 'mark out' ideas in the space around you or illustrate the relationship of one thing to another. You might, for instance, talk about the past, and gesture with your left hand, then about the future, and gesture with your right hand. This routine is great for making contrasts of all kinds: 'finance says we need to cut costs (left hand moves to one side), marketing believes we need to invest in the future' (right hand moves in the opposite direction). As you discuss five points you can count them off on your fingers. Or you can use one hand to denote a high price point (head), a medium price point (chest) and a low price point (waist).*

▶ **Allow you to emphasize ideas that are important** *The more forceful a gesture is, or the faster you do it, the more you underscore a message, which helps the audience know what to pay most attention to.*

▶ **Are an outlet for nervous energy** *You can channel it effectively rather than have it express itself through distracting mannerisms. People who try to stand still when presenting are often the ones who shuffle and sway the most.*

GESTURING EFFECTIVELY

Gestures are most effective when they're smooth and slow. Imagine you're moving your arms through water, so they travel with a steady, even flow. Avoid jerky movements because they look rushed and awkward.

Most of the time you want your hands at the same height as your elbows or higher. If you allow them to drop below it looks weak, particularly if you gesture below waist height. And give your arms permission to move freely. Sometimes we see presenters with 'Velcro' arms – they're extremely close to the body as if stuck there. Their gestures, as a result, are small and restrained. Sometimes the 'Velcro' only goes as far as the elbow, allowing the lower arms to move. This can make presenters look like puppets. On some people it goes all the way down to the wrist, so only the hands move. Because the gestures appear timid, the impact is negative (see Figure 15.3).

Figure 15.3 Velcro arms.

Unless you have a specific reason to do so, avoid showing your hands with your palms upwards. If you're not careful it can look as if you're begging or pleading. If you want an open, welcoming gesture, don't tip the hands back beyond 45 degrees. Gestures in which the palms are face down or only partially revealed are perceived as being stronger.

Figure 15.4 The open gesture.

Most of the time you'll want to keep your hands open and loose. For obvious reasons you should avoid making them into fists – once you start gesturing you can all too easily come across as aggressive (see Figure 15.4).

Be careful, too, of pointing at people, even if it's to acknowledge a point they've made or to ask a question. Pointing is a universal gesture that's associated with blaming and accusing, and can unconsciously trigger a negative response in your audience. Some politicians get round this by forming a loose fist with the thumb resting on the forefinger. They use this when they want to emphasize a point (see Figure 15.5).

THE IMPORTANCE OF VARIETY

What's most important is that you have variety in the way you gesture. One figure in the business world who regularly appears on television has only one gesture, which he repeats over and over again. It quickly catches your attention and begins to distract from

Figure 15.5 Fist and thumb.

what he's saying. We'll consider in a moment ways in which you can expand your repertoire of gestures to make your presentation more interesting to watch and to give you greater impact.

CHOOSING AN EFFECTIVE RESTING POSITION

You can't gesture all the time. Nor would you want to. If your arms and hands were constantly on the go it would be tiring for you and for those listening. It would also mean you were gesturing when you weren't actually speaking, and you do need to pause regularly to let the audience take in what you're saying.

What you need, therefore, is a comfortable resting position for your hands – a 'base' to which they return when they're not in action. Some people are happy to have them hang down by the side of their body, lightly resting on the outer part of the thigh (see Figure 15.1). Seen from the audience's perspective this looks confident and professional, providing you don't hold the position too long, when it starts to look as if you're lined up for a firing squad, and it starts to violate the 'your hands must be above the elbow' rule.

An alternative approach, which is widely used by television reporters, and which many presenters also favour, is to hold both hands in front of the navel, lightly touching each other or overlapping, with the fingers bent slightly inwards towards the body. From this position it's easy to gesture in all directions and quickly return. But don't hold your hands too high – you'll look like a hamster or a squirrel (see Figure 15.6).

Figure 15.6 Good posture.

COMMON ARM AND HAND MISTAKES

Here are some of the common mistakes presenters make with their hands:

▶ **Putting their hands behind their back** *Because they don't know what to do with their hands, some people place them behind them. We call this the Military Posture because it's how sergeant majors often stand when inspecting their troops. It's formal, rigid and makes it impossible to gesture effectively. Sometimes you get the impression they've been handcuffed. The other disadvantage is that the person's weight is thrown forward, which creates an imbalance (see Figure 15.7).*
▶ **Stuffing their hands in the pockets** *We often see presenters put one or both hands in their trouser pockets (see Figure 15.8).*

Figure 15.7 Military stance.

Figure 15.8 Poor posture – hands in pockets.

This looks relaxed and casual, which is fine for certain kinds
of presentation, but should be avoided in formal settings when
it can look as if you're not taking it seriously enough. Men
are more guilty of putting their hands in their pockets than

Figure 15.9 'Fig leaf flasher' or footballers' pose.

women and, because their pockets often contain change they sometimes become 'pocket janglers' who absent-mindedly fiddle with coins while talking. This can become immensely distracting for the audience.

▶ **Fig leaf flasher** *In this pose the person's hands are clasped together in front of the groin, like footballers preparing to defend against a direct free-kick on goal. They also act as a 'fig-leaf' covering the private parts. When the presenter moves his or her arms to gesture, they appear to be 'flashing'. This sounds amusing, but appears defensive, and should be avoided (see Figure 15.9).*

▶ **Placing hands on hips** *When animals meet rivals in the wild they often make themselves look as big as possible in a bid to scare off the rival. One way that humans do the same thing is to place both hands on their hips. This is widely recognized as a 'macho' dominance gesture, though women sometimes do it as well. Because it can make you look aggressive, belligerent and arrogant, this is one to avoid most of the time. Curiously, placing one hand on your hip has the opposite effect (see Figure 15.10). Start to gesture with the other hand and you become a 'teapot', which can appear rather amusing.*

Figure 15.10 Poor posture – hands on hips.

▶ **Gunfighter's pose** *Some people adopt a pose that's similar to the 'high noon' scenes in Wild West films where there's a showdown between gunfighters. When presenters have both arms out and a little away from their body it looks like they're about to draw their six-shooter. This pose displays quite a lot of muscular tension and obviously comes across as aggressive, so we don't recommend it (see Figure 15.11).*

Figure 15.11 Gunfighter's pose.

▶ *Arms folded or across the body* Everyone knows that folding your arms is defensive, and the same is true of any posture in which the arms cross the body, such as one hand reaching over and grasping the opposite wrist or arm. Avoid such poses. Open body language conveys a feeling of ease and should be adopted as standard. Another defensive variation is the 'Napoleon Bonaparte' where one hand is tucked into a jacket with the other is behind the back (see Figure 15.12).

Figure 15.12 Arms folded across the body.

SPECIFIC GESTURES

Gestures, then, should be natural, and relate to what you're saying. But sometimes we end up with an impoverished repertoire of things we do with our hands and arms. As we observe other people we notice they gesture more effectively than we do.

Just because what we currently do feels 'natural', it doesn't mean it's not possible to enlarge the range of options available to us. Average tennis players can take coaching lessons and develop skills they didn't have before. Aspiring cooks who lack understanding of culinary techniques can learn to turn out gourmet meals with practice. And it's the same with public speaking.

You can greatly improve the impact you have by expanding your range of gestures.

Watch several politicians and business leaders speak and you'll start to notice similarities in the way they stand, move and use their hands. That's because many of them have received considerable training in communication and presentation skills. They may have started out with a certain amount of 'talent', but in most cases this has been enhanced by study and practice. They weren't always able to wow an audience, they learnt how to do it.

And you can do the same. Simply copy the gestures used by some of the world's leading communicators and you'll get the same results they do. Yes, it will feel strange, unnatural even, for a while. But it doesn't take long to create new habits – and you'll quickly find it becomes automatic.

Here are some tried and tested gestures that are worth learning and incorporating when you want to come across with authority and conviction. The first time you try one you might want to save it for a specific moment when you say something of particular importance. But once you've mastered it you can use it whenever seems appropriate.

▶ **The two-handed stab** *Politicians favour this short, stabbing motion when they want to ram a point home. It can be used with one hand or both for extra emphasis. The hands are in front of the body with fingers pointing forwards (parallel to each other in the two-handed version). Wrists are straight and stiff (see Figure 15.13).*
▶ **Coming together** *This gesture is especially for when you're talking about things coming together or groups working in partnership. The hands start facing each other about 45 cm apart, in front of the body (as if showing the length of a fish) and then move towards each other. It often looks at the end as if the presenter is holding a ball.*
▶ **The Leveller** *With palms facing down, the hands move downwards and outwards starting from a central point in front of the chest. Imagine you're smoothing out a bag of*

Figure 15.13 The two-handed stab.

flour. The message this conveys is that 'This is the way things are', 'I'm levelling with you', or 'These are the facts'. The Leveller asserts authority and helps calm people down (see Figure 15.14).

Figure 15.14 The Leveller.

▶ **The bare knuckle** *In this gesture both hands are held at chest height with the knuckles, as the name suggests, facing* outwards. *When you use this you're perceived as powerful and dominant. It suggests you're in charge and have something important to say (see Figure 15.15).*

Figure 15.15 The bare knuckle.

▶ **The Visionary** *This gesture is ideal when you want to inspire people and works extremely well with large audiences. Hands are around the level of the chin, and arms slightly away from the body, with palms at 45 degrees (see Figure 15.16).*

Figure 15.16 The visionary.

Facial expressions

When we watch people speak we pay attention to lots of things –
what they say and how they say it, their posture and body language –
but it's their face we observe most closely. The reason is simple, it's
the part of them that most readily expresses what they're thinking
and feeling. Expressions, like gestures, reinforce the points being
made. And they're one of the principal ways an audience decides
whether it likes and trusts the speaker.

So when you give a presentation you need to make sure your
expression conveys what you want it to. This is crucial, because
if there's inconsistency between what your face says and what
your mouth says, it's your face people believe every time. Some
presenters hide their emotions in an attempt to appear professional.
This is a mistake. You'll come across as lacking in passion. Instead,
let the conviction behind your ideas show on your face.

What kinds of expression should you display? Well, it depends,
quite obviously, on the topic of your presentation. If you're
delivering bad news it would clearly be inappropriate to smile.
You need a certain amount of gravitas. But if you're presenting
something upbeat and positive, you don't want to look as if your
dog just died. You probably do want to smile.

Smiling shows that you're happy to be there and suggests that
you're confident. It's the most obvious sign of happiness. Cheery
expressions are infectious, and a good way to start because you
make a positive connection from the outset. But don't try to fake a
smile. The audience will see through it in an instant. A genuine smile
is difficult to manufacture, because it uses the zygomatic muscles at
the corner of the eyes, which are not under conscious control.

Eyes and eyebrows are another vital form of expression when
you're presenting. They give your audience vital clues about how
you're feeling. Eye contact is extremely important (see Chapter 14)
but eyebrows, believe it or not, are central to conveying what
we're thinking. We're not suggesting you mimic Jim Carey when

speaking, but varying your facial expressions will help to keep people engaged enormously. This is particularly important when you're behind a lectern and the audience can't see your body.

Adapting to the audience and situation

The crucial rule for gestures and expressions is to match them to the situation. When the room is large, or you're far away from your audience, you need to amplify your movements. They just won't carry if you keep things small. But when you're right in front of the people you're speaking to, and in a standard room, you need to tone things down.

It's also important to think about the audience. What kind of people are they? Imagine the look on the faces of a quiet, staid audit committee when a presenter turns up and starts his presentation in a bold fashion with flamboyant body language. It's unlikely to go down well. Equally, a meek and mild speaker using minimal gestures will bore the pants off a lively group of strong-minded extroverts.

Most organizations evolve a culture, they expect people to behave in a certain way. If you want to connect with them it's important to match their world view. The same is often true of country cultures.

In Morocco, standing with arms behind the back is considered the right way to deliver a presentation. In Japan and some countries in the Far East, people don't make as much eye contact. In some cases, the audience will close their eyes during a presentation to show they are listening carefully to the speaker. The bottom line here is that you need to adjust your approach to meet their needs.

Insight

I (Amanda) know only too well about the importance of facial expressions when presenting. I have quite large eyes

(Contd)

and if I'm not careful I can come across as a bit too intense even when I don't feel that way inside. In my case I make an effort to blink and take care not to look at any individual for too long. Steve can sometimes look worried or even grumpy when thinking, so he has to remember to smile, especially when co-presenting, and planning what to say next. If you identify an aspect of your behaviour that's open to misinterpretation you can take action to change it.

Body language matters

Body language is a vital element in communication. There can be a lot to think about for a presenter who wants to be effective and make a positive impact. While it's useful to review what you do, if you're constantly worrying about how to stand and what to do with your hands you won't relax. When you forget your body and let the message and your passion for the subject drive you the audience won't notice either.

TEN KEY POINTS TO REMEMBER

1 *When we're with other people – especially when we present – we reveal what we're thinking and feeling through 'silent messages' we give off.*

2 *The best way to stand at the start of a presentation is with your feet shoulder-width apart and your toes turned slightly outwards.*

3 *When you move make sure it's purposeful and not random. Random movement is distracting and makes you look uncomfortable.*

4 *Posture is important when you present. You need to stand tall, as if there's a piece of string attached to your head pulling you up with your shoulders back, and stomach tucked in.*

5 *Hold your head upright with your chin parallel to the floor.*

6 *Make sure your gestures are motivated by what you want to convey so they look natural and authentic.*

7 *A good resting position is to hold both hands in front of the navel, lightly touching each other. Alternatively let your arms hang loosely by the side of your body.*

8 *When you give a presentation you need to make sure your facial expression conveys what you want it to.*

9 *When giving a seated presentation, sit upright with your bottom at the back of the chair. Rest your lower arms on the table so it's easy to make gestures.*

10 *Adapt your gestures, movements and expressions to match the audience and situation.*

16

Maximizing your voice

In this chapter you will learn:
- *how to avoid common voice problems*
- *about voice projection, clarity, intonation, pace, pitch, resonance and rhythm*
- *why breathing well is important*
- *about the power of the pause*
- *how to look after your voice.*

Your voice is not what it seems

Most of the time we don't hear our voice as others hear it and it can be a shock when we do. That's because we normally experience it reverberating through the flesh and bone of our head and as a result it sounds deep and resonant. When we do hear it as others hear it – via an audio or video recording – we're often surprised. We don't like the way it sounds. It's usually 'thinner' and weaker than we thought.

As the sound passes through the air, it loses some of its power. This means other people hear something very different. When we hear a recording of our voice many of us are dissatisfied with the sound we produce. Sometimes it's so soft and quiet it's hard to detect, or flat, dull and monotone.

In this chapter you'll find ways to add variety to your voice, answers to common voice problems, and techniques for maximizing the impact you have with your voice when presenting.

Ways in which your voice can be different

The human voice is like a finely tuned instrument capable of producing beautiful sounds. There are an infinite number of different voices. Some are deep, others shrill. Some people are softly spoken while others are brash and loud. Each individual voice is capable of rich variety in the level of volume, pitch, intonation, pace and rhythm. Some of us make more use of the range available to us than others. It isn't just changes in modulation and inflection of the voice that make a difference. Some of us speak clearly and distinctly while others mumble and sound muffled. Resonance enriches the sound, animation brings it to life, and emphasis tells those who listen to us which words or phrases are important. In everyday conversation voice is extremely important for communication. When you're presenting it's vital. As the saying goes 'it ain't just what you say, it's also the way that you say it' that matters.

What kind of problems can there be?

If the human voice is capable of such richness why is it that we don't all speak beautifully? There are a number of common problems presenters experience that prevent them from maximizing their voice.

- ▶ **Being too quiet** *If the audience can't hear, you're unlikely to get your message across.*
- ▶ **Limited projection** *Even if your voice is at a reasonable volume the audience won't all hear you if you don't project your voice in their direction.*
- ▶ **Speaking too fast** *If you gabble everything out at 90 miles an hour the audience may hear but are unlikely to understand a word you say.*
- ▶ **Monotone delivery** *If everything you say is delivered at the same pitch with no variation it will be dull in the extreme.*

- **Running out of breath** *When you run out of breath before you complete a sentence and gasp like a swimmer between strokes for air.*
- **Hesitating** *If you appear unsure of yourself, your audience may think you're either unprepared or lacking in confidence.*
- **Presenter's voice** *If you try too hard to do a professional job it can come across as lacking passion and conviction.*

Some of these problems are simply habits, and unless you hear a recording of your voice or receive feedback from someone you may not even realize there's an issue. Others are caused by anxiety and once you've dealt with your nerves using the techniques in Chapter 12 they'll start to disappear. The way you feel about yourself affects your vocal delivery. Soft speakers are often unconsciously holding themselves back.

Using your voice as a tool

On our courses we regularly ask people, 'How old were you when you decided to speak how you do today?' The response we get is often bemused and confused. Most people never make a conscious decision to speak the way they do. Biology, of course, plays a part, but we're also enormously influenced by how our parents, friends and teachers speak – as well as the country, region and culture – and we end up with a particular voice.

Just because that's how things are now doesn't mean that's how things have to stay. Once you learn how the voice works you can make changes and create a new, improved way of speaking. One way of thinking about your voice is as a tool that will give you the results you want. If you're happy with it as it is, fine. If not, then you can change it.

Insight
Some of the people we work with are reluctant and resistant to changing their voice because they somehow think of it as

being part of who they are – rather than something they do. This is understandable – we've had a lifetime of hearing our voice – but not useful. We're only talking about adapting your voice to make it more effective when presenting, so it's not a huge compromise, if you think of it that way.

DEVELOPING YOUR VOICE

If you want to develop your voice you need to create a regime that helps you put in place the changes you want to make. One way is to practise exercises that establish new patterns. Some of the exercises encourage you to add variety or simply become aware of your current speed of speaking and compare that with a recognized, desired rate. It's not how long you practise that matters, it's how often. The best way to form a new habit is to fit it into your daily life, such as when driving or in the shower. The most important thing is to find a way that works for you and suits your lifestyle. You'll be surprised and delighted at how fast you make progress once you make a commitment to yourself to transform the way you speak.

Creating variety

If you get only one thing from this chapter, and we believe you'll get much more, we want it to be an understanding that variety is vital. It's one of the key ways of making your delivery interesting and engaging. Aim to do this in as many ways as possible. Speed up to express enthusiasm and excitement. Slow down when you want to say something serious. Reduce your voice to a whisper as if sharing a secret and increase the volume when you want to emphasize an important point. If you simply make this small change you'll improve your voice enormously. One of the easiest ways to do it is by letting your passion for the topics you speak about guide your delivery. When we care about the subject we're speaking about we naturally adapt our voice to convey the emotion we feel about it.

Volume

There's nothing wrong with speaking quietly, but if the volume is not sufficient for your audience to hear what you have to say you obviously won't be able to communicate effectively. Some people seem unable to adjust their volume. It's like the volume knob is permanently stuck on low, and no matter how big the room or the occasion is, they're unable to turn it up higher. This is even true when there's a lot of background noise such as air-conditioning inside, traffic outside. Members of an audience will not strain to hear for long before they give up and stop trying, preferring instead to entertain themselves by checking their BlackBerrys or making a few notes ready for their next meeting.

You can use volume for emphasis by raising your voice slightly to highlight a key word or phrase. If you tend to speak loudly most of the time you may want to go down a notch for some parts of your presentation to make sure there is some differentiation.

PROXEMICS AND ORIENTATION

When you're presenting it's useful to take into account proxemics – the study of the effects of spatial distance between people who interact with each other, and of their orientation toward each other. If you're some distance from your audience your voice obviously has farther to travel. Don't stand too far away from the people you're communicating with. Some presenters turn away from their audience slightly, especially when they're using PowerPoint, and the volume is lost. For maximum impact you need to face those you're speaking to.

Make sure the volume is appropriate for the size of the room and the number of people in it. Take account of the room's acoustic properties as well. If there are no carpets or soft furnishings to absorb the sound there may be an echo. The height of the ceiling can make a difference too.

The importance of posture

Posture is vital for an effective speaking voice. If you stand with your shoulders slumped and your head down your voice won't be as powerful. Our bodies have a number of cavities – vocal tract and nasal and oral cavities – which fill with air. The air we breathe in moves out from the lungs, passes up through the trachea and into the voice box or larynx. The vocal cords vibrate producing sound. Standing up straight like an opera singer places the vocal cords, lungs and diaphragm in the right position to send your voice across the room. You may find it useful to look back at the section on good posture in Chapter 15.

Exercise

Practise the opening of your presentation in front of a mirror so you can keep an eye on your posture at the same time. Say it once at whisper, then at normal conversation level and finally as if you're presenting in front of a large group.

Voice projection

Experienced speakers, actors and singers recognize voice projection to be an essential skill. This doesn't mean raising your voice or shouting. Volume and projection are not the same but they are connected. When you choose to speak louder or more softly you're changing the volume. You can project your voice even at a whisper. To project your voice effectively you need to:

▶ *have good posture so you can breathe effectively and have enough air available to you*

- *face the direction you want the sound to go – this means looking at your audience rather than your slides, the ceiling or floor so your voice travels towards your audience*
- *manage your breathing well*
- *speak at an appropriate pace*
- *clearly pronounce your vowels and consonants.*

We've mentioned some of these key components already, such as posture and orientation. We'll now go to explain why breathing, pace and clarity are also crucial. Before we do, try the exercise below to help you practise projecting your voice without straining.

Exercise

1 Locate a point about an arm's length in front of you.
2 Take a deep breath and exhale with the intention of reaching this point without straining.
3 Choose a short sentence from a presentation and do the same thing while expressing your message.
4 Select a second point approximately two metres ahead.
5 Say the same sentence again, letting the words flow out as you exhale.
6 Continue to repeat this sequence until you reach the back of the room.

The importance of breathing well

Good breathing technique is vital for voice projection. In fact, if you find it difficult to project your voice, poor breathing may be the root cause. Every breath you take needs to provide enough air for each phrase or sentence. It's all too easy for your voice to tail off at the end of sentences, especially where a word ends with a consonant. When you reach a point where your breath runs out, pause and take another breath. Allow your words to flow out as you exhale.

In normal conversation we tend to use air from the upper part of our lungs. For public speaking, shallow breathing like this doesn't provide sufficient air to project our voices. We need air that comes from a deeper level. You know you're accessing the deeper level when you can feel your rib cage expand and your diaphragm contract as you breathe in. This process enlarges the chest cavity. It's important to maintain good posture when you're speaking. It's all too easy to lean backwards slightly as you take a breath in and then lean forwards again as you speak while exhaling. Breathing is easier if you avoid this by remaining upright. Slowing down your delivery rate and pausing will also assist your breathing.

Exercise

1   Stand up and adjust your posture
2   Inhale
3   Pause
4   Recite the alphabet while breathing out

Your goal is to get to the letter 'h' with an even flow of breath. Make sure you maintain good posture throughout.

This exercise can help you to prevent your voice trailing off at the end of sentences. You need enough breath to get through your first phrase.

Clarity of diction

Clarity of diction is a vital component of voice projection. You need to be both audible and intelligible. People may be able to hear your voice but if they can't understand what you're saying your message won't get through. To be clear you need good articulation and pronunciation. Some presenters have a habit of mumbling their words, which can make it difficult for their audience to comprehend. Saying things clearly involves using the teeth, lips and tongue. Moving your tongue when you speak helps you articulate and prevents your voice from sounding muffled. Make sure you position your tongue at the front of your mouth and use it to enunciate clearly. Check your jaw is relaxed because this helps articulation. Yawning can relieve tension in the jaw and throat. Mispronouncing words will reduce clarity. If you're not sure how something should be said, check first. Most dictionaries explain how words should sound.

PRONOUNCE CONSONANTS CLEARLY

Clarity and good pronunciation come from precise use of language. Speak slowly and clearly, making sure the consonants in each word are clear, particularly at the beginning and end of words. Pay special attention to plosive consonants such as b, d and g, which are produced by stopping the flow of air and suddenly releasing it. The 'ng' at the end of some words is also often omitted. Take a look at the example below. The first sentence is typical of some conversational language. The second is much clearer.

> *We wanna succeed an start sellin*
> *We want to succeed and start selling*

Although this is important, you don't want to overdo it. If you take this advice too far your voice may start to sound 'clipped' or even false rather than articulate.

Insight

Lack of clarity, diction and enunciation of words is a common problem, says Amanda. You don't have to sound like the Queen, but saying those Bs, Ps, Ds, etc. is crucial. This is especially true when the audience is listening to you speak in a non-native language – which is frequently the case in business today. It requires much more concentration from them.

Pace

The pace at which people speak varies. Some are slow, others fast and most somewhere in between. The speed at which you speak reflects the speed at which you think. Those who present at 100 to 120 wpm (words per minute) will sound ponderous to those who speak faster. The danger here is that they may get bored, irritated or even fall asleep. Those who race along at 180 to 200 wpm will leave slow talkers struggling to keep up. After a while they zone out – it becomes just noise to them.

If you're at one of the extremes, 100 wpm or 200 wpm, you need to speed up or slow down to around 130 to 170 wpm if you're to be able to communicate effectively with most people.

Fast speakers should also consider increasing the length and number of pauses between sentences to give the audience time to catch up.

Variety in pace is important. If you say everything at one speed you make it hard for people to listen to you. If you continue to talk at a fast pace, and a high pitch, they may think you're nervous. In practice, this simply means slowing down from time to time for emphasis if you naturally speak quickly and speeding up to add energy and enthusiasm if you usually talk slowly.

If you get it wrong, people will stop listening. If this happens all you have to do is change your pace for a while.

Exercise (with thanks to Clare Willis)

Read the following passage (150 words) as if you were giving a presentation and time yourself. If you get through it in less than 60 seconds, you're speaking too quickly.

(Contd)

Practise inserting longer pauses until you can fill 60 seconds, and then 80 seconds.

Many inexperienced speakers find it hard to pause, but it is an extremely effective way of holding your audience's attention and of conveying a confident impression. Pauses are powerful only if they are silent. Speakers who can't bear silence fill it with the noise of their brain working as they search for the exact word or phrase. While their brain is getting into gear, it emits the sound of 'er' and 'um' and 'mm' – non-words that convey nothing and distract listeners. Learn to think silently. In your everyday conversation you may find that you are using other non-words such as 'I mean', 'basically', 'you know', 'actually' and 'you know what I mean'. Try to eliminate these altogether as they are unnecessary and indicate a lack of concentration on your part. Sharpen up your conversation and eventually you will be sufficiently confident to pause when you are speaking in public.

The power of the pause

One of the most powerful ways of improving your impact is to use regular 'power pauses'. Stop speaking – for one, two, sometimes three seconds – even when you know what to say next. Pausing gives you time to think and your audience space to take in your ideas. It gives the impression you're in control and comfortable with being the centre of attention. Silence conveys confidence.

Some people are afraid of pausing because there's a time distortion when you're presenting – one second can seem like ten seconds. But you quickly get over that, and grow comfortable with the silence.

One great advantage of pausing is that it helps you to eliminate 'fillers' such as 'um', 'er', 'okay' and 'so'. These are words we use in everyday conversation to let the other person know we haven't finished talking. But they become redundant in a presentation because the audience isn't expected to take turns in the same way.

You can incorporate more pauses in your presentation by inserting them at the end of sentences or phrases where you want to emphasize a key point. One obvious place to pause is before a change of topic.

When you're using PowerPoint slides you can pause as you turn to look at the slide and then speak when you're facing the audience. As we discussed in Chapter 10, this also helps you maintain eye contact.

Pitch

Human beings have a range of notes available to them when they're speaking, from low to high. The term pitch, sometimes referred to as intonation, is used to describe which note they're actually using. Varying your pitch makes your speaking voice more interesting and engaging. Our 'modal pitch' is our default or baseline that we return to after pitch variations. When we speak at a lower pitch than normal it suggests that what we're saying is serious and can add gravitas. When our voice is higher it conveys energy and excitement. There's also a relationship between volume and pitch – typically as our voice gets louder so it gets higher and vice versa. Nervous speakers sometimes have tension in their vocal chords, resulting in an unintentionally higher pitch. Relaxation and breathing exercises can help with this (refer to Chapter 12 for ideas).

DIFFERENCES BETWEEN THE SEXES

As we all know, male voices are generally lower in pitch than female voices. This is because a man's vocal cords are longer and as result produce a deeper sound. Deeper voices are associated with authority and have greater credibility. When women join the legal profession in America their voice typically drops by an octave between starting to train to starting to practise.

HOW TO AVOID COMING ACROSS AS MONOTONE

To avoid coming across as monotone – staying on the same note for a long period of time – you need to vary your pitch when speaking. This maintains variety. You need, though, to be careful to avoid the pitch rising at the end of a sentence. This upward inflection sounds like a question, and can suggest that someone is uncertain and seeking agreement or approval. When your voice remains on one level it sounds like a simple statement of fact. When your voice tone drops at the end of a sentence it comes across as a command, conferring instant authority.

Emphasis

Certain words or phrases will be more important than others in getting your message across. By placing emphasis on them we indicate their importance. When you do this you also add variety. It's simply a matter of pausing slightly before the word you want to highlight and then delivering it with more volume. The effect is like putting words in bold in a report. But if you take it too far, and over-emphasize, it sounds wooden and false.

Exercise

Practise by reading the following sentences aloud and adding emphasis to the word in bold.

That's what friends are for.
That's **what** friends are for.
That's what **friends** are for.
That's what friends **are** for.
That's what friends are **for**.

Whichever word you stress becomes more important than the others.

Resonance

Resonance makes your voice sound deep and rich. You achieve resonance through good breathing and by speaking at the right pitch. Resonance occurs when the source of vibration (the vocal chords) sets up vibration in your teeth, hard palate, nasal bone, cheekbones, sinuses and cranium. Some people are aware of this resonance in different areas of their body, such as chest, neck, throat, head and body. Most of us are not aware of this and don't make the most of our voices.

Your voice reveals a lot about how you're feeling and conveys a certain impression on others. Here are a few examples of how voice resonance can be affected:

▶ *When you feel shy or inhibited your voice tends to be restricted to the areas around your neck and throat. Because there are no deeper tones it lacks impact.*
▶ *If your voice resonance comes mainly from your head your voice can lack conviction. At the extreme people may think you sound childish or immature.*
▶ *Chest resonance conveys confidence and conviction. If you worry about what others think this is likely to be missing.*

These examples show the impact voice tone and resonance have on an audience. By becoming aware of where our voice resonance comes from we can adapt what we do to create the results we want.

Rhythm

One way we differentiate one piece of music from another is by the rhythm. It's the same with the human voice. Some voices are staccato. They sound jerky and spiky. Other voices are smooth and flow steadily. There's no right or wrong, but the effect is quite different. As with every other aspect of speech we've discussed in this chapter, when it comes to rhythm variety is important. A change in 'beat' makes the 'music' you create more interesting and entertaining.

If you have an accent

We live in a world where diversity is the norm. Most companies have workers from many different countries and cultures. You no longer stand out like a sore thumb if you have an accent.

But you need to take care if you have a strong accent and you'll be presenting to people not familiar with it. This is especially true if you're presenting to people who do not have English as their first language. They have a double challenge: the language itself and the accent. The most important thing to do is slow down. If you're worried about being understood, ask someone to listen to you when you rehearse your presentation. They can give you feedback on any areas that need more work.

IF YOU SPEAK ENGLISH AS A SECOND LANGUAGE

Many people who attend our courses are asked to present in English when it's not their first language. Even though their grasp of English is extremely good they're often concerned about their accents. Most people find accents charming and attractive. It makes a speaker more interesting to listen to because it's different from the norm. Don't worry about it. Concentrate on clarity and speaking slowly. Rehearsing with an English speaker can be helpful because you can ask for feedback on pronunciation.

Getting a voice coach, going on a course

More by luck than judgement, some people have a voice that's 'naturally' great for presenting. Most have a voice that's 'okay', though it might benefit from some development. If you have a voice that you know needs a lot of work, either from your own judgement or from feedback from others, and which could be holding you back, then it could be worth investing in a specialist voice coach. Be aware that it can take months, and lots of practice, to reap the full benefits. Most good presentation skills courses will include time spent on developing your voice. You'll also gain from hearing a recording of your voice and receiving feedback to give you a clear idea of which areas you need to improve.

Speaking when using a microphone

The most important thing to be aware of when using a microphone is that all it does is amplify your voice. You need to speak normally and allow the microphone to do the work. Having said that, you still need to be clear, emphasize key words, pause, and vary your pitch, volume and rhythm. In other words, everything you would normally do to get the best from your voice. If you're using a fixed or handheld microphone, make sure it's not too close to your mouth or too far away. If you want more hints and tips on using microphones refer to Chapter 13.

Warming up your voice

Whenever possible take the opportunity to warm up your voice. You wouldn't go straight into a game of badminton or advanced yoga movements without warming up first. The same is true of presenting, especially if you're going to be talking for quite some time. Start by relaxing your jaw. Open and close it to get some movement going. Then clean the outer edge of your teeth with your tongue. Your voice will sound better and stronger once you've started to use it. Do some tongue twisters to help you pronounce your words so that you will be crisp and clear when you present. Here are a few well-known ones to get you started.

Red lorry, yellow lorry, red lorry, yellow lorry.

She sells sea shells by the sea shore.
The shells she sells are surely seashells.
So if she sells shells on the seashore,
I'm sure she sells seashore shells.

Peter Piper picked a peck of pickled peppers.
Did Peter Piper pick a peck of pickled peppers?
If Peter Piper picked a peck of pickled peppers,
where's the peck of pickled peppers Peter Piper picked?

You may be wondering where to do all of this. Pop to the washroom but make sure there's nobody from the audience in a cubicle! Or, go outside if possible and find a quiet place where you won't be overheard.

Looking after your voice

Looking after your voice is fairly simple. All you have to do is avoid things that are likely to cause you problems.

▶ **Smoke** *An obvious one is smoking and smoky environments, because they not only damage your health in the long term but can also affect your ability to control your breathing.*
▶ **Milky drinks/dairy products** *It's best to avoid drinking tea, coffee and any other milky drinks before or during your presentation. Don't eat cheese or lots of butter either. Dairy products are mucus-inducing and make your voice sound thicker. Some medicines dry mucus up, which can also be*

a problem because you need some but not too much to speak well.

▶ **Alcohol** *Take care with alcohol as it can affect the blood flow to the vocal cords. Plus you don't want to risk slurring your words!*

It's a good idea to have water to hand to prevent your mouth from becoming too dry. Sip water as you go along to keep it lubricated. If you present regularly or have a sore throat make sure you rest your voice as much as possible.

A finely tuned instrument

Your voice is a finely tuned instrument that needs care and attention. If you look after it and use it effectively it will serve you well. One of the keys to great presenting is to have a varied and interesting voice. Powerful pauses, emphasis, clarity, pace, pitch, resonance and rhythm are vital ingredients that help to create great presentations.

TEN KEY POINTS TO REMEMBER

1 *Your voice doesn't sound the same to others as it does inside your head.*

2 *Many people develop habits of speaking which mean they don't use their voice to its full potential.*

3 *Variety is vital. It's one of the key ways to make your delivery interesting and engaging.*

4 *If you speak with insufficient volume your audience may give up trying to listen. Experienced speakers recognize the value of projection and the importance of good breathing.*

5 *Clarity is crucial when you're presenting. You need to be both audible and intelligible.*

6 *Variety in pace is important. If you continue to speak too fast people will find it hard to listen to you. If you're too slow they may become bored or irritated.*

7 *We have a range of notes available to us. Pitch is the term used to describe the note we use. A lower pitch suggests gravitas and a higher pitch excitement.*

8 *Placing emphasis on important words or phrases indicates their importance. Add a pause to provide even more impact.*

9 *You can achieve resonance through good breathing. Most people are not aware of this and don't make the most of their voices.*

10 *To look after your voice avoid things that are likely to cause you problems such as smoky environments, dairy products and alcohol.*

17

Language matters

In this chapter you will learn:
- *about style and substance*
- *how to be clear, concise, coherent, credible and compelling*
- *how to choose powerful words with high impact*
- *about the importance of grammar and active language*
- *how to use rhetorical techniques.*

Style and substance

In this book we've devoted a lot of space to helping you make sure your presentation is delivered in an engaging, effective and compelling way. Style is extremely important. When you receive a beautifully wrapped present in attractive paper, with ribbons and bows, you look forward to seeing what's inside. If when you open it the contents are dull or not right for you, such as gardening gloves when you live in a flat with no outside space, you'll be disappointed. On the other hand, when you receive a gift in a plain paper bag that someone hasn't bothered to wrap, it may be a wonderful present but it lacks impact. You don't get excited about it.

It's the same with presentations. You can have lots of style – energy, gestures, passion, voice and so on – with no substance. Other presentations have lots of 'beef', with unrelenting facts and figures, but you don't want to listen because they are tedious and dry. To achieve success you need both style and substance. The words you use form the substance of your presentation. How you string them together and make them compelling to listen to is all about style.

Words matter

Words are important because they are the main tool you have for communicating your messages. The more effective you are at selecting and using them the more successful you'll be as a presenter. It's all too easy to choose the wrong phrase or incorrect grammar and create a negative impression. This chapter explains the importance of effective communication, which means being clear, concise, coherent, credible and compelling. It reveals the magical potential and power of words.

Be clear, concise and coherent

Speech is an imperfect medium for communication. You may have worked out your structure and a smooth flow of ideas but if the words you use aren't clear you won't transfer those ideas into your audience's minds. Rather than saying, 'It's not small and it's not big and a brownish colour …' you might say 'It's one metre high and made from pale beech wood.' To get through, your message needs to be expressed clearly using meaningful communication. Keep your language simple too. Say what you mean. Rather than saying 'sales are diminishing' say 'sales are down'. Many people are irritated by flowery words and phrases because they find them pretentious. Short sentences have greater impact. Whenever possible choose words with one or two syllables. They are packed with power. Good speakers use lots of them. The table below contains some examples of flowery waffle vs. crisp and concise words and phrases that get to the point.

Flowery waffle	Crisp and concise
Prior to	Before
Due to the fact that	Because
To be honest	Leave this out, it implies you weren't before

Flowery waffle	Crisp and concise
The fact of the matter is	The point is
In close proximity	Near
In the event of	If
A propos	Regarding
At the present time	Now
Are in agreement with	Agree
Employ	Use

It's not just words that need to be simple. Short, concise sentences are easy for audiences to follow. Some people include superfluous details because they fear being caught out. A presenter's job is to summarize. The details belong in a written document. Every presenter wants to be articulate. If you waffle and talk round and round the main point, going this way then that, the audience will have little chance of following you. Your presentation will sound disjointed and the audience will think you're unprepared.

Insight

The big difference between hearing a presentation and seeing the same content written down is that you only get one chance to hear the presentation. If it's not clear, you've got a problem. You don't have a second chance to gain clarity. When it's written down you can go back and re-read it. That's why your presentations need to be crisp and clear – so your audience gets the message first time.

AVOID OR CLARIFY MANAGEMENT SPEAK

Be careful about using management speak that sounds impressive when you hear it but lacks substance when you think about it. High level, big picture statements need to be backed up with detail. 'We need to downsize our capacity.' 'We plan to upskill our workforce to deal with the challenges of the re-engineered competitive environment.' What do they actually mean? What will they do in practical terms? The devil, as the saying goes, is in the detail.

'We intend to attract, retain and motivate top talent.'
What this means, in practice, is, 'We will bring on board
25 graduates by the end of this financial year and ...'

STEER CLEAR OF JARGON

Audiences dislike jargon, acronyms, abbreviations and management speak. Instead of 'The IOD and NAB are working with the CFO', say 'The Institute of Directors and National Association for Board Members are working with the Chief Finance Officer'. Terminology like this excludes people not 'in the know'. It's easy to assume that most people will understand and it's one of the quickest ways of isolating members of your audience. Colloquialism and slang can add interest if it reflects who you are. Take it too far, though, and you'll turn some people off. Clichés such as 'every cloud has a silver lining' and 'no pain, no gain' are fine as long as they fit your message and you don't overdo them.

Be credible

What you say has to be believable. One way to achieve this is to be articulate, which comes from being clear about the words you want to use and planning how to structure your thoughts in an effective way. It's also about the words you choose. Some convey doubt and others certainty. Some people habitually use tentative, 'puny' phrases and others opt for 'punchy' language that is full of conviction. Take a look at the lists below to get an idea of what we mean.

Puny	Punchy
Possibly	Definitely
May	Can

Puny	Punchy
Try	Will
I think	I know
Suggest	Recommend
Did	Achieved
Quite well known	Renowned
As soon as possible	Immediately

USE ACTIVE VS. PASSIVE LANGUAGE

To communicate with authority and conviction you need to use active rather than passive language. Instead of 'The target will be met by the sales team' say 'The sales team will achieve the target'. The second sentence is much stronger and more believable. Instead of 'Mistakes have been made' say 'We made mistakes'. The latter phrase gives the sense that management is in control and taking action. Passive expressions often sound too formal, as if you're reading from a legal document and want to achieve a neutral effect.

ACTUALLY SOME WORDS TO BASICALLY AVOID

Some people have a habit of using words or phrases such as 'actually', 'basically' or 'you know what I mean'. This can be irritating in everyday conversation, but gets downright annoying and distracting when you're speaking in public. We once heard a presenter say the word 'actually' 27 times in the course of a five-minute presentation – five times in just one sentence! When you get to the stage where people are counting your verbal fillers they've stopped listening to what you're saying.

Insight

The first step towards getting rid of unnecessary words or phrases such as 'actually' is to recognize you're using them, says Amanda. You can then actively work on eliminating them. If you don't make the effort you'll drive your audience crazy. Some people have been known to start counting the number of times you use a word and stop listening to what you're really trying to communicate.

KEEP SOFTENERS, PLATITUDES AND APOLOGIES TO A MINIMUM

'I may be wrong', 'I'll make sure later', 'You could interpret this as …'

Avoid platitudes such as 'rise to the occasion' and 'face the challenges ahead'.

Don't apologize or explain, 'I'll go through this very quickly', 'This is a busy slide', 'I'll skip through the next few slides'…

GRAMMAR

Some people don't care about grammar, but those who do care, care a lot – and will make judgements about what they hear. If your sentence structure or syntax is poor they'll think you're careless or clueless. Your credibility can be shot to pieces when you make a simple grammatical mistake. If you think it's an issue you need to address we recommend you buy a good book that covers the basics. Here are a few common examples to get you started.

Haitch	Aitch	Many people pronounce the eighth letter of the alphabet incorrectly. It should be said 'Aitch' without, curiously, an 'H' sound. But many people insist on saying Haitch, which is wrong.
If you have any questions, ask Dave or myself	If you have any questions, ask Dave or me	Only use the word 'myself' if previously in the sentence you've used the word 'I'–'I went to the meeting by myself'. People often use myself in the belief that it sounds more sophisticated.
There were less people recruited last month	There were fewer people recruited last month	If you can count it use 'fewer', if not use 'less' (there were fewer cars on the road today, which means less traffic).

This set-up is different than the one at Head Office	This set-up is different from the one at Head Office	The rule is simple – 'similar to' and 'different from'. The use of 'different than' is American in origin. Some people also use 'different to', which is also incorrect.
Ahmed and me went to Glasgow	Ahmed and I went to Glasgow	The easy way to work out which one is correct is to take out the other person and ask yourself if the sentence still makes sense.

TAKE A STAND

Credibility and authority go hand in hand. Your audience will expect you to take a personal stand and own your statements. There's an art to doing this without sounding arrogant. Declare your view and then put forward other options. For example, if you believe the best course of action is to increase the sales team by three people this year, you could say 'Some people may argue the money should be spent on marketing …'

Be compelling

Language provides a rich resource for you to draw upon to inspire and motivate your audience. To be effective, communication needs to be compelling, using words that attract, persuade, cajole and stimulate your audience. Conversational language is more inviting and interesting than something 'professional' and formal. You can use contrasts to add variety such as conflict vs. harmony or challenge vs. giving in. All it takes is a little forethought and trying different phrases out in the moment. Words like all, never, none, always, everything, everybody, totally, and the only way show conviction and they can provoke resistance. You'll be able to tell from the reaction you get which ones hit the spot and which fall on stony ground.

Some words distance you from your audience and others bring you closer to them. When you use 'I' language the focus is on you, the presenter's perspective. When you use 'we', 'you' or 'us' it involves the audience and draws them in. There's a sense of collaboration. These examples illustrate this point:

- ▶ *'Now I will explain how this works' – presenter focused*
- ▶ *'Let us explore how this works' – audience focused*

When people feel part of something they're automatically more engaged and emotionally attached to what you're saying.

Rhetorical techniques

In the 1970s, the phrase 'naughty but nice' became part of the English language following a televised promotion for fresh cream cakes. Such was the power of this simple catchphrase that people still say it today, even though the advert has long since disappeared from our screens. Rhetorical techniques can work in a similar way in presentations because they make ideas memorable, assist you in influencing others and help you get your message across with impact. They're easy to learn and are widely used by great speakers. It can, however, be a challenge to weave them into your presentation at first. If you decide where you want to use them in advance you'll start to build confidence in including them.

THE ORIGINS OF RHETORICAL TECHNIQUES

There's nothing new when it comes to presenting. Rhetorical techniques were first used over 2,000 years ago in ancient Greece when people learnt the art of rhetoric in order to speak in public and persuade others. Those same methods are still used today because they work so well and increase the chance of an audience recalling key messages. Experienced public speakers know how to use them to make their messages memorable, stir up emotion and create impact.

Rhetorical techniques come in many different forms, around 70 in total. We've listed some of the most useful ones below together with examples of how they can be used to get you started.

REPETITION

Examine almost any famous speech over the years and you'll find examples of repetition – Winston Churchill, Malcolm X, Bill Clinton and Tony Blair have all used this technique.

Martin Luther King is famous for his use of rhetoric and, in particular, repetition, in his 'I have a dream' speech in 1963. Most people recall the repetition of 'I have a dream' but he used repetition in other ways. 'Let freedom ring from Stone Mountain of Georgia. Let freedom ring from Lookout Mountain of Tennessee. Let freedom ring from every hill and molehill of Mississippi. From every mountainside, let freedom ring.'

The reason this technique is so powerful is that the act of saying it again and again burns it into the audience's brains. Some forms of repetition are not acceptable in written communication but they add impact when you're speaking. If the key words are not repeated they don't make such a lasting impression on the audience. There are various ways of using repetition.

▶ **Anaphora** *Repeats the same word(s) at the beginning of a series of phrases or sentences. The restated words or phrases are the part you want to emphasize, perhaps a key message you want to communicate.*
We'll find ways to make sure our customers are happy.
We'll find ways to better understand what's important to them.
We'll find ways to wow them so they never want to leave.

We must not let this get to us, we must not give up, and we must not let them win.

▶ **Epistrophe** *Similar to anaphora but it repeats the last word(s) in one phrase or sentence at the end of successive phrases or sentences instead of the first.*

The way we tackle this problem is **obvious**, really **obvious**. The database records **need to be reviewed**, the client's comments **need to be reviewed**, in fact, our whole approach **needs to be reviewed**.

▶ **Symploce** *Combines anaphora and epistrophe by repeating the first and last word(s) in phrases, clauses or sentences.*

We will complete the research **on time. We will** develop the products **on time. We will** deliver them to you **on time. Our sales** in Europe **are increasing, our sales** in Asia and America **are increasing** and this means that **our sales** around the world **are increasing.**

These are classic examples. In reality you can repeat anything providing it's intentional rather than sloppy or slapdash.

▶ **Anadiplosis** *Repeats one word or phrase that ends one clause or sentence and begins another. The immediacy of the repetition reinforces the chosen word.*

The way forward is **simple**. It's **simple** because we have the solution.

Every day we get **closer – closer** to achieving our goals.

▶ **Diacope** *Repeats a word or phrase after an intervening word or phrase.*

The people we met last week **want to work with us** – yes, you heard me right – they **want to work with us**.

The project is **overdue three months** – can you believe that? – **overdue three months**.

You need to repeat the right words to create focus and a smooth flow of ideas. Anadiplosis and diacope are two ways you can do this.

Emphasis

Some rhetorical techniques are especially useful when you want to emphasize a word or phrase. We've included two types: amplification and expletive. In Winston Churchill's *Fight Them on the Beaches* speech he uses expletives. 'I have, myself, full confidence that if all do their duty ...'

EXPLETIVE

Expletive is a short word or phrase that breaks up the sentence and places emphasis on the words next to it. The fact that the expletive forces you to pause adds additional weight to it.

> *The project is, indeed, vital to the success of this company.*

> *In brief, there is no more money available for advertising.*

There is a natural tendency to emphasize 'is' and 'vital' in the first example above. Expletives can also be placed at the start of short sentences to indicate that the whole sentence is important.

AMPLIFICATION

Amplification clarifies your communication and adds emphasis to your message. It repeats a word or phrase, adding more detail to it.

> *The board is united on this point. Every single member is fully behind it.*

> *The office is getting very untidy – it's a complete mess.*

THE RULE OF THREE

The rule of three gives the listener a sense of rhythm and completeness. Well-known examples are time, quality and cost, and faith, hope and charity. Mahatma Gandhi used this technique, 'Happiness is when what you think, what you say, and what you do are in harmony.' The longest word or phrase is usually at the end of the sentence and the most important.

We need to take account of cost, quality and customer service.

We must talk to sales, marketing and finance.

This is going to be tough, exciting and rewarding.

REVERSAL

Some rhetorical techniques reverse the order of repeated words and phrases. Chiasmus is an example of this. It's often used by experienced public speakers and presenters. It's useful for bringing two things closer together for emphasis or to highlight contrast. The words in one phrase or clause are reversed in the next.

A well-known example comes from Albert Schweitzer: 'Success is not the key to happiness, happiness is the key to success.'

And Kevin Costner: 'When a defining moment comes along, you define the moment or the moment defines you.'

Contrasts

Sentences that strike a chord with an audience are far more likely to be recalled afterwards. When you use contrasts such as antithesis you're tapping into a powerful way of showing how one idea is different from another (not *this* but *that*). You start by saying what something is like and then say what it is not like. One famous example comes from the astronaut Neil Armstrong when he first landed on the moon: 'That's one small step for man; one giant leap for mankind'.

Last month's target was challenging; this month's will be easier.

We may not be big, but we have great ideas.

We met the deadline, but there were too many errors.

Insight

Many people find it challenging to include rhetorical techniques at first, says Amanda. They worry about remembering the exact wording at the right moment. They're then surprised at how effortlessly they can start to use them to highlight a key message. Plan to use one or two at first and then using them will soon become a habit.

Combining techniques

Be creative when you're preparing your presentation and combine these techniques to achieve greater impact. You'll find transcriptions of many well-known speeches on the internet from some of the best speakers, both now and in history. When you examine them you'll see that they're filled with rhetorical techniques of different types. This excerpt is from George W. Bush's 9/11 Speech:

> *... Tonight I ask* for your prayers **for all those who grieve, for the children whose worlds have been shattered, for all whose sense of safety and security has been threatened** *[ANAPHORA]. And I pray they will be comforted by a power greater than any of us spoken through the ages in Psalm 23.* **Even though I walk through the valley of the shadow of death, I fear no evil for you are with me** *[DIACOPE].*
>
> *The project is, in fact,* [EXPLETIVE] *making progress. All we need to do now is cut costs, increase output and hit target* [RULE OF THREE].

Time and effort pay off for you and your audience

The more time you spend working on the language you use in your presentation, the more impact you'll make. In practice this means being clear, concise, coherent, credible and compelling. Rhetorical techniques provide a great way of helping your audience remember the most important points you want to communicate. The effort you make to produce not only beautifully wrapped but magnificent gifts for your audience will undoubtedly be rewarded.

TEN KEY POINTS TO REMEMBER

1 *The words you use form the substance of your presentation and how you make them compelling is all about style.*

2 *Words matter – the more effective you are at choosing them the more successful you'll be as a presenter.*

3 *Aim for short concise sentences and clear coherent language that's easy for audiences to follow.*

4 *When you're articulate and use words that convey certainty you'll come across as credible.*

5 *To be effective communication needs to be compelling, using words that attract, persuade and stimulate your audience.*

6 *Rhetorical techniques make ideas memorable and help you to influence others and get your message across with impact.*

7 *Some rhetorical techniques are useful when you want to emphasize a word or phrase, such as amplification, reversal or the rule of three.*

8 *Using contrasts such as antithesis is a powerful way of showing how one idea is different from another.*

9 *Combine the use of rhetorical techniques to create greater impact.*

10 *The time and effort you put into working on language will pay off.*

18

Handling questions successfully

In this chapter you will learn:
- *how to prepare for questions*
- *when to take questions and how to manage the process*
- *what to do when you don't know the answer*
- *about the importance of closing with impact.*

The art of managing the Q&A

'Any questions?' That's what most people say when they've finished giving a presentation. Often those two words are uttered automatically, without thinking, because it's customary – almost compulsory – in many companies to give the audience a chance to raise any queries they might have at the end.

For some presenters this is an exciting, liberating moment. Leaving their slides and notes behind they relish the opportunity to speak without having to worry about remembering what they planned to say. They come alive, communicate spontaneously, and enjoy the experience.

For others this is the part of the presentation they find most scary. 'They could ask me anything! What if I don't know the answer?' Some people worry they will be 'found out', and are petrified at opening things up to the audience.

Do you feel like this? If so, you don't have to. Once you've mastered the easy-to-use techniques we cover in this chapter you'll feel comfortable in your ability to handle questions successfully and will never have to be anxious about them again.

Why do people ask questions?

People ask questions for a variety of reasons. Some genuinely want to clarify aspects of the presentation they don't understand, get more information on things you've covered, or raise concerns they might have. Dealing with them is relatively straightforward because their agenda is open and transparent. Questions like these should be welcomed as they assist in making sure your messages are communicated accurately.

Others ask questions for murkier reasons – because they want to steal some of your limelight or, worse, undermine or discredit you. We discuss strategies for dealing with saboteurs, hecklers and snipers in Chapter 19.

Anticipate and prepare

One of the easiest and most effective ways of feeling more confident about the Q&A session is to prepare ahead of time. It seems obvious, doesn't it? If you've thought about what you might get asked, and how you would reply, you're more likely to handle it successfully. Yet, surprisingly, many presenters fail to take this elementary precaution, and end up sounding uncertain and unprepared. As a result their impact and influence is greatly reduced.

And it's no exaggeration to say that how you handle your Q&A session can make or break your presentation. If you struggle to get your point across, or stumble over your answers, the success you had in the structured, planned part of the proceedings can be squandered. And it's the same the other way round. If your presentation was less than stunning, but you give a storming performance when taking questions, you can leave an extremely positive impression of your skills.

So put yourself in the shoes of your audience. Will they be in agreement with what you have to say or will they challenge you? What questions are they most likely to ask? Which areas of your presentation might they struggle to understand? Where might they want more detail?

Just ten minutes spent brainstorming every question you're likely to be asked will pay handsome dividends. If you have time, it's worth getting colleagues to come up with suggestions as well. Be exhaustive. Don't give up too soon. And don't ignore the simple questions – they're often the ones that catch you out because you spend time preparing the difficult stuff. How many can you generate? Then go on to consider which questions you'd hate to be asked. If you can come up with answers to them, you'll go into the Q&A session feeling much more resourceful.

If you think you might need to look things up on the day to be able to answer some questions – things such as financials, specifications or dates – make sure you have the relevant information in an accessible, printed form. Frantically searching for files on your laptop for what you need is not going to give a favourable impression.

Insight

Anticipating questions is an essential part of your preparation, says Amanda. I often find myself looping back and making adjustments to the content at this stage. It provides a good double check that everything is clear and that I have dealt with what is most important to my audience. This process highlights anything that's missing, and allows me to go back and add it.

PREPARING FOR TEAM Q&As

If you're presenting as part of a team you'll need to prepare for the Q&As together as well. Decide who will act as leader and who will answer questions on which topics. The leader will field the questions and pass them on to the team member with the most appropriate experience. The leader will usually tackle anything that falls outside the prepared plan. The great thing about this arrangement is that you can help each other out and offer to take a question if you know the answer.

Say what areas you'll be able to answer questions on

One simple way of protecting yourself from a gruelling 'third degree' is to state at the beginning of your presentation what you will and won't be able to answer questions on. If there are certain areas where you don't have the necessary expertise, knowledge or experience, say so. If you're a marketing specialist introducing some new products, for instance, you may not be able to discuss in detail technical aspects of their operation or manufacture. Being pro-active in this way prevents you appearing defensive when issues arise outside your field of competence.

Say when you'll take questions

Should you take questions throughout the presentation or just at the end? That's one of the key things you need to communicate at the beginning of your presentation. It's a tough call, as there are advantages and disadvantages to both approaches. Sometimes you won't get the choice because in certain companies senior managers will stop you in mid-flow anyway. There's more on how to handle situations like this in Chapter 19.

Leaving questions to the end means you can deliver your presentation as it was planned, without interruption and without distraction. It's also easier to control time. If you have 40 minutes in total, and want to speak for 30 minutes, that leaves 10 minutes for questions. Once the 10 minutes are up, you have to bring things to a close.

The major disadvantage is that if anyone in the audience finds what you're saying confusing or perplexing they have to go through the whole presentation before they can let you know. What if they're not alone? What if several people are like that? Inviting them to ask questions as you proceed means you can sort out any problems they may have along the way – and keep them with you rather than losing them. Where there's a training/instructional aspect to your presentation this can be an important consideration. If someone gets left behind, it's hard for them to catch up.

The principal advantage of taking questions during the presentation is that the session becomes much more interactive, and helps to keep the audience's attention span longer.

You may, however, be asked about things you're about to discuss and could endlessly find yourself saying, 'I'll be covering that shortly'. You can minimize this problem by providing a clear route map at the beginning of what you'll be covering. But people do forget, and inevitably you'll be asked about things that are scheduled for later.

Taking questions as you go along can also disrupt your flow – you just get into your stride and there's an interruption, which makes you lose your thread, and you find yourself struggling to remember where you were. This can be especially problematic for those new to presenting. Those with more experience will find it easier to keep on track.

Then there's the issue of time. Unless you're extremely disciplined, it's all to easy to get drawn into protracted discussions arising from questions, only to find you're running out of time and you end up having to rush the last few slides or cut back on some important material.

One in-between option is to stop every few minutes, where there is a natural transition from one section of your presentation to another, to take questions. This potentially gives you the best of both worlds: you maintain full control, but people have the chance to raise issues periodically.

Insight

Where does a six-foot gorilla sit? Anywhere it wants.
The same is true of many senior managers I've (Amanda) come across. They make up their own mind when and if they'll interrupt you mid flow. I'm happy to manage questions as they arise. After all my purpose is to communicate my message and answering questions is a vital part of that process.

Signal a willingness to answer questions

We once saw a presenter fold his arms, take a step backwards and frown as he said, 'Any questions?' Not surprisingly he didn't get any. His entire body language signalled, 'Don't ask me anything'. If you genuinely want people to ask questions, you need to make it clear that you welcome them. One simple way of doing that is to step towards your audience and use open body language. With smaller groups some presenters sit down and join the audience. If you're standing behind a podium or near a projector, there's no reason to stay there once you get to the Q&As. Move closer to the audience. Voice tonality is also important. You need to sound like you genuinely want people to speak.

Respect the question and questioner

People don't always listen carefully to presentations. Their attention drifts in and out. As a result they may ask 'dumb' questions about something you discussed in detail only minutes earlier. You might be tempted to respond by saying, 'I thought I'd covered that, but I guess I can go over it again', but you must resist the urge. The audience will know it's not the smartest of questions, and you'll rise in their estimation if you're polite in the way you deal with it. There's nothing to be gained by disrespecting or embarrassing your questioner. Do so and you make yourself look small. There's no mileage in making enemies in your audience. If you're sharp or sarcastic, no one will dare to ask anything else.

Always be respectful of the question and the questioner. But don't go over the top and gushingly say, 'That's a good/great question' every time, as some presenters do. Having said it once you've set a precedent, and other people might be mildly offended: 'Are you saying *my* question wasn't good?'

Sometimes the questions you get will be unfocused and not particularly articulate and you may have to help the person formulate them. Once again, if you do so with a smile and a friendly manner you have an opportunity to win the audience over.

Use the person's name if you know it

People always appreciate being addressed by name, and if you know it you should use it. 'Thank you, Richard' makes it more personal. If you don't know their name you can always ask, and then use it when you go back to them to check you've answered the question to their satisfaction. Always be on the lookout for ways of building rapport with the audience.

Listen carefully to the question – and repeat it

When you know someone is about to ask a question, fix your attention on them and listen carefully. If you didn't hear what they said clearly, don't guess. Ask them to repeat it. And if you don't understand the question, ask for clarification. One simple way of checking you have the question correct before you begin to answer it, is to repeat it yourself. This has two other advantages:

▶ *It lets everyone else hear it. There's nothing more frustrating for someone sitting in a group to hear the answer to a question but not know what the question was. This is more of an issue in larger groups, where the person's voice may not carry, or when you have someone who is quietly spoken. With big groups arrange for someone to pass a handheld microphone around to each questioner to make sure everyone can hear. If this isn't possible make sure you repeat the question every time so the whole group is clear about what has been said.*
▶ *It gives you time to think. It may only be a few seconds, but that's enough to gather some ideas together. The part of the brain that repeats the question isn't the same as the part that comes up with the solution, so it saves time.*

Paraphrase the question only if it's long and it would be impossible for you to repeat exactly what the other person said. Whenever possible use precisely the same words they did.

Make sure you answer the question that's asked. When sitting an exam it can be tempting to answer the question you wish you had been asked rather than the one on the paper – and it's the same with presentations.

Divide up multiple questions

Some people ask two, three or more questions at the same time, all bound together. You may not have time to answer them all. Point out what's happening and either pick just one question or ask them to. 'You're asking three things there. What's your main question/ I'll take your point about logistics'. If you have time you can come back later to the other questions, but you need to give others the opportunity to raise their points.

Take a moment before you answer

Don't feel you have to rush in and answer the question immediately. Take a moment to gather your thoughts and what you say will be more lucid and coherent. You'll also come across as more composed and in control. People want presenters to think before they speak, rather than say the first thing that comes into their mind. But don't take too long – if you wait any more than five seconds before you start talking you'll give the impression you don't have an answer.

Don't get emotional

Some questions can be extremely challenging, and you may find yourself starting to get emotional, either defending your position or attacking the other person. Nothing good ever comes of this. Keep cool, detached and calm. Once you lose your composure there's a danger you'll say or do something you'll later regret. That doesn't mean backing down. If someone disagrees with what you've said, you'll obviously want to argue your case. But make sure you do so in a positive, detached, professional way that reflects positively on you.

Insight

The secret to not getting emotional is to not take the question personally, says Steve. But that's easier said than done. I know from my own presenting that when people ask sharp, barbed questions I tend to get defensive, because I feel they're 'having a go'. Most of the time, though, they're just looking for clarification not challenging you.

Avoid waffle mode

You've planned your presentation carefully and practised (haven't you?) so it runs to time, and you need to be just as crisp, clear and concise when answering questions. It's all too easy to go into 'waffle mode' and answer at length. The last thing people want at the end of a presentation is another presentation. Get to the point. Keep it brief. If they want more detail when you've answered, they'll ask for it.

You also need to control people who ask long, rambling questions. While you would normally wait for the person to finish speaking you need to be prepared to interrupt them if they go on and on and on. 'So what you're asking is …?' If you don't stop people it will reflect badly on you. The rest of the audience will be delighted when you take decisive action.

Never get drawn into having a long conversation with people during 'question time'. Audiences don't have an inexhaustible supply of patience, and they'll quickly zone out. If someone insists on asking another question, and you don't have sufficient time or you think it won't interest other people, politely say you want everyone to have a chance, break eye contact and move on. Another option, to retain a positive mood, is to suggest the person speaks to you afterwards, when you'll be happy to discuss things at greater length.

Never feel you have to answer a question that's not relevant to your presentation. If it won't interest the audience, be prepared to 'take it offline'.

What if you don't know the answer?

What do you do when someone asks a question and you don't know the answer? For many presenters this is the ultimate nightmare. They feel as if they've been 'found out' and have failed. But no one can possibly have all the answers. And there will often be people in an audience who know more than you do. So there will be times when you don't have the answer. Obviously, since you're the one giving the presentation – and supposedly an expert on the subject – you need to prepare as effectively as possible, so you minimize the possibility of getting caught out by a curve ball.

Here are some tried and tested ways of handling the situation when you don't have an answer:

- **Say 'I don't know'** *But say you'll get back to them as soon as possible. Yes, it can be hard. And you might feel silly. But honesty really is the best policy. Never, ever, guess. And don't try to bluff it or wing it. The consequences of trying to get away with it and being found out are usually far worse than confessing you don't know the answer. Your credibility and reputation will be shot to pieces.*
- **Ask someone else in the audience to respond** *If you know a particular person in the audience who is an expert on the subject, you might refer the question to them. 'I know, Susan, you've studied this area in some depth, and you're better qualified than I am to answer.' You can only get away with this once. Try it a second time and you give the impression you're always playing 'pass the parcel'. Another option is to throw the question open to the audience. 'What does anyone else think?' Once again this only works once.*
- **'I'm not 100 per cent sure'** *When you say this you're not saying 'I don't know', you're saying 'I'm not completely sure', which is a totally different thing. Another option is 'I don't want to rely on memory for something as important as this. I'll get back to you later'.*

Eye contact

When answering questions don't limit eye contact to the person who asked the question. Give them your full attention up to the point where they've finished speaking, and for the first few seconds of your answer, then widen your focus and respond to the entire room. Don't get into an intimate little 'tête-à-tête' with anyone, because the rest of the group will switch off. You also increase the odds of that person continuing to ask you a series of questions.

Check it's landed

It's good practice when you've answered a question to go back to the person who asked it to check they're satisfied with your response. A simple 'Does that answer your question?' is usually sufficient to elicit a 'yes' or a nod. If you haven't told them what they wanted to know, it's an opportunity for them to clarify what they do want.

What if no one asks a question?

The period between you asking 'Any questions?' and someone speaking can sometimes seem like a lifetime. But you must avoid the temptation to fill the void by asking again. Take a sip of water at this point, so you don't feel the need to rush, and wait. Some people are nervous about being the first to speak, and will hold back. Once someone else has asked their question, they feel more confident about joining in.

So how do you get things started? The way you ask is important. Instead of the more usual 'Any questions?' you might use language that presupposes questions will follow: 'I'm sure you all have lots of questions', 'What questions do you have?'

Sometimes – this is done more easily on internal presentations – it's possible to arrange for a colleague to ask the first question. Choosing something that's credible but which you can answer well will often get the ball rolling.

Another effective ploy is to raise the first question yourself: 'I'm often asked about ...' Then ask for other questions, which tend to be more forthcoming.

Leave them with your key messages

The great advantage of placing the Q&A session before your close, as we suggested in Chapter 6, is that if no one has asked a question after a reasonable period of time you can simply move on to your summary, repeat your key points, call to action and closing 'bang'. You're not left with an awkward, low-impact close, you retain full control over the proceedings.

TEN KEY POINTS TO REMEMBER

1 *People ask questions to clarify aspects of your presentation, get more information, raise concerns or steal some of the limelight.*

2 *If you anticipate questions and prepare ahead of time you'll feel more confident.*

3 *Let people know what areas you'll take questions on and whether you want questions throughout or at the end. Signal your willingness to answer.*

4 *Always be respectful of the question and the questioner without being too gushing in your acknowledgement of them.*

5 *When someone asks a question focus your attention on them and listen carefully. Repeat the question so everyone hears it. When you answer look at the questioner for a few seconds then broaden your eye contact to include everyone else. Look back at the questioner at the end to make sure it's landed.*

6 *Keep your composure and avoid being defensive when faced with challenging questions.*

7 *Make sure your answers are brief and avoid getting into long conversations with one person.*

8 *If you don't know the answer say, 'I don't know', 'I'm not 100% sure' or ask someone else to respond.*

9 *Instead of asking 'Any questions?' say 'What questions do you have?'. Take your time and wait for someone to speak.*

10 *After the Q&A move on to your summary, repeat your key points, call to action and close with a 'bang'.*

19

Dealing with problems

In this chapter you will learn:
- *how to handle problems in the moment*
- *about managing equipment issues*
- *what to do when there's limited time*
- *how to deal with disruptions*
- *how to cope with difficult behaviour.*

The best laid plans sometimes go wrong

Have you ever had one of those days when nothing seems to go right? The alarm doesn't go off, the shower runs cold, the traffic seems to have doubled and it looks like you're about to miss your train.

Well, the same thing happens with presentations. There will be times when the best laid plans go wrong. It could be a relatively small problem with the equipment when you're in mid-flow, content you didn't anticipate, people arriving late, or dealing with disruptions and interruptions. The most important thing is to keep calm, solve what you can, and move on. You can even, where it's appropriate, make light of the problems as they occur. The more experience you have of handling situations like these, the easier it gets. In the meantime here are some tried and tested strategies you can use to get you out of trouble.

What to do when the equipment goes wrong

Dealing with equipment that goes wrong in the middle of a presentation may sound like your worst nightmare but this kind of situation rarely happens. When it does you can often recover quickly and win the admiration and respect of everyone present. Most equipment problems are avoided by checking everything carefully before you start. Nevertheless, things sometimes go wrong. Don't apologize, panic or fumble around desperately. Instead calmly take control.

In most everyday presenting situations it doesn't matter too much if you take time to get the equipment working or even reschedule if that seems the best option. You can easily arrange for another projector, lead or whatever you need to solve your problem. If you're presenting off-site it's a good idea to take spare equipment with you. If not you'll need assistance.

HOW TO HANDLE A LOST CONNECTION BETWEEN A LAPTOP/COMPUTER AND THE PROJECTOR

Electrical equipment is prone to problems from time to time. The most common issue with laptops and other computers is loose wires. This can be the cable providing the electricity supply or the VGA lead connecting the laptop with the projector.

Never rely on laptop battery power alone unless you want to risk running out of 'juice'. When equipment goes wrong check all the cables are firmly in place. It's easy for them to work free, especially if something gets moved. If that doesn't work switch everything off and then on again. Sometimes a simple reboot is all you need to reset the system.

WHAT IF A BULB BLOWS IN A PROJECTOR?

It's a rare occurrence to have a bulb blow in a projector because they have life of 2000–3000 hours. But eventually, of course, they do blow and it could be when you're presenting. If all else fails, and there's no one around who can help, you may have to continue your presentation without slides. If you've prepared well this shouldn't be a problem, just an inconvenience. It's handy to have a paper copy of your slides as a reminder of what you plan to cover.

> ### Insight
> Don't panic! That's the secret of crisis management in a presentation. Things can go wrong and will go wrong. Panic may be natural, especially when you're in front of a crowd, but it doesn't help. Everybody will feel for you, and be on your side, so you can take heart – however uncomfortable you feel – that people will be understanding while you sort things out.

Dealing with equipment issues at large events

Equipment issues at larger events are often easier to manage because there's usually AV support available. It's far simpler and less stressful to let someone else fix the equipment, leaving you to concentrate on communicating with the audience.

WHAT TO DO WHEN THE MICROPHONE DOESN'T WORK

Sometimes handheld microphones develop a buzzing sound. If this happens move your mouth slightly away. If the mike stops working altogether, turn it off and step closer to your audience. You'll obviously need to project your voice more. If you're using a lapel microphone, which is ideal, you're likely to have AV support available to sort the problem.

Managing content problems

When you've prepared your presentation thoroughly and rehearsed properly you're unlikely to experience any content problems. Life, though, isn't always like that. You may have to present at short notice, or you may have so much work to do that the time you set aside for rehearsing has disappeared. On the day you need strategies you can use in the moment so you can continue with confidence if something goes wrong.

WHAT TO DO ABOUT SPELLING MISTAKES

You won't be the first or the last person who spots a spelling mistake on a slide part way through your presentation. Our advice is to ignore it. If you make a fuss about it all you do is draw the error to everyone's attention. If someone points it out thank them for mentioning it and move on. Obviously the best way to avoid this is to get someone else to check your slides beforehand.

HOW TO COPE WITH MISSING SLIDES

If you're expecting a slide to appear and it doesn't, press the 'B' key to black out the screen without mentioning there's something wrong. Tell the audience what the slide was meant to cover. Rather than diminishing your point, this action is more likely to emphasize it. Then press the 'B' key again and continue with the next slide. If you can't remember what was on the missing slide, or you lose your way, the best approach is to pause and then say something. Once you start to speak you'll quickly get back on track. If you leave something out the audience won't know. Whatever you do, don't apologize because that draws unnecessary attention to the omission.

HANDLING UNEXPECTED ADDITIONS

While it's disconcerting to discover something's missing, it can be equally disquieting to find an extra slide tucked into the set. This sometimes happens when you intend to 'hide' a slide or borrow a file from someone else that you're not familiar with. If you really don't know what the slide is about, don't try to talk your way out of it. Move on to the next one instead. If you feel the need to explain why, keep it brief and say, 'I won't cover this now so we have plenty of time for ...'

WHAT TO DO WHEN ANIMATION AND VIDEO CLIPS DON'T WORK

If, against our advice, you decide to use animation and it doesn't work it's best to move on to the next slide once you've covered the point you intended to make. The simpler you keep your slides the less likely it is that things will go wrong. Occasionally embedded video clips don't work. It's a good idea to have a back-up copy loaded on your laptop, ideally on your desktop so it's easy to find. All you need to do is minimize PowerPoint and then click on the relevant icon.

If you want to use the internet to show something as part of your presentation there's always a danger the connection will fail at the crucial moment. If this happens you obviously need to reconnect. If that doesn't work, talk about something else and come back to it at a later point or have paper copies of the pages you wanted to show people in the form of a handout as a back-up.

What to do when you say something you shouldn't

Have you ever had one of those moments when you wish the ground would open up and swallow you whole? If so, you can imagine just how challenging it is to deal with such an instant in the middle of a presentation. It's all too easy to say something that upsets one or more people in your audience. Maybe what you say isn't politically correct, such as implying in a distracted moment that all women are secretaries or only men are directors.

Even if what you say is accurate, some people could react negatively. Obviously you can avoid this by being aware of the potential offence this kind of statement can cause. If, however, the words pop out of your mouth and the look on their faces tells you they're not happy you can't ignore it. If you don't deal with it you'll lose credibility.

One way to do this is to dissociate yourself from the other you who made the *faux pas*. Step away and look at the space where you were standing and say 'I can't believe s/he just said that …'. In a seated presentation you can stand up briefly and point to the chair where you were just sitting.

The same strategy works when you tell a joke that falls flat. When you move away point to where you were standing and say something like 'Would you believe a story like that?' or 'Call that funny …' You can then go on to explain your point in a different way in case people weren't able to make a connection with the main body of your presentation.

Troubles with time

We're often asked by presenters how to cope when the time available for your presentation changes. Sometimes your slot will be reduced at the last moment. Maybe your audience needs to squeeze in another important meeting, leave early to catch a plane or a previous speaker over-runs and you're left with half the time you thought you had. Sometimes it's because the audience asks more questions than you allowed for and you suddenly realize you've got important issues to cover and only a few minutes left. The key to success in this type of situation is to have a Plan B.

WHAT TO DO WHEN YOUR TIME IS CUT SHORT BEFORE YOU BEGIN

If, despite your careful preparation, you discover you've underestimated how long your presentation will take, or your session's cut at the last minute, you need to be clear about what you can leave out. Don't try to cram it all in by talking faster. If you do this you're less likely to communicate your message effectively. People need time to take in what you're saying.

You may be able to miss out a quote, video clip or detailed case study as long as they're not central to achieving the outcome you want. Make sure you don't get rid of all the interesting bits of 'flavour' though, or your presentation will end up dry and dull.

And don't cut the conclusion – it's important to leave the audience with your key messages ringing in their ears.

If you suddenly find you only have five minutes for a 20-minute presentation, a well-crafted introduction should contain all you need. Being able to reduce your presentation to a few minutes is great because it helps you be clear on what your most important key messages are.

At larger events where there are several speakers, you may find your time is eroded as each person over-runs. If this happens, check what the organizer wants you to do. They may be prepared to extend the time by reducing a coffee break or ask you just to cover the essentials. If you find time-keeping a challenge make sure there's either a wall clock clearly visible or take a small one with you that you can glance at from time to time.

Dealing with disruptions

No matter how well prepared you are, your plans can be thwarted by external forces beyond your control. Some disruptions will be caused by people, whether they intend to do so or not. Experienced presenters learn to cope with a crisis and are flexible enough to think on their feet and adapt their approach at a moment's notice. We've included some of the most common disruptions.

FIRE ALARMS

Fire alarms are just one of the things that will stop you in your tracks. They're a frequent form of interruption. Not, of course, because you come across a lot of fires, but you may be disturbed by the weekly test. If you're sure that's what it is, wait until the alarm stops ringing. There's no point in battling with the noise. From time to time you'll be faced with a full fire drill and occasionally the building will be cleared because of a false or real alarm and you'll obviously have to ask everyone to leave in an orderly fashion.

Depending on how long it takes, you may be able to reconvene. If not you'll have to reschedule.

....

Insight

I've had to break off mid-flow in a presentation a number of times over the years because of fire alarms, says Amanda. While it's less than ideal, you can often use the situation to add a bit of humour when everyone has trooped back inside. It also gives you valuable time to take stock and chat to some of the audience to get a feel for how your presentation is going.

....

THE HUMAN FACTOR

The most unpredictable element of any presentation, though, is the audience. Obviously they're an essential element so you need to be aware of how to manage the human factor. Some people arrive early, others late, travel arrangements go awry, and mobile phones or BlackBerrys intervene at inopportune moments.

ARRIVALS AND DEPARTURES

When you're presenting to a small group in your own office you're likely to have fewer issues with people arriving late or saying, 'I have to leave in 20 minutes to attend another meeting'. Or are you? To some extent this depends on the culture in your organization.

If you're speaking to two or three people and only one turns up on time, it's obviously best to wait for the others to arrive. If they're so late you're not sure how you'll fit your presentation into the time left you could gain agreement for extending the session. If that's not possible you either need to reschedule or find a way to leave something out.

If you're presenting to a medium or large group and missing one or two people at the outset it's less of an issue. If, however, it's crucial that someone who is delayed be there you may choose to wait for them. If you can, find out when they're likely to turn up. It's obviously easier to make a decision when you have facts to go on.

Keeping people who arrive on time waiting more than five minutes will be irritating for some of them. Status plays a part here too. Most speakers are more comfortable making a prompt start when they're the boss and some of the team is late arriving. If the tables are turned they may feel obliged to wait a little longer. The same is true if you're holding on for a client to arrive.

Some people will turn up for a presentation and let you know they have to leave early. What you do next is a judgement call. If you're presenting to a small group and this person is key to the proceedings you may decide to cut some material and ensure they get all the key messages by reducing the overall time. If not, you can offer to send them a handout afterwards or brief them at another time.

It's harder to deal with those people who slip out without saying anything part-way through. This usually only happens when you're speaking to larger groups. With smaller audiences people usually feel obliged to explain their actions before leaving. It can be a little disconcerting if you don't know why someone's leaving. If the rest of the group appears engaged it's unlikely to be about anything you've done. The crucial thing is not to take it personally. At larger events you may even want to make a joke of it by saying 'It's no good trying to get away. I've locked the doors'.

WHAT TO DO ABOUT PHONE CALLS

The number one rule about mobile phones is to make sure you switch your own to silent mode or off altogether. This may sound obvious but it's easy to forget. It can be embarrassing if it rings when you're presenting, particularly if you have a loud ring tone.

More commonly it will be someone in the audience, unless you remind everyone to switch them off. In small meetings people usually let you know if they're expecting an important call before you start. If they don't, it's best to wait patiently while they complete the call and then ask them nicely if they'd mind turning it off. With medium- to large-size groups it's better to carry on.

If the noise of them speaking is distracting everyone you can always ask them to step outside, which they may do of their own accord anyway. One presenter we know was so fed up with this that he carried a goldfish bowl around with him, complete with gravel, water and a couple of fish. At the bottom of the bowl in place of the usual ornate bridge sat a mobile phone. He jokes that this is where phones end up if they ring during his session. When people use phones at large events, walk to the other side of the stage until they hang up. This will draw the audience's attention away from the distraction and towards you.

HOW TO DEAL WITH CRACKBERRYS AND TEXT ADDICTS

Some people are so addicted to their BlackBerry they're nicknamed CrackBerrys because they can't bear to be parted from it. If you notice people checking their email or sending text messages while you're in mid-flow we recommend you ask them politely to put the device to one side until the end of your presentation. If you allow them to continue you can't guarantee they will have taken your message on board.

Dealing with disruptive behaviour

In Chapter 14 we emphasized the importance of observing energy levels, noticing body language and asking questions to check how engaged your audience is. If you make your presentation interesting and stimulating your audience will normally stay with you and you won't have any problems. Most of the people who disrupt, ask challenging questions or interrupt are genuinely seeking more information or clarification. More often than not people are unaware their behaviour is difficult for you to deal with. This means they respond best if you use empathy and understanding. Ignoring them will only make matters worse because they take this as a license to continue or even escalate their behaviour. The important thing is not to be defensive or argue with them. The rest of the audience will be on your side if you take action and respond with compassion.

WHEN THEY WANT TO BE IN THE SPOTLIGHT

Sometimes people simply enjoy being in the spotlight. They hog the air space at every opportunity and this not only affects your timing but also sometimes forces you to discuss topics before you're ready. If you're likely to be covering the material later in your presentation, say so, for example: 'Could I ask you to hold that thought for now as I think all will become clear in a moment'. If answering the question will cause the audience to lose the thread of your argument, suggest you postpone your answer until the conclusion. Answering questions can disrupt a well-structured presentation and you have to judge whether your audience will gain from hearing unplanned material at a specific stage in your presentation. Answer succinctly. If it requires a longer response suggest taking it offline. Tie the answer to part of your presentation where possible. Questions, no matter how challenging, help reinforce and clarify your message.

MANAGING THE EXPERTS

Some people want to draw attention to their experience, or greater knowledge, and this manifests itself through interruptions, questions or comments. If possible, gain their support and acknowledge their expertise in a meeting or over coffee before you speak to the group. During your presentation, stick to your experience and include well-documented evidence that cannot be disputed. They often talk a lot because they want to show off what they know. When they pause for breath, thank them and refocus the audience by coming back to the point you want to make. Don't embarrass them. Your aim is to show empathy and stay in control.

Sometimes these characters continually interrupt with, 'Yes but ...' questions or observations, designed to showcase their knowledge.

It can be useful to have one or two of these to expand/clarify issues, but it can be disruptive and time-consuming particularly if asked in a challenging manner or they start to monopolize. When they ask a question turn away from them when you answer and address the whole group. If necessary, let them know that you want to hear other people's views. Occasionally, people deliberately behave in a manner that could jeopardize the outcome of your presentation. When you suspect this is happening, you need to take control by reminding the audience of the objective and time limits of the meeting, for instance: 'We're here to decide on the reorganization of the department and we only have this morning to complete the exercise'.

HANDLING INTERRUPTIONS FROM SENIOR PEOPLE

Many presenters in business will experience tough questions and interruptions from senior people. The Drivers among them think nothing of stopping you in your tracks to discuss a challenging issue. This can be embarrassing unless you're well prepared to answer each point raised. In our experience these people respect you more if you get to the point quickly and push back if you know you will be able to answer their query in the next few minutes. The most important thing is to stand your ground.

HANDLING SIDE CONVERSATIONS

Side conversations tend to happen less when there are only two or three people. It's easier for them to feel comfortable about chatting to a neighbour when they're part of a larger group. People engage in side conversations for a variety of reasons. They may:

▶ *not understand what you said and are seeking clarification from a colleague*
▶ *be sharing an experience that was triggered by your presentation*
▶ *be talking about something unrelated to what you're saying*
▶ *be translating for someone who doesn't speak the language well*
▶ *be bored and want entertainment.*

Whatever the reason, be aware that it may be genuine rather than deliberately disruptive.

If it becomes distracting, stop talking, wait for them to stop and then ask if they have any questions or a comment to add. Make sure your tone is neutral because it's easy to come across as sarcastic. With large groups you could try a joke such as, 'I work alone'.

COPING WITH CRITICISM AND HOSTILITY

It's not fun for most of us to receive criticism, especially in public. We learn most from constructive feedback. Thankfully it's rare to experience this or any form of open hostility. If your audience research leads you to believe they'll be negative or likely to raise arguments against your case, make sure you plan to answer them during your presentation. If possible lobby for support and meet with potential dissenters beforehand. If you find out their concerns you'll be better equipped to deliver answers and compromises.

If you think there may be problems, gauge the feelings in the room while you speak. Be careful not to tune in to one or two negative people or your emotion may start to match theirs, even if they're in the minority. Instead, find someone who seems upbeat and positive. It's all too easy to focus on the person you want to win over instead of the whole group. If you do that the rest of the audience may feel neglected.

Keep cool in the moment if someone is hostile towards your ideas. The way you react will be remembered more than what you say. Listen attentively to them, show compassion and stay calm. It's important to be able to see things from their point of view.

A useful way to think about this is that there's a positive intention behind every behaviour, even if the benefit is more for them than it is for you. Thinking this way helps you understand what motivates them to behave the way they do. If you get angry or defensive you'll lose the audience's respect. Move forward towards them and invade their space without showing emotion. Acknowledge their viewpoint with empathy, as if you are speaking to a friend.

Always be prepared to respond, no one likes an avoider. Don't use language that's likely to inflame the situation. Agree with the criticism to take the sting out of it and look for areas of common ground. Be specific and stick to the facts. Acknowledge their point and make it clear you're moving on without dwelling on it. Make a statement that shows you're confident this can be overcome if that's the case.

If you feel they're being petty, or what they said has no validity, acknowledge their point and let them know you don't feel it's central to the topic. If they continue to ask difficult or loaded questions say you're curious to learn what led them to ask that question. They will probably modify or withdraw it. If not, suggest taking it offline and speak with them afterwards.

COPING WITH ILLNESS

There will be times when your presentation is disrupted by people who are ill. It may be as simple as lots of coughing or sneezing. This can be distracting for you and for the other people present. Offer the person some water. If you're presenting to a small group you may even wait for them to recover before continuing. If someone faints or is taken ill in a more serious way you obviously need to stop and get help.

Handling problems that are harder to anticipate

No matter how well prepared you are you can still encounter problems that are harder to anticipate. If you're one of a series of speakers, for instance, you can never be sure how the previous presenter will be received or what they will do. How they leave the audience affects their mood and this determines how you approach your opening when it's your turn to speak. If someone steals your lines you need to think quickly and put a different angle on the same topic. If the audience is angry, bored or simply overloaded with information by the time you present it can be challenging to turn things around. If you've followed the guidelines we gave you in preparing an engaging presentation full of flavour you're likely to provide light relief from what has gone before. Always sit in on previous sessions so you get a sense of the audience's mood. If for some reason you can't, you'll need to adapt your approach in the moment. If they're angry, acknowledge their mood and then move on.

Take problems in your stride

The more experience you have as a presenter the better able you'll be at taking problems in your stride. Many issues can be ironed out with good research, preparation and practice. In some ways you learn more from difficult situations than the straightforward ones. Over time your confidence will grow and you'll be ready to face any challenge.

TEN KEY POINTS TO REMEMBER

1 *When best laid plans go wrong keep calm, solve what problems you can and move on.*

2 *If equipment goes wrong in the middle of your presentation take the time you need to fix it. Check cables are in place and reboot the system if needed.*

3 *At larger events you're likely to have AV support. If microphones buzz move away from amplifiers and, for handheld microphones, move it away from your mouth.*

4 *If you notice a spelling mistake, a slide's missing or there's an additional one you intended to hide, take it in your stride. Don't apologize because that draws attention to the error.*

5 *If you realize you've inadvertently said something that's upset your audience, dissociate yourself from the other you. Step away and say 'I can't believe s/he just said that...'*

6 *If your time is cut short have a Plan B. Reducing your presentation forces you to get clear on your key messages.*

7 *Disruptions come in many forms – fire alarms, late arrivals and mobile phones – and you need to think on your feet and take control.*

8 *Disruptive people respond best if you avoid being defensive or arguing with them.*

9 *Show empathy and stay in control when people talk a lot or draw attention to their expertise.*

10 *You learn more from difficult situations than straightforward ones and learning helps you grow more confident.*

20

Presenting in different situations

In this chapter you will learn:
- *how to present to a variety of groups*
- *about being a Master of Ceremonies*
- *how to present effectively as part of a team*
- *about the importance of influencing, persuading, inspiring and motivating others.*

Narrowing the focus

If you started at the beginning of *Present with Impact and Confidence* and worked your way chapter by chapter to the end, you should by now have a solid grasp of the theory and practice of public speaking. Our aim has been to cover as comprehensively as possible the common problems people have, and supply effective solutions to give you more impact and confidence.

We'd like to end by narrowing our focus and leaving you with more detailed advice on how to make the most of specific situations. This will give you a handy reference section you can quickly turn to whenever you have a particular type of presentation to do. If, for instance, you don't present to conferences very often, and have one come up, you don't need to flip through the whole book. It's pretty much all in one place. Some of what we say will intentionally reprise what we've covered earlier but, where appropriate, we've also added some new information.

Large groups and conferences

Many presenters find large groups intimidating, particularly at conferences where the audience can number hundreds or thousands. Having all those pairs of eyes trained on them can make even experienced speakers nervous. But in some ways large groups are easier because when everyone is farther away they're more anonymous. One simple way of reducing anxiety is to mingle with those who will be in the audience before you speak. As you start to think of them as friends, rather than strangers, so you will become more relaxed.

When there are more than around 25 people present it can be a challenge making eye contact with them all and once you go beyond 50 it's impossible. Instead, move your gaze around the room in either an 'M' or a 'W' shape, focusing on a cluster of 6–20 people, depending on the size of the gathering, before moving on. That way they still feel as though you're giving them individual attention. Unless you absolutely must use notes or a script, use your slides as a prompt and make sure you prepare well. When you read your material you cut yourself off from your audience, and they'll quickly switch off.

When you're one of a series of speakers, and several others have gone before you, energy levels may be low and you'll need to work harder to keep them alert. This is particularly an issue when you're presenting after lunch. Most of us experience a dip in our energy after we've eaten.

The most important thing when you've got a big group is to make everything you do larger and louder. Your gestures need to be more expansive and your voice needs to project more. Keep things punchy and upbeat. It's also a good idea to move around more than you would in a smaller setting. If you're static and rooted to the spot on a stage, you come across as lacking in passion and enthusiasm. That means, whenever possible, coming out from behind a lectern or table. If the venue is narrow and deep, and some of the people in your audience are so far away you can't really see them, you may want to consider 'working the room' by moving in among them if the seating arrangement allows it. If you're using PowerPoint you'll obviously need either to use a remote mouse or have an 'assistant' who changes the slides as necessary.

Multicultural audiences

These days you'll often find yourself presenting to multicultural audiences. Many conferences are international, and increasingly companies have a diverse workforce drawn from several countries and continents. That means your language may not be their first language, and you'll need to adapt your content and delivery if you are to be sure of communicating effectively. So use simple words ('use' rather then 'employ'), shun colloquial expressions ('over the moon'), and avoid long and complicated sentences. It's your responsibility to make sure you're understood, so you need to speak slowly and articulate your words clearly but without, of course, seeming to patronize anyone.

On occasions you may find yourself speaking to an audience that has little or no comprehension of your language, and will be relying on a translator. You need to allow for the time it takes to relay what you are saying. Typically you will only get half as much across as you would normally, which means either speaking for longer or reducing your content accordingly. If you don't speak their language at all, spending a few minutes learning some local phrases and expressions ('Hello, I'm delighted to be here', 'Thank you very much') can be useful in building rapport.

Gestures have different meanings around the world, and you might like to check whether there are any you should avoid based on who is likely to be in your audience. In the West, for example, when we gesture for people to come over to us we have our palm upwards and curl fingers in but in some Asian cultures this is considered vulgar.

Master of ceremonies (MC)/Introducer

It's an honour and a privilege to be a Master of Ceremonies (MC) at any function. People rely on you to make sure the event runs smoothly. You're also responsible for introducing speakers, which means doing your homework so you can say something meaningful about them where necessary. How much you say and how formal/ informal you are depends on the event. You need to keep things upbeat and moving along while never doing anything that might make the audience feel uncomfortable. Preparation, as with any presentation, is vital. Many MCs become deeply involved in planning the event, rather than simply turning up on the day. Ask people to give you a description of themselves ahead of time when you have to introduce them. The key to success lies in sounding like you're talking 'off-the-cuff' and knowing what you want to say.

Accepting awards

If only all acceptance speeches were modelled on the *Webby Awards* – presented for the world's best websites – where you're only allowed five words. Meg Whitman from eBay's speech was 'Bidding starts at 99 cents'. It's all too easy to go on too long. Keep it brief, and to the point. This is especially important when there are lots of awards. After a while it gets tedious for the audience. If the recognition means a great deal to you, and you get all emotional, take care you don't start to gush. What follows is often rambling and incoherent – as is often the case at the BAFTAs and EMMYs – and infinitely regrettable. So have something prepared that you can read if necessary. Ideally what you say should be amusing or inspiring. Unless you're noted for your lively, spontaneous wit, that means preparing ahead of time.

Team presentations

If you're presenting as part of a team, there are some additional things you need to consider over individual presentations. One crucial step is to elect a leader who is responsible for allocating roles and co-ordinating every aspect of preparation and delivery on the day. He or she will also have the final say if there's a dispute. Don't simply assume that this will be the most senior person in the team. Instead choose the person who has the best skills to handle it. The team leader often opens and closes the presentation.

Obviously it's essential that you agree who does what and swap notes as often as necessary to ensure there are no unnecessary overlaps. Whatever you do, don't skip rehearsals. You need to practise handovers and be clear about how everything flows as a whole. Where you can, make reference to previous content/speakers so the audience can clearly understand the links between each section. Whenever possible rehearse in the room where you'll be delivering so you know the layout and can plan where everyone will sit when they're not speaking. If not, arrive early so you can check things out well in advance. Sometimes it's appropriate to set up a table for everyone to sit at or just a row of chairs to one side at the front. This way they form a panel when the focus of attention switches to the question and answer session. The team leader fields the questions and also takes responsibility for dealing with any queries that the rest of the team can't handle.

Presenting at a distance – web/video/ teleconferencing

Presenting at a distance not only requires all the skills of face-to-face, it also provides you with some additional challenges. For a start it can be harder to build rapport and engage with people. If you're using a webcam or video conferencing at least you'll be able to see the other person. Staring at a screen can make you appear more passive so you need to articulate more obviously the emotion in what you say. Make sure that other participants can see you by staying in view of the camera, and don't make rapid movements because they can appear exaggerated. To some extent you'll rely more than usual on your voice. If the person at the other end is using a microphone you may hear your own voice relayed back to you, almost like an echo. One way round this is to pause more frequently.

Teleconferencing is commonplace and it's fairly easy to get used to it. The main thing is to allow everyone plenty of air time. Sometimes more than one person will attempt to speak at once and you may have to stop and let them talk first.

Selling and pitching

The most important thing about sales presentations is to know your audience. The modern approach to selling is consultative. This means matching the way individuals want to buy. The interactive style allows you to forge close relationships where you work in partnership with your clients. Your role is to identify and solve their problems.

There is sometimes, but not always, a stage in the sales process where you will be asked to pitch. Sometimes it will be just you and your company the client wants to see. At other times you'll find yourself taking part in a 'Beauty Parade'. This can take the form of a standing or seated presentation delivered by an individual or team of people. Often you'll be allocated a time slot that you have to keep within. When you plan your presentation you need to divide the time available so you achieve a balance that allows you to adequately present your ideas and allow plenty of time to answer their questions. In a 45-minute slot allow around 25 minutes for your presentation and leave the rest for questions. If time is really at a premium, consider sending a document in advance. If you decide to use PowerPoint make sure you don't include too many slides. It's better to create another document with all the details to leave behind.

As with any presentation, a strong opening is vital. Get straight to the point. Less is more when you have limited time available. Make sure you back up your claims with evidence, facts and case studies that are relevant to the situation. Include not only the features of your proposed solution but also the advantages and benefits too. Speak with conviction and be convincing – you need to get them excited about it. If possible get them to experience something. It may be handling the product or showing them a video if it's something less tangible. Create a compelling vision of how things will be when they buy your solution. Close the deal if this is appropriate.

Insight

We regularly pitch for business and know that for a sales presentation to be successful it must meet the wants and needs of the audience. Always, always, always ask yourself what's important to them, and what would be their criteria for saying yes. If you're in doubt, ask them. Then focus as much of your presentation as possible on that. The single most important word when selling is 'you'.

Influencing and persuading

When you're presenting there is frequently an element of influencing and persuading involved. If people are to buy into your ideas, or purchase your products and services, you need to tap into not just the logical brain but also the emotional brain. This idea is far from new. People have been perfecting the art of influencing others through public speaking for centuries. More than 2,000 years ago Aristotle put forward the view that there are three rhetorical techniques that can be used to convince an audience:

▶ *ethos (ethical/credible/likeable – can I trust this person?)*
▶ *pathos (emotional – do I feel moved by what I have heard?)*
▶ *logos (logical – do the arguments/figures stack up?).*

A presenter has to be credible for the audience to accept what's said as being true. Aristotle claimed there are three elements to credibility: intelligence, a virtuous character and good will. Today, presenters often establish their credibility through their track record, qualifications or published works. Equally important, though, is whether they're likeable or not.

Speakers also need logos – to provide their audience with facts, data, evidence, logical arguments that substantiate the case being made. You can, however, be credible and logical and still not convince your audience. The missing ingredient is Aristotle's pathos. If logos is the head, pathos is the heart. Every presentation needs heart. When you believe in your message your passion for it shines through and you touch your audience at a deeper level. All three of these ingredients need to be included in your recipe for a successful and influential presentation.

Running a training session

While presentations and training sessions have some things in common, there are important differences. You need all the skills of a presenter, preparation is equally essential for success, and you need to manage your audience's attention span. Just like a presentation you're seeking to make your messages stick. Most trainers vary their approach. They may use PowerPoint for input sessions, or flipcharts when they want to build up ideas.

One of the biggest differences is that trainers often take a facilitative approach, even when conveying information, on the basis that people learn best when they're involved. One way to achieve this is to make it interactive. Take questions and comments as you go. After each new concept include an activity or exercise so your participants can experience it.

Think about different learning styles. Some people need time to think (reflectors), others have to see a practical application for it to sink in (pragmatists), some want to experience it (activists) and others want the underpinning theory (theorists). You need to incorporate something for everyone. When people are learning they need to take regular breaks. This gives them time to digest each chunk of new information before moving on. Monitor the emotional state of your participants, be prepared to change things if people are not engaged and zone out. Be aware of group dynamics too. When you put individuals together to form a group they're affected by each other's behaviour. One strong character can influence the views of the whole group. If people are negative, stroppy, or simply don't want to be there you need to deal with them. If you don't, you'll lose the respect of the whole group. Many of the ideas in Chapter 19 are equally applicable in a training situation.

Motivating and inspiring

One of the advantages of a presentation over a document is that you can inspire and motivate people. To achieve that yourself plan how you want your audience to feel. This may seem an odd thing to suggest and yet, when you present, you're like a film director who takes people on an emotional journey that taps into all of their senses. Decide how you'll connect with them, arouse their interest, keep their attention, make them feel something.

We delivered a presentation to a multicultural group of managers in Sofia, the capital of Bulgaria. The group was made up of representatives from individual companies that had formed an international alliance. They were in the process of finding ways to deepen the relationships between participating organizations. Our presentation purpose was to help them develop their presentation and networking skills, so they were better equipped to grow their businesses faster.

For the overarching theme of our presentation we used the metaphor of building a cathedral. We took them back in time to when Sophia cathedral was built. We reminded them of the knowledge, skill and effort that must have been required. The implication was that the same was true of them as individuals and as companies. By working together and developing their skills they could create something greater than the sum of the parts. They were building a 'cathedral' by working together to enhance their skills.

By linking to common interests and values, the speaker and audience become one. People relate what they hear to what they know already. The words combined with the emotion expressed by the presenter are contagious.

Impromptu speaking – at the drop of a hat

Sometimes the need may arise for you to speak with the minimum of preparation. You may be asked by clients, your boss or colleagues to give a verbal report or a summary of your views 'at the drop of a hat'. Or perhaps you'll find yourself in a situation where you need to respond to something another person has said, perhaps offering a 'vote of thanks' or something similar at an industry event. How do you handle moments like this, particularly if you're someone who likes to have time to prepare?

Well, the secret lies in keeping things simple and not worrying about making mistakes. Since you're speaking off the cuff, you're clearly not going to be able to deliver a perfectly structured presentation, so don't set your expectations of what you'll achieve unrealistically high. There's every chance your mind will go blank at least once or you will get stuck for words. It's not a big deal.

The most important thing is to decide quickly what you want to say, then come up with no more than three key messages that communicate your core idea. Once you've put them in order, you're pretty much ready to go. If you start out strong you'll grow in confidence, and the rest will fall into place so be clear exactly what you're going to say in that first crucial sentence.

There's always a danger of waffling and rambling when you speak in a spontaneous manner, since you haven't had a chance to think things through. You need, therefore, to be disciplined. Keep it simple. Less is more. Stay focused, and avoid going 'off-piste', and you'll succeed.

An excellent way of developing this skill is to practise using a presentation you set yourself. Imagine you've been asked to report on a project you've been working on and you have two minutes to prepare. Then quickly pull together your thoughts, and actually deliver them out loud. If possible, record what you say either on tape or video, and then review the recording afterwards. What worked? What could have been better? It's like practising your scales when you have to play a musical instrument in public. The more you practise the more fluent you'll become.

Insight

The key to speaking off the cuff lies in trusting you'll have something worthwhile to say. I (Amanda) have discovered over the years that the more I find myself speaking spontaneously the easier it gets. The first few times I did this and then reflected on what had happened I thought, 'Got away with that one!'. With each positive outcome I achieved I became more confident. Nowadays I think of myself as someone who can get up and speak in this way with ease.

Social speaking

This is a book that's first and foremost about business presenting. But you'll sometimes also need to speak at social occasions such as weddings and celebrations, so we'd like to end by giving you some tips on how to tackle them successfully.

It goes without saying that most of the techniques we've described in this book will be as useful when presenting in a non-work context as they are in a professional setting. You need to:

▶ *think about your audience and your outcome*
▶ *structure your ideas in an interesting and engaging way*

- *write for the spoken rather than written word, if you use a script*
- *stand well, move purposefully and use effective body language*
- *project your voice powerfully and persuasively*
- *use language that is clear, concise, coherent, credible and compelling.*

But you need to do more than that if you are to give a good speech in a social setting. You need to gather facts and details relevant to the occasion. Your research should uncover sensitive areas to avoid such as family feuds at a wedding or someone present who was turned down when they applied to join a committee. Your aim should be not to embarrass or offend anyone. Don't:

- *start by saying, 'Unaccustomed as I am to public speaking' – it's not funny any more*
- *swear or tell jokes more suitable for the stag night or an all-male gathering*
- *talk about anything that will embarrass anyone present*
- *be too formal – social events lend themselves to a little levity*
- *speak for more than five to ten minutes unless you want everyone to start yawning.*

A never-ending journey of discovery

We started this book by saying 'Everything's a Presentation'. We've ended it by giving you hints and tips for a variety of situations where you may find yourself speaking in public. We could write a whole book on this area alone if space allowed. In between we've packed in loads of information drawn from our personal experience and learning from others. We believe that one of the best ways of becoming a great presenter is to practise and get feedback on your style.

The process of learning about presenting is a never-ending and enjoyable journey of discovery. There's always something you can improve, experiment with or change. We wish you every success with your presentations now and in the future.

TEN KEY POINTS TO REMEMBER

1 *When you present to a big audience make your gestures expansive, project your voice and own the space by moving around more than you would with a small group.*

2 *When speaking to people whose first language isn't the same as yours use simple words, avoid colloquial expressions, articulate your words clearly and speak slowly without patronising them.*

3 *If you're in the role of Master of Ceremonies make sure you introduce people in a meaningful way.*

4 *When presenting with a webcam or via video conferencing make sure remote participants can see you by staying in view of the camera and avoiding rapid movements that can appear exaggerated.*

5 *The most important thing about sales presentations is to know your audience.*

6 *For people to buy your ideas, products or services you need to connect with their emotional brains.*

7 *To motivate and inspire people you need to plan how you want your audience to feel.*

8 *When asked to speak 'off the cuff' keep it simple, don't worry about making mistakes, come up with three key messages that communicate your core idea.*

9 *Gather relevant facts and details when you're asked to speak at a social event. Aim not to embarrass or offend anyone.*

10 *One of the best ways of becoming a great presenter is to practise and get feedback on your style.*

Taking it further

This section contains a list of resources that will help you become a great presenter. It contains details on how to choose a training course, and where to go for more information, including useful organizations, books, websites and newsletters.

How to choose a training course

There are a number of questions you need to ask before deciding on the right presentation skills training course for you.

- ▶ *Do they use video with freeze-frame coaching?*
- ▶ *What is the group size? Will I get individual feedback and attention from the trainer?*
- ▶ *Is the course aimed at the right level to match my skills and experience?*
- ▶ *Will I be learning with people who have a similar level of experience as me?*
- ▶ *Does the course cover the areas I want to focus on, such as dealing with nerves or managing attention span?*

Our highly practical presentation skills training courses will give you great tips to improve your skills and lead you to a new level of excellence whatever your starting point. We offer three different levels of course that are open to the public:

- ▶ **Confident Presenter** *Two-day course for those new to presenting focusing, as the name indicates, on developing confidence.*
- ▶ **Advance Your Presentations** *One-day course for people with some experience of presenting who are seeking to refresh*

their skills. It's designed for experienced speakers who need stimulus and new ideas to be even more effective.

▶ **Presentations Masterclass** *One-day course for managers who have to give persuasive and motivating presentations, deliver in challenging situations, and for those in a leadership role.*

We also offer **individual coaching for presentation skills** and tailor-made courses run to meet the needs of your company.

Please call us today to discuss your learning needs on 020 7253 2117 or email us at info@speak-first.com

Organizations

Toastmasters International www.toastmasters.org

Books

Atkinson, R.C. and Shiffrin, R.M. (1968) 'Human memory: A proposed system and its control processes', in K.W. Spence and J.T. Spence (eds), *The Psychology of Learning and Motivation*, vol. 8, Academic Press

Atkinson, Professor Max (2004) *Lend Me Your Ears*, Random House

Bavister, Steve and Vickers, Amanda (2010) *Teach Yourself NLP*, Hodder Headline

Berkley, Susan (2004) *Speak to Influence*, Campbell Hall Press

Boothman, Nicholas (2002) *How to Connect in Business*, Workman Publishing

Clarke, Boyd and Crossland, Ron (2002) *The Leader's Voice*, The Tom Peters Press and SelectBooks Inc

Cohen, Steve (2005) *Win the Crowd*, HarperCollins

Covey, Stephen (1999) *The Seven Habits of Highly Effective People*, Simon & Schuster

Decker, Bart (1993) *You've Got to be Believed to be Heard*, St Martin's Press

Denning, Stephen (2005) *Leader's Guide to Storytelling: Mastering the Art and Discipline of Business Narrative*, Jossey Bass

Gallwey, Tim (2001) *The Inner Game of Work*, Random House

Glanzer, Murray and Cunitz, Anita R. (1966) 'Two storage mechanisms in Free Recall', *Journal of Verbal Learning and Verbal Behaviour*

Heath, Chip and Heath, Dan (2007) *Made to Stick*, Random House

Jeary, Tony (2004) *Life is a Series of Presentations*, Fireside

Luntz, Frank (2007) *Words that Work: It's not what you say, it's what people hear*, Hyperion

Merrill, David W. and Reid, Roger H. (1999) *Personal Styles & Effective Performance*, CRC Press

Morgan, Nick (2003) *Working the Room*, Harvard Business School Publishing

Naistadt, Ivy (2004) *Speak without Fear*, HarperCollins

Payne, Richard (2004) *Vocal Skills Pocketbook*, Management Pocket Books Ltd

Pearce, Terry (1995) *Leading out Loud*, Jossey-Bass Books

Stuart, Cristina (2000) *Speak for Yourself*, Piatkus

Walters, Lily (1993) *Secrets of Successful Speakers*, McGraw Hil

Weissman, Jerry (2006) *Winning Presentation: The Art of Telling Your Story*, Prentice Hall

Wilson Learning Library (2004) *The Social Styles Handbook*, Nova Vista Publishing

---

Websites

The authors' training company www.speak-first.com

Patricia Fripp, award-winning speaker www.fripp.com

Newsletters

Speak First's monthly newsletter contains valuable articles on a range of communication-related topics including presentation skills. And it's absolutely free of charge. To sign up go to www.speak-first.com

Index

switch off, why audiences, *68, 120, 179, 188–90, 267, 287*

symploce, *250*

table, use of, *110, 111, 288*

team presentations, *133, 259, 290*

'teapot' pose, *212*

teleconferencing, *290–1*

teleprompter *see* autocue

'tell 'em times three' structure, *57–8, 65, 68, 83, 84*

testimonials as 'flavour', *100, 102, 111*

text addicts, dealing with, *279*

'the leveller' gesture, *215–16*

Theatre room layout, *168, 172*

Thoughts, Feelings, Actions, *146–7*

time
    audience expectations of, *38*
    control of, *6, 7, 260*
    for mingling and chatting, *48–9*
    needed for rehearsal, *119, 130*
    needed to present, *37, 111, 132–3*
    for preparation, *21, 24–6*
    when cut short, *275–6*

tongue twisters, *238*

training sessions, running, *293–4*

travel and presenting, *172*

'two-handed stab' gesture, *215, 216*

'um' (filler), *10, 145, 232–3*

'Velcro arms' gesture, *207*

video clips in slides, *127, 172–3, 274*

video conferencing, *290–1*

videoing for feedback, *132, 134–5, 140, 196–7, 296*

'visionary, the' gesture, *217*

visual aids, *114–28*
    reasons for using, *114–15*
    types of, *115–18*

visualization, *74, 89, 152–3, 154*

vocal impact, *xxi*

voice in presenting, *xxi, 222–40*

volume of voice, *6, 18, 201, 223, 224, 226, 227, 233–4, 237*
    described, *226*

waffle, *44, 242–3, 264–5*

'warming up' the voice, *237–8*

web conferencing, *290–1*

weddings, speaking at, *296–7*

'what's in it for them' (WIIFT), *61–2*

whiteboard as visual aid, *115–16, 131, 162*

'winging' it, *22, 23, 131, 144, 266*

'working the room', *172, 288*

yawning to relieve tension, *156, 230*

zoning out (definition), *59*